The Law Lords

Also by Maxwell Barrett

CHILD LAW INDEX: Case Precedents 1900–97

CRIMINAL LAW INDEX: Case Precedents 1900–97

FAMILY LAW INDEX: Case Precedents 1900–97

LAW OF EVIDENCE INDEX: Case Precedents 1900–97

LAW OF TORT INDEX: Case Precedents 1900–97

MARRIAGE BREAKDOWN LAW INDEX: Case Precedents 1900–97

ROAD TRAFFIC LAW INDEX: Case Precedents 1900–97

SENTENCING INDEX: Case Precedents 1900–97

The Law Lords

An Account of the Workings of Britain's Highest Judicial Body and the Men who Preside Over It

Maxwell Barrett

First published 2001 by
MACMILLAN PRESS LTD
Houndmills, Basingstoke, Hampshire RG21 6XS
and London
Companies and representatives
throughout the world

ISBN 0–333–72519–0

A catalogue record for this book is available
from the British Library.

This book is printed on paper suitable for recycling and made from fully managed and sustained forest sources.

10 9 8 7 6 5 4 3 2 1
10 09 08 07 06 05 04 03 02 01

Printed and bound in Great Britain by
Antony Rowe Ltd, Chippenham, Wiltshire

For Agapi and Athena

Contents

List of Plates

Acknowledgements

I am very grateful to the various Lords of Appeal past and present and to the retired Lord Chancellor who generously agreed to let me interview them for this book during the summer of 1997.

On a more personal level I would like to thank my family and friends for their kindness towards me throughout the period that I was writing this work. My wife, Agapi, has been a tower of support. My parents, Della and Michael Barrett, have afforded me every encouragement. My brother, Dr Gavin Barrett, BL, has been particularly helpful, especially as regards making comments on the final text. My other brother, Conor, has also been supportive. My good friend Jennifer Powell has generously worked as a one-woman Reuters agency for the last year or so, trawling through the newspapers and the Internet each day to find anything that might be of relevance to this book. My college friends, Dr Jonathan Rush and Stefano Pistillo, have been consistently helpful. Finally my daughter, Athena, has done what she and her mother seem to do best – make everything seem so worthwhile.

Notwithstanding the assistance I have received from the above-mentioned people, any views expressed in this book are entirely personal, and the responsibility for any factual errors which may occur in the text rests with me alone.

Maxwell Barrett,
Dublin

Introduction

The nearly 700-member House of Lords is not only a legislative body. It is also a court. In fact it is the final court of appeal for most cases decided in the United Kingdom. Because of this there has been a long tradition of appointing senior judges to be members of the House. These judges are often referred to as 'Law Lords'. Twelve of the Law Lords are full-time members of a committee of the House of Lords known as the Appellate Committee. This is the body that hears and decides the various appeals that come before the House. Its decisions do not actually have legal effect until they are approved by a full meeting of the House – albeit a full meeting that only the relevant Lords of Appeal attend. The fact that this approval has to be sought is simply a reminder that it is technically the House of Lords which is the final court of appeal even though it is actually the Appellate Committee that does all the work.

The twelve Law Lords who are full-time members of the Appellate Committee are known as the Lords of Appeal in Ordinary. They usually sit in panels of three or five when hearing cases but it is not unknown for seven of them to sit together when a case merits particular attention. Each year the Lords of Appeal in Ordinary hear and decide between 70 and 80 appeals cases. They are sometimes assisted by the Lord Chancellor and they are occasionally joined by one or two of the Law Lords who are not full-time members of the Appellate Committee. However it is the Lords of Appeal in Ordinary who do the bulk of the Committee's work.

In some respects the role of the Appellate Committee is similar to that of the United States Supreme Court. Its interpretations of the law are binding on all other courts in the United Kingdom. Indeed unless the law is changed by Parliament or the Appellate Committee itself revises its own interpretation of the law (perhaps on foot of a decision of the European Court of Human Rights) its judgments *are* the law and can remain the law for many years. This makes the men who work on the Appellate Committee very powerful individuals. Yet unlike the United States where members of the federal Supreme Court are prominent public figures, the members of the Appellate Committee are very much unknown to the British public. This book aims to change that. It looks at the lives of the Lords of Appeal in Ordinary and the Lord Chancellor both on and off the Appellate Committee. It is intended for anyone who is interested in discovering a little more about the men who form what is the most eminent judicial body in the United Kingdom. In this respect it is a very timely book. Over the last couple of years the Appellate Committee has been the subject of considerable public interest. In part this may be attributable to the enactment of the Human Rights Act 1998 and the consequences of that Act for the Appellate Committee. When the Act comes into force in October 2000 the judiciary will for the first time acquire the power to determine the compatibility or otherwise of UK legislation with a written body of human rights, the European Convention on Human Rights, which the Act incorporates into British law. Although judges will not acquire the power under the Act to set aside legislation in the way that the US Supreme Court can declare legislation to be unconstitutional, any decision by the Appellate Committee, the most eminent judicial body in the United Kingdom, that certain legislation contravenes the basic human rights and freedoms contained in the Act will almost inevitably lead to the amendment or repeal or revocation of the legislation, or portion of the legislation, concerned. This means that Appellate Committee members will be very powerful individuals indeed. So it is not surprising that a certain degree of interest has arisen regarding their background and qualifications. That said, it is just possible that the coming into force of the Human Rights Act – though a significant event in itself – might not have excited the same degree of interest about the men who man the Appellate Committee, had not the interest of the public in Appellate Committee members already been prompted by the burst of publicity to which the Appellate Committee was exposed in late 1998 and early 1999 as a result of certain appeals brought by General Pinochet.

General Pinochet is the former leader of Chile. During the time that he was in office some four thousand of his opponents disappeared or were killed. Many of them were tortured. A number of these opponents were Spanish citizens. Because of this the General is wanted for trial in Spain. For legal and political reasons there was never any possibility that the General would be extradited to Spain from Chile. But in October of 1998 the General left Chile and flew to London for some surgery. A Spanish magistrate learned of the General's visit to London and decided to see if he could have the General extradited from England to Spain. He issued an international warrant of arrest against the General. Later he thought that the wording of this warrant might be defective. Concerned that the General would escape his grasp the Spanish magistrate decided to issue a second international warrant of arrest. This second warrant alleged that the General was guilty of a variety of crimes including genocide and terrorism.

In order that the two international arrest warrants might be lawfully enforced in England they were presented by the British police before London magistrates who checked to see if the warrants appeared to be in order and then issued two English arrest warrants. These English arrest warrants were dated 16 October and 22 October respectively. Acting on the two English warrants the police arrested General Pinochet in the London clinic where he was staying. The General quickly employed some lawyers to defend him. These lawyers decided to bring a case before the English Divisional Court challenging the validity of the General's arrest.

The General's lawyers asserted that an error on the face of the first international arrest warrant tainted the first of the two English arrest warrants – the 16 October warrant – and rendered it invalid. The General's lawyers also raised a more fundamental problem. They claimed that even if both of the English warrants were valid neither of them was enforceable. This was because the crimes for which the General was arrested were said to have occurred at a time when he was the leader of Chile and under English law heads of state enjoy immunity from civil or criminal liability in respect of their official actions.

The Divisional Court accepted these contentions. It decided that the 16 October warrant was invalid. It also decided that the General enjoyed immunity from arrest and prosecution for the crimes alleged against him in the 22 October warrant. If the Divisional Court decision had been allowed to stand the General could have flown straight home to Chile. However lawyers for the prosecution requested that they be allowed appeal the question of immunity to the Appellate Committee of the House of Lords. The Divisional Court acceded to this request. Pending the outcome of this appeal it ordered that General Pinochet should remain under arrest.

On 5 November, 1998 the Appellate Committee began to hear the appeal. It was presided over by five Lords of Appeal in Ordinary.

Because the issues involved were of considerable legal and political significance the Lords of Appeal allowed additional submissions to be made by human rights lawyers and by lawyers renowned for their expertise in international law. Some of the lawyers who argued against General Pinochet were employed to do so by Amnesty International, the human rights organisation. This was later to be of great significance, but at the time of the appeal it did not attract particular attention.

The appeal focused exclusively on the issue of whether General Pinochet was immune from arrest and prosecution for the offences alleged against him in the 22 October warrant. The General's prosecutors claimed that the High Court was wrong to find that the General did enjoy such an immunity. They did not appeal the decision of the High Court that the 16 October warrant was invalid. That decision still stood. So if the Appellate Committee decided that the General enjoyed immunity from arrest and prosecution for the offences alleged in the 22 October warrant he would be free to return home as each of the two warrants issued against him by the London magistrates would have been found by the courts to be unenforceable. If, however, the Lords of Appeal rejected the claim of immunity that had succeeded in the Divisional Court then it would follow that the arrest of the General pursuant to the 22 October warrant was valid.

On 11 November, after five days of hearings involving more than sixteen barristers, the Lords of Appeal retired to consider what General Pinochet's fate would be. Two weeks later they entered the chamber of the House of Lords to announce what they had decided. Upstairs the galleries were crowded with onlookers. On the streets of Westminster opponents and supporters of the General broke from shouting at each other to watch the proceedings on live television. Across the world in Chile the events inside the House of Lords were broadcast live by all five of Chile's national television stations. Outside the gates of the London clinic where the General was staying campaigners and protestors fell silent as they too turned to the television and watched the Lords of Appeal prepare to give their speeches. At the front door of the clinic a police motorcade stood prepared to whisk the General away to a nearby airbase where there was a Chilean government jet waiting to fly him home if the Lords of Appeal decided in his favour. Inside the clinic the General sat in a wheelchair ready to leave. He too was watching the television.

The first Lord of Appeal to rise and speak was Lord Slynn of Hadley. In line with practice he did not make an extensive speech explaining the reasons for his decision. He simply indicated what way he would be voting and referred interested listeners to a printed speech in which he had set out the rationale behind his judgment.

"My Lords" he said, "I would hold that the respondent [General Pinochet], as a former head of state is immune from arrest in respect of the matters alleged in the warrant of October 22, 1998, and I would dismiss the appeal."

1–0 to the General. And something of a bad start for the General's opponents. But with four judges to go it was far too soon for either side to be certain how their Lordships had decided this case.

The next Lord of Appeal to speak was Lord Lloyd of Berwick.

"My Lords" he said. "In my opinion the State of Chile is entitled to claim immunity on behalf of... [General] Pinochet... I would therefore dismiss the appeal."

2–0 to the General. And yet another disappointment for the General's opponents. Still, with three judges left to go it was just possible that the General would not go free – provided all three judges voted that the General should not enjoy the very extensive immunity from civil or criminal liability which acting and retired heads of state were argued by his lawyers to have long enjoyed under international law.

The third Lord of Appeal to rise and speak was Lord Nicholls of Birkenhead. With all the judges thus far having voted in such a way as to ensure the General's release his lawyers could be forgiven if they thought as Lord Nicholls of Birkenhead rose to his feet that their client had won his appeal. This was certainly the view among those supporters of the General who had taken to the streets of London. Whether they were outside the Palace of Westminster or outside the clinic where Pinochet was staying they now began to cheer what they thought was the General's imminent victory. In their excitement they almost missed what Lord Nicholls had to say.

"My Lords," he started. "For the reasons set out in a speech which I have prepared in draft, and of which copies are available in print, I would reverse the decision of the... [High] Court, allow this appeal and hold that the respondent... [General] Pinochet is not immune from the criminal process of this country."

2–1. The case was still going in the General's favour but this was a dramatic turn. With only two Appellate Committee members left to speak there was now a glimmer of hope for those opposed to Pinochet that the General would not now be released to fly home. The Lords of Appeal were certainly providing a nailbiting end to weeks of speculation as to what General Pinochet's fate would be.

Lord Steyn now rose to speak.

"My Lords" he said. "For the reasons contained in my speech, copies of which are available to the parties, I would allow the appeal. The effect of my speech is that, in a correct interpretation of the law, General Pinochet has no immunity whatever."

2–2. Now there was no predicting which way this case would go. After Lord Steyn there was only one Lord of Appeal left to speak. This was Lord Hoffmann. As he rose to his feet to speak the only people in the chamber of the House who cannot have been waiting with bated breath for what he had to say were his four fellow Lords of Appeal in Ordinary who already knew what Lord Hoffmann had decided.

"My Lords" he began. "I have had the advantage of reading in draft the speeches of my noble and learned friends, Lord Nicholls of Birkenhead and Lord Steyn. I agree with them that ... [General] Pinochet does not have immunity from prosecution, and I too, therefore would allow the appeal."

Shock from the General's supporters. Glee from his opponents. By the slimmest of majorities the Appellate Committee had decided that the General did not enjoy immunity from arrest and prosecution for the offences alleged against him. In short the General had been validly arrested on foot of the 22 October warrant and was one step closer to facing trial in Spain.

After Lord Hoffmann had resumed his seat Lord Slynn of Hadley stood up once more. As the most senior Lord of Appeal present it was his duty to ask this full meeting of the House of Lords to give its approval to the decision of the Appellate Committee. This the House did. The five Lords of Appeal then left the chamber. It had been an occasion of high drama but the greatest drama was yet to come ...

1
The Origins of the Appellate Committee

The Norman king as the fount and source of justice – House of Lords appeals in the early nineteenth century – the reforms of 1824 – the trial of Daniel O'Connell – the appointment of Lord Wensleydale – the enactment of the Appellate Jurisdiction Act 1876 – the creation of the Appellate Committee

It is a principle of law, long established, that the British Sovereign is the fount and source of all earthly justice within every territory where the British Crown holds sway. It is a matter of fact that this is too great a responsibility for any Sovereign to discharge alone. In Norman times the Kings of England performed their duties in this regard with the aid of a council of advisers. But being the fount and source of justice (or even being the adviser of the fount and source of justice) is a fairly time-consuming task and in the war-strewn Middle Ages there was enough for the King and his council to do without having to act as final arbiter in every legal dispute that arose within the King's dominions. As a result the responsibility for deciding cases was devolved onto various other bodies which in time became the courts we know today. The King and his council of advisers remained the ultimate source of justice. And they continued to hear the most important cases. But less significant cases were tried by the lower courts and only went to the King and his advisers on appeal. Over time the King's council of advisers evolved into the House of Lords and the Privy Council. These two bodies jealously guarded their judicial responsibilities and did not share them with the House of Commons whose members were never considered to possess the divinely-given power of justice which the King and his nobles claimed to enjoy.

By the early nineteenth century this constitutional framework had changed considerably though not so much as to be unrecognisable.

The House of Commons had a vastly more significant role than in Norman times but the monarch and the House of Lords continued to enjoy real power. Down at Oxford and Cambridge academics sought to justify this system of government by speaking of the Monarchy, the House of Lords, and the House of Commons as embodying respectively the three great virtues of power, sensibility, and democracy. They suggested that the balance between these three institutions of government had prevented Britain from descending into the vices of tyranny, faction and tumult, which plagued other nations. They conveniently ignored the fact that outside their dreaming spires the system was in fact hopelessly imbalanced, and was plagued by corruption, inequality, unrepresentativeness, and occasional violence. Still, change was afoot. In 1832 Parliament passed the first of four great reform Acts aimed at remedying the worst excesses in the British system of government. A new political vocabulary was also seeping into the political vernacular at this time. Inspired by the American and French Revolutions it abandoned traditional ideas about the fluctuating balance of power between the monarchy, the aristocracy and the plurality. It spoke instead of the need for checks and balances between the Executive, the Legislative, and the Judiciary, each of which was considered to be a separate but equal organ of government. In this new environment a House of Lords which was both a legislative and a judicial body quickly came to be viewed by many as a feudal anachronism ill-suited to modern times. Voices were soon heard suggesting that the House of Lords ought to be stripped of its judicial responsibilities and turned into a purely legislative body with the dispensing of justice left exclusively to the courts.

Not everyone supported the idea of reforming the House of Lords. But those arguing in favour of the status quo were not helped in making their case by the shambolic manner in which the House approached its judicial responsibilities at this time. These responsibilities were discharged in a like manner to any other piece of business that fell to be transacted by the Lords. Any or all peers could sit in judgment on a case regardless of whether they possessed legal qualifications or not. Any or all peers could vote on what way a case was to be decided regardless of whether they had attended the full hearings or not. While some peers with judicial experience such as Lord Chancellors, former Lord Chancellors, and the Lord Chief Justice did have seats in the House there was no requirement that they be present when a case was heard or decided. Even when peers with judicial experience were present there was no tradition in the House of yielding to the opinions of a legally experienced peer. The vote of any such peer was just one among many and carried no special weight. Very occasionally the House might seek the advice of eminent lower court judges on how best to resolve particularly complex questions. But on the whole the House preferred to resolve matters by itself – with very mixed results.

Legal amateurism was not the only problem which afflicted the House as a judicial body in the early nineteenth century. The enormous delay in bringing appeals to the House was another serious defect. This delay was almost entirely the result of an Order made by the House in 1709 forbidding the execution of any sentence or decree made by a Scottish court if an appeal against that sentence or decree was made to the House of Lords. In theory this seemed a perfectly sensible Order for the House to make. After all, there was not much point in bringing an appeal if the court order or decision being appealed against had already been put into effect. But in practice the Order was wide open to abuse. It was barely in place before every Scottish litigant from John O'Groats to Gretna Green whose case had gone against him was instigating a House of Lords appeal. After all, the delay and expense in bringing an appeal the whole way from Scotland to Westminster meant there was a good chance that in the period between the launching and hearing of the appeal the other side to an action could be browbeaten into accepting a compromise solution different to what a Scottish court had ordered. Even if the other side was not prepared to do a deal the launching of an appeal was an effective way of putting off the awful day when the relevant Scottish court order would have to be put into effect.

The enormous number of cases emanating from Scotland was not something which the House of Lords could really have anticipated. However where the House could be (and was) roundly criticised was that it took no real steps to eliminate the massive backlog of appeals awaiting hearing until more than a century had passed. At last in 1824 the House finally decided that some action was indeed necessary. It agreed that for the time being appeals would be heard by the Lord Chancellor (a lawyer) or a nominated deputy (who also had to be a lawyer) along with up to three other peers (who were not required to have legal qualifications). Together they were to hear cases on a continuous basis for six hours a day, five days a week, until all outstanding appeals had been resolved. Any decisions arrived at by the panel were to be treated as decisions of the whole House. Those peers required to make up a panel were to be nominated on a rota basis by the Lord

Chancellor who was authorised to fine any peers who were listed on the rota but who failed to turn up.

In so far as streamlining the appeals process was concerned the 1824 reforms were an unqualified success. But in so far as effecting justice was concerned they turned out to be an unmitigated disaster. First of all the panel of peers required to attend the appeals saw their presence as being very much for show – they felt that they were there simply to make up numbers. They did not like being given a choice of either showing up or paying up. They considered that judicial work was really a matter for the Lord Chancellor or his deputy. So they turned up, they sat down, and they did very little else. This type of attitude can have done little to persuade an appellant coming before the House that he was getting a fair hearing of his case. A second and more serious difficulty was that each panel of peers was only required to sit for a single day. Then another panel of peers would be called upon to do their duty and so on, so forth until all eligible peers had done one day's service. At this point the first panel would be called back again and the cycle would begin once more. Consequently in a case which lasted two or more days the hearings were conducted before the Lord Chancellor (or his deputy) and a different set of peers on each successive day. To cap it all, when it came to voting on which way the case was to be decided only those peers present on the final day had the right to vote. So in any case which went on for more than a day the Lord Chancellor or his deputy could, when it came to making a decision, be out-voted by two or more peers who had not heard all the facts, who had not sat in on all the hearings, and who had no legal qualifications. Even if the case lasted less than a day litigants still ran the risk that the Lord Chancellor or his deputy, each of whom was experienced in the law, could be out-voted by a few old duffers who had never seen the inside of a law book. A third problem arose when the Lord Chancellor was not a member of the House of Lords.[1] Under the post-1824 system of hearing appeals only the Lord Chancellor or his deputy (who was rarely a peer) ever had the benefit of hearing entire appeals from start to finish. So obviously what the Lord Chancellor or his deputy had to say regarding the merits of a particular appeal was of great value to peers who had neither the advantage of having heard a full case nor in most cases the benefit of a legal education. The problem, however, was that even if peers wanted to listen to what the Lord Chancellor or his deputy had to say – and it was by no means invariable practice that they did – they could not do so in the chamber of the House if the Lord Chancellor or his deputy were not themselves peers as only peers may speak in the chamber of the House of Lords. To overcome this difficulty a compromise was reached whereby any Lord Chancellor or his deputy who did not happen to be a peer would walk over to one of the peers at the end of the hearings and quietly inform him what he thought of the issues raised. This peer would then repeat the opinion of the Lord Chancellor or his deputy to the House. The various peers present would then discuss the opinion or they would simply take a vote on the case.

Delivering judgment by way of Chinese whispers was hardly an inspired fashion in which to run a court of final appeal. Still in some ways the 1824 reforms did mark a step in the evolution of House of Lords appeals towards the form in which they are conducted today. They established the pre-eminence of the Lord Chancellor and they established a precedent for having a legally qualified person present at all hearings. That said, it continued to be the case that the peers who made up the majority at any appeal were not legally qualified. Moreover, many peers perceived the 1824 reforms as a temporary measure introduced to alleviate a temporary problem. Once the large number of cases pending before the House had been dealt with these peers sought a return to the old way of doing things. Indeed by the mid-1830s the House was again hearing some appeals without any legally qualified peers being present. Then two things happened. First, a rapid turnover of government administrations led to there being a lot of legally qualified ex-Lord Chancellors with peerages swanning about the House of Lords. Second, a number of professional judges were also elevated to the House for one reason or another at this time. So it just happened that there were enough legally qualified peers to make up a quorum of the House in appeals cases without there being any need for peers without legal qualifications to be present.[2] Even so, the odd peer who did not have legal qualifications and who did not care about the need for a clear division between the legislative and executive branches of government continued to turn up and vote in appeals before the House. At least, that was, until the case of Daniel O'Connell.

O'Connell was one of the foremost Irish politicians of his generation. In the 1840s he launched and led the Repeal Association. This was an organization dedicated to securing the repeal of the legislation which joined Britain and Ireland together under one government in 1801. O'Connell was convinced that the only way of relieving the very great poverty that afflicted Ireland in his day was to put in place an Irish government that would be exclusively responsible for the Irish economy. He travelled the length and breadth of Ireland advocating this idea and urging people to join the Repeal Association. His efforts were tremendously successful: within two years of forming the Association he was attracting crowds of up to a quarter of a million people at some of his meetings. Across the water in London the Conservative administration of Sir Robert Peel, was forced to sit up and take notice. The administration did not like what it saw. It was prepared to address specific Irish grievances but was vehemently opposed to any suggestion that there should be an end to direct rule of Ireland from Westminster. It resolved to crush the Repeal Association and in 1843 it got its chance. On 8 October of that year O'Connell was supposed to address a vast public meeting in a place just outside Dublin called Clontarf. This was a highly emotive venue at which to hold a meeting demanding self-government for Ireland. Eight centuries previously Clontarf had been the place where Brian Boru, the 'Emperor of the Irish', had inflicted a crushing defeat on the Viking invaders who had for long attacked and settled the island of Ireland. The symbolism of all this was wasted on nobody, least of all the people who drafted the advertisements for the meeting which O'Connell was to attend. In a fit of patriotism they referred to the ceremonial parade of horsemen which would accompany O'Connell's carriage to Clontarf as "repeal cavalry". Over in London the Peel administration seized on this wording, saying it showed that the real purpose of O'Connell's meeting was to launch an attempt to overthrow British rule in Ireland. An order was issued banning the meeting. A number of soldiers were rushed to Clontarf. And a gunboat was sent into Dublin Bay. It was make or break time and O'Connell broke. Fearing bloodshed if the meeting went ahead he cancelled his speech and published a notice urging people to stay at home. 8 October came and went and nothing untoward happened. The Peel administration had won the day. But now it overplayed its hand. Determined to put an end to unrest in Ireland it had O'Connell and several other leaders of the Repeal Association arrested, brought to Dublin and charged with conspiracy to bring down the government. But still the administration was not satisfied. If it was to avoid looking foolish it had to secure a guilty verdict. Happily it knew one sure way to get this. The administration was aware that Protestants in Ireland had been afraid if the Repeal Association was successful they might end up being trapped in a nation whose government was dominated by Catholics and headed by O'Connell, himself a devout Catholic. The administration decided to use these Protestant fears to its own ends. When O'Connell's case came before the courts in 1844 it ensured that the trial was conducted by a panel of Protestant judges before an all-Protestant jury. Not surprisingly O'Connell was found guilty as charged. Equally unsurprisingly O'Connell launched an immediate appeal against the decision to the House of Lords. His case was to bring about a sea-change in British constitutional history.

By the time O'Connell's appeal got to Westminster the members of the House of Lords were in a fever of excitement. Many of them saw the Irishman as little more than a rabble-rouser and were determined to see him get his comeuppance. But the Peel administration was alarmed. Since O'Connell's conviction Ireland had been teetering on the verge of massive civil unrest. Crowds were marching through the Irish cities and towns and countryside demanding that O'Connell be released. The administration was concerned that the situation would escalate beyond control but many in England and some within the administration itself were baying for O'Connell's blood. In short, if O'Connell's appeal failed there was the very real possibility of serious trouble in Ireland, but if O'Connell was released as an act of executive clemency there was the very real possibility of serious trouble within the Peel administration and the Conservative party. What the Peel administration needed was for O'Connell to be released but by somebody other than the administration.

On 8 June 1844, O'Connell's appeal came before a thronged House of Lords. The arguments of counsel were heard and the House then paused to consider its verdict. Of the five legally qualified peers present in the House three voted for O'Connell's release and two for his continued imprisonment. A number of peers without legal qualifications then sought to vote with the minority of legally qualified peers in order to ensure that O'Connell went straight back to prison. At this point Lord Wharncliffe intervened. He was the Lord President of the Privy Council, a senior member of Peel's government. He urged those Lords who did not possess legal qualifications to abstain from voting. His speech struck a chord with the House. The peers who did not have legal qualifications abstained from voting and by the slimmest of majorities O'Connell was granted his freedom. Ireland heaved a cry of triumph. Peel and the bulk of his administration heaved a sigh of relief. And the House established a convention that only legally qualified peers can vote in an appeal. It was a small jump from this convention to the practice of appointing senior judges as peers specifically in order that they might hear House of Lords appeals. At first the unusually high number of legally qualified peers present in the House during O'Connell's day made any such appointments unnecessary. But it was only a matter of time until this changed. At last in 1856 Sir James Parke who had previously sat on the Court of Exchequer was elevated to the House of Lords as Lord Wensleydale. As a peer Lord Wensleydale's brief was simple. He was to aid the House in the discharge of its judicial responsibilities. He was not expected to play a part in the legislative proceedings of the House. In this Lord Wensleydale was different from all other legally qualified peers who had been appointed to the House before him. They had been appointed to help make laws. Lord Wensleydale had been appointed solely to decide cases. Because of this difference in capacity it was initially intended that he would only be given a life peerage. But die-hard blue-bloods in the House of Lords did not want to see the hereditary principle diluted in this fashion. They blocked Parke's appointment until the government reluctantly arranged for him to be given a hereditary peerage.

The practice of bestowing hereditary peerages upon Law Lords continued unabated until 1876. From that time on hereditary peerages tended to be granted to Lord Chancellors only.[3] The reason for the change in practice was the coming into force of the Appellate Jurisdiction Act 1876. This piece of legislation was passed by the second Disraeli administration. At the time it was passed there was a feeling within the House of Commons and among senior members of the judiciary (including Disraeli's Lord Chancellor, Lord Cairns) that the United Kingdom would be better served if the appellate powers of the House of Lords were transferred to a separate supreme court which would be the court of last resort for all cases emanating from England, Ireland, Scotland, and Wales. It was thought that this would tidy up the messy overlap of legislative and judicial powers enjoyed by the House of Lords and help restore flagging public confidence in the courts system. However the idea met with stiff opposition from members of the Upper House who were sick and tired of what they considered to be an apparently endless assault on their traditional prerogatives and responsibilities in the judicial sphere. Between 1873 and 1875 they made it clear that they were not prepared to see the appellate functions of the House of Lords transferred to some new-fangled supreme court. But Disraeli and his government were determined to implement their reforms. They decided that if the peers did not want a separate supreme court *outside* the House then the only solution was to have a separate supreme court *inside* the House. And this in effect is what the 1876 Act did. It provided for the appointment of two Lords of Appeal in Ordinary selected either from senior members of the judiciary who had held high judicial office for at least two years or from senior barristers who had been in active practice for at least fifteen years.[4] All Lords of Appeal were to belong to the House of Lords but only for so long as they held office. All appeals made to the House of Lords were to be heard and determined by the Lords of Appeal along with the Lord Chancellor or any other peers who held or had once held high judicial office. Serving Lords of Appeal were to enjoy the rank and privileges of an ordinary member of the House of Lords and so could participate in House of Lords debates. Regular members of the House of Lords were not to be allowed share in the judicial powers enjoyed by the Lords of Appeal, the Lord Chancellor and those peers who held or had once held high judicial office. Thus there were in effect to be two Houses of Lords. The 'legislative' House was to deal with the ordinary political business of the House. It was to consist of the Lord Chancellor and the ordinary peers and occasionally be attended by the Lords of Appeal.[5] The 'judicial' House was to be concerned solely with the hearing and resolving of appeals and was to be composed of the Lords of Appeal who were sometimes to be chaired by the Lord Chancellor and occasionally be assisted by a select group of other peers with experience of high judicial office.

The efforts of the Disraeli administration to establish a professional court of last resort for the United Kingdom were so successful that the Appellate Jurisdiction Act remains substantially intact today. Of course there have been some changes. New Lords of Appeal are now automatically granted full life peerages rather than the working-life peerages envisaged by the 1876 legislation.[6] Moreover their numbers have slowly been creeping up over the last century and a quarter so that instead of the original two Lords of Appeal there are now twelve of them at any one time. There has also been one significant practical change which has served to heighten the distinction between the 'judicial' and 'legislative' sides of the House of Lords. During the Second World War the roof of the House of Commons was damaged by a bomb. Because of this the House of Commons moved its proceedings into the main chamber of the House of Lords. The Lords in turn moved into the Royal Robing Room, at least for legislative purposes – appeals hearings were shunted off to one of the many committee rooms upstairs. It was soon after this that the panel of peers who conducted these appeals came to be known as the Appellate Committee. The members of this Committee quickly discovered that it was far more comfortable to hear cases in a committee room and that there were far fewer interruptions to their work than had been the case in the main chamber of the House of Lords where judicial business had previously been conducted. So when the legislative side of the House of Lords finally returned to the main chamber in 1951 the Appellate Committee remained upstairs in the committee rooms and now only conducts hearings in the main chamber for one week each summer when all the other peers are away on summer holiday. Hence, contrary to the position which existed after the 1876 Act whereby there was a notional but not a physical separation between the 'legislative' and 'judicial' sides of the House of Lords, nowadays the discharge by the House of its twin responsibilities – legislative and judicial – generally transpires in different places (albeit within the same Palace).

The physical separation of the Appellate Committee from the main body of the House of Lords has meant that those Lord Chancellors who have served since the end of the Second World War have been required to choose between acting as speaker of the House of Lords on the one hand, and head of the Appellate Committee on the other when both the main body of the House and the Appellate Committee have been sitting at the same time. Of the post-Second World War Lord Chancellors only Lord Simonds has elected to concentrate on his judicial responsibilities though Lord Hailsham of St Marylebone did try particularly hard during his two terms in office as Lord Chancellor to sit in on as many House of Lords cases as possible out of a belief that it was important for the Lord Chancellor as head of the judiciary in England and Wales to actually exercise his judicial powers.

Oddly enough the general absence of Lord Chancellors from Appellate Committee hearings in the last 55 years has not been entirely unbeneficial. Lord Chancellors unlike other Appellate Committee members are very much political appointees so the fact that these days they are rarely present at Appellate Committee proceedings has rather helpfully served to disengage the Appellate Committee from the political side of the House of Lords and make it more like what was envisaged in the 1876 Act – a professional court staffed by professional judges. Still, not all has changed. There is one significant feature which has endured since the trial of Daniel O'Connell. To this day it is nowhere written into law that non-legally-qualified members of the House of Lords are excluded from exercising influence over cases that come before the House. It is only the precedent that was set in the O'Connell case which precludes non-legally qualified members of the House of Lords from voting in such appeals. Needless to say, it is a rigidly enforced precedent. Indeed it has only ever been challenged once. In 1883 in something of a last hurrah for the good old days Lord Denman, who had no legal or judicial experience, sought to vote in an appeal case that had come before the House.[7] But when it came to counting the votes Denman was, it seems, ignored by the Lord Chancellor of the day, Lord Selborne. The message was clear. The judicial members of the House would take care of judicial business themselves. The message has not been forgotten.

2
The Lords of Appeal in Ordinary

Family background – nationality – education – early career at the Bar – becoming a Queen's Counsel – marriage and children – appointment to the bench – promotion within the judiciary – the procedure of appointing a Lord of Appeal – elevation to the House of Lords – biographical details of the Lords of Appeal who have served since 1876

The average Lord of Appeal in Ordinary is usually the first person in his family to have been elevated to the House of Lords. That said almost one in fifteen Lords of Appeal have had a father who sat in the House of Lords before them. Lord Asquith was a younger son of William Herbert Asquith, the Liberal Prime Minister who led Britain into the First World War and later became the first Earl of Oxford and Asquith. Lord Thankerton and Lord Keith of Kinkel had fathers who were themselves Lords of Appeal in their day.[8] Lord Oaksey was the son of a former Lord Chief Justice of England. And the second and third Lords Russell of Killowen came from a quite amazing family that has provided no fewer than three Lords of Appeal in the past.[9]

Of the other Lords of Appeal who have been appointed since the office was first established in 1876 roughly three in twenty have had fathers who were lawyers, almost two in twenty have had fathers who were clergymen, about one in twenty have had a father who was a military man, and around one in twenty have had fathers who were doctors.[10] Indeed coming from a privileged background seems almost a prerequisite of appointment. There have been Lords of Appeal whose fathers were judges, merchants, landowners, baronets, architects, Members of Parliament, even one whose father was a Fellow at Cambridge University. And there is no sign that the backgrounds of the Lords of Appeal are becoming any less privileged. In the period since the Second World War ended only one Lord of Appeal in Ordinary – Lord Mackay of Clashfern – could be described as coming from a non-middle class background.[11] As yet there have been no 'Ladies' of Appeal.

The first Lord of Appeal in Ordinary was Lord Blackburn. By nationality Lord Blackburn was Scottish but as a young man he qualified as an English barrister and only ever practised in London. Of the 102 Lords of Appeal who have served since Lord Blackburn, 71 have been Englishmen, 19 have been Scotsmen, 9 have been Irishmen and 3 have been Welshmen.[12] Of the 9 Irishmen, 3 have been Northern Irishmen appointed since the division of Ireland in 1922.

Of the 71 Englishmen who have served as Lords of Appeal, 7 of them – Lord Atkin, Lord Du Parcq, Lord Hoffmann, Lord Pearson Lord Steyn, Lord Uthwatt and the (at the time of writing) soon to be appointed Sir Richard Scott – have been members of the English bar and were appointed English judges but were not actually born in England. Lord Atkin and Lord Uthwatt were born in Australia. Lord Du Parcq was born in Jersey. Lord Pearson was born in Canada. Lord Hoffmann and Lord Steyn – both of whom are presently Lords of Appeal – were born in South Africa. And Sir Richard Scott, who is due to join the Appellate Committee in October 2000, was born in India.

The disproportionately large number of Scotsmen who have served as Lords of Appeal is principally attributable to the fact that Scotland has a different legal system to the rest of the United Kingdom and so it has always been deemed necessary for there to be at least one, and more recently two Scottish Lords of Appeal, to help deal with Scottish points of law that come before the Appellate Committee. It has also been considered important that the Appellate Committee should be representative of the different nations that make up the United Kingdom.

Of the 6 Irishmen who were appointed as Lords of Appeal before 1922, Lord Carson ought really to be counted as an honorary Northern Irishman. Indeed he might rightly be considered the father of Northern Ireland as it was his masterful leadership of the Unionist cause in the early years of the twentieth century which ensured that Ulster – or at least two-thirds of it – remained within the United Kingdom. Not surprisingly Lord Carson was (and still is) revered by Unionists to the extent that they actually erected a statue to him in his own lifetime outside the Parliament Buildings at Stormont, near Belfast – Lord Carson himself performed the unveiling. It is something of a surprise to discover that such a staunch Unionist followed a distinctively southern Irish career path in so far as being a lawyer was concerned: he received his university education at Trinity College Dublin, trained as a barrister at The King's Inns in Dublin, and was called to the Irish Bar in 1877.

Nearly all Lords of Appeal have attended university. However not all those who have attended university have gone on to obtain a degree. For any of them who did not this is usually because they went to university during the nineteenth century when exposure to the rigours of university life was considered to be more important than getting a formal qualification. A small minority of Lords of Appeal in Ordinary have not initially studied law at university. Lords Cohen, Keith of Avonholm, Roskill, and Shaw all studied history. But the most popular alternative to law has been maths. Lord Denning was a mathematician before he became a lawyer. So too were Lords Atkinson, Davey, Mackay of Clashfern, Moulton, Romer, and Upjohn. Lord Moulton was perhaps the most outstanding mathematician of them all. As a student he seems to have won every prize in mathematics there was. And like Lord Denning and Lord Mackay of Clashfern after him he went on to become a university maths teacher before switching career to become a barrister.[13] One of the many Lords of Appeal who did study law at university was Lord Devlin, but this was after he abandoned his studies for the religious life at a Catholic seminary.[14]

Most Lords of Appeal who have studied at university have gone to Oxford or Cambridge, Oxford having the slight edge. However this overall figure hides some interesting regional variations. Of the 9 Irishmen who have served as Lords of Appeal, 5 of them had an exclusively Irish university education, 2 of them went to an English and an Irish university, one of them had an exclusively English education, and one of them did not go to university at all.[15] Each of the 3 Welsh Lords of Appeal in Ordinary had a primarily English university education. Lord Griffiths studied at Cambridge University. Lord Morris of Borth-y-Gest also attended Cambridge University although he did go on to spend a year at Harvard University. Lord Edmund-Davies broke the mould a bit by studying law at London University before doing postgraduate work at Oxford University. In so far as the 20 Lords of Appeal in Ordinary from Scotland are concerned, 14 of them spent some time at an English university, 7 of them at Cambridge University and 7 of them at Oxford University. Among those Scottish Lords of Appeal in Ordinary who have attended university in Scotland, the University of Edinburgh has been the undoubted favourite. To date only 7 Scottish Lords of Appeal have studied at another Scottish university and all 7 of them attended the University of Glasgow.[16]

Most Lords of Appeal tend to be homebirds when it comes to university study. Only 8 of them have ever studied outside the United Kingdom and 3 of those 8 were born and grew up in the countries where they studied, only coming to reside permanently in England sometime after they had finished their primary studies back home.[17] A paltry 4 of the 103 Lords of Appeal in Ordinary appointed since 1876 have left the United Kingdom to study abroad. Lord Hannen studied at Heidelberg. Lord Normand studied at the University of Paris. And Lord Lloyd and Lord Morris of Borth-y-Gest each studied at Harvard University for a year.[18]

Some Lords of Appeal have pursued an academic career before turning to a full-time career in the law. This is not especially surprising given that the first few years of a barrister's life – and Lords of Appeal are still exclusively drawn from the ranks of barristers – can be very lean indeed. What is interesting, however, is that university teaching experience seems to be on the increase. In the last 10 years alone five onetime academics – Lord Goff of Chieveley, Lord Hoffmann, Lord Lloyd of Berwick, Lord Mackay of Clashfern (who went on to serve as Lord Chancellor) and Lord Slynn of Hadley have served as Lords of Appeal. Lord Hoffmann and Lord Lloyd of Berwich taught at Oxford University, Lord Goff of Chieveley taught at Cambridge University, Lord Mackay of Clashfern taught at St Andrew's University, and Lord Slynn of Hadley taught at the London School of Economics.

Regardless of whether they have attended university or obtained a degree all Lords of Appeal in Ordinary ultimately take a professional qualification in the law. Any Scottish Lords of Appeal who have practised in Scotland will have trained as Scottish advocates. However an overwhelming majority of the Lords of Appeal – 80 of the 103 appointed so far – have trained as barristers in London. On arriving in London each future Lord of Appeal will have joined one of the four Inns of Court (Gray's Inn, the Inner Temple, Lincoln's Inn or the Middle Temple), the medieval bodies to which all prospective and practising barristers must belong. Ten of the 80 Lords of Appeal who have studied in London to become a barrister initially became members of Gray's Inn, 28 initially became members of the Inner Temple, 21 initially became members of Lincoln's Inn and 21 initially became members of the Middle Temple.

Of those Appellate Committee members who have not trained in Edinburgh or London, 5 are Irishmen who trained in Dublin before what is now the Republic of Ireland parted company from the rest of the United Kingdom and 2 are Northern Irishmen who, in the years since the division of Ireland in 1922, have been called to and practised at the Northern Irish Bar.[19] Both Northern Ireland and the Republic of Ireland have one Inn of Court each. The Northern Irish Inn of Court is known, aptly enough, as the Northern Ireland Inn of Court. The southern Irish Inn of Court is known as The King's Inns. As the Republic of Ireland has not had a monarch as head of state since 1937 one might have thought that the Irish Bar would consider re-naming the Inns to which all of its members belong but it would appear that while the life of the law is logic, the life of its practitioners is not: the name remains unchanged and there are no plans to alter it. There is no Inn of Court for Wales as barristers called to the English Bar are entitled to practise in England and Wales. Thus all three of the Welshmen who have served as Lords of Appeal in Ordinary studied to become barristers in London, 1 of them at Gray's Inn and 2 of them at the Inner Temple.

The average Lord of Appeal is called to the Bar about the time he turns 25. Raising this average figure are the four Lords of Appeal who commenced their professional careers after they turned 30.[20] The oldest when he was called to the Bar was Lord Wright who became a barrister at the ripe old age of 31.[21] Curiously Lord Wright does not hold the record for being the oldest future Lord of Appeal to start practising at the English Bar. That record goes to Lord Steyn who is one of the present Lords of Appeal. He commenced practising at the South African Bar at the age of 26 and went on to become the South African equivalent of a Queen's Counsel. However he decided to quit his career in South Africa and, at the age of 41, he emigrated to the United Kingdom where he took up work at the English Bar.

After qualifying as an advocate or barrister the 'average' Appellate Committee member in the last century and a quarter has waited in or about 16 years (or until an average age of around 41) before going on to become a Queen's Counsel, the highest rank that it is possible for an advocate or barrister to attain outside judicial office.[22] Barristers who have become Queen's Counsel are often said to have 'taken silk'. This is a reference to the silk or silk-like robes that Queen's Counsel wear to distinguish themselves from their more junior colleagues.

The practice of ranking barristers dates at least as far back as the reign of Queen Elizabeth I when the select body of barristers who helped the Attorney-General and the Solicitor-General to perform their duties were known colloquially to the world at large as 'Her Majesty's learned counsel'. King James I – the man who gave the world sirloin steak – formalised the colloquial term when he recognised Sir Francis

Bacon as Britain's first officially designated 'King's Counsel'. The practice of appointing King's Counsel was emulated by James' son, King Charles I, until the untimely severance of Charles from his position as monarch and his even more untimely severance from his head. After Charles' death and the rise to power of Cromwell and the Roundheads the title of King's Counsel went the way of Christmas and theatre performances, falling into abeyance until the restoration of King Charles II to the throne. Charles II did more than any of his predecessors to emphasise the distinctiveness of the title of King's Counsel. He issued an order that bestowed a special degree of precedence on those barristers who became King's Counsel. By making the title a matter of rank and by allowing more and more barristers to achieve the rank Charles quickly loosened the traditional connection which had existed between holding the title and performing a particular service for or to the Crown. Instead it became and remains a mere badge of distinction for eminent barristers, though until 1920 holders of the title were precluded from arguing a case against the Sovereign unless they obtained a Crown licence allowing them to do so, and, at least until recently, all Queen's Counsel were required to declare upon appointment that they would 'well and truly serve' the monarch – at the time of writing this particular requirement has been the subject of a successful High Court challenge by two Northern Irish barristers who objected to a decision by the present Lord Chancellor that the declaration should be retained in Northern Ireland. The barristers in question claimed that leaving the declaration in place discriminated against them as nationalists. The decision of the High Court aroused a certain consternation among Unionists.

Although Queen's Counsel no longer have any particular duties the title is more than a mere bauble for senior barristers. It is also a promise of things to come. Most of the 600 judgeships which fall vacant each year are filled by the Lord Chancellor from the ranks of Queen's Counsel. And for those who do not succeed in advancing to judicial office, the title is almost a licence to print money as Queen's Counsel are able to charge enormously greater fees for their services than their junior colleagues.

So what must a future Lord of Appeal do to become a member of this elite rank? As it happens becoming a Queen's Counsel is a rather tortuous business. Barristers who think they have what it takes must apply for the honour from the Lord Chancellor. They are allowed make one application each year. Unsuccessful applicants may re-apply though a previously failed application can jeopardise later chances of success if it is seen as indicating an undesirable lack of judgment on the part of the barrister concerned. As a result knowing quite when in one's career to make the necessary application is something of a test of nerves. All applications received by the Lord Chancellor are kept on file by his officials until after the summer vacation. Then the names of the various hopefuls are sent to the Lords of Appeal, the next roughly one hundred and fifty most senior judges in the country, a sprinkling of leading Queen's Counsel and some barristers' societies. Their observations on the merits of individual applicants are sought and once received are assembled together along with any additional information such as letters of recommendation from existing Queen's Counsel which candidates may arrange for the Lord Chancellor to be sent. All of the material which has been gathered is then sifted through by the Lord Chancellor's officials and a draft list of approved applicants prepared. The list then goes before the Lord Chancellor and a panel which includes several senior judges. Together with this panel the Lord Chancellor whittles the proposed names down into a final list of successful applicants by reference to such criteria as intellectual ability, skill in advocacy and conduct in court (whatever that means), with annual earnings being taken into account as a crude indication of just how prominent a barrister the individual applicant really is. Finally, after months of consideration the Lord Chancellor's Department publishes the names of the lucky few on the Thursday before Easter. After the Easter vacation the new Queen's Counsel are invited along to a swearing-in ceremony at the Palace of Westminster.

It really is open to question whether a more efficient system of choosing Queen's Counsel could not be put in place. After all it is difficult to imagine any commercial enterprise asking someone who had sought promotion to wait several months before making a response and then insisting that the response be given on a particular day simply because it seemed a nice day on which to give it. It is not as if the existing system meets with general approval. First of all there is the question of cost. In early-1999 a Parliamentary question by a backbench Labour MP prompted the revelation from the Lord Chancellor's Department that the process of selecting Queen's Counsel was costing the taxpayer in the region of £80,000 a year. With some barristers applying many times – one had applied 25 times – to become Queen's Counsel there was, not surprisingly, a degree of consternation that ordinary taxpayers should be asked to finance the appointments process, so much so that as of 1 September 1999 a new statutory order was put in place which, at the time of writing, requires aspiring QCs to pay £335 per application. Notwithstanding this change, however, there are still concerns about the system of selecting Queen's Counsel which has been widely alleged to be open to abuse. Stories are told of particular individuals being blocked from advancement through the animosity of a single judge with whom they have had the misfortune to cross swords in court. And there can be some surprise appointments. Until recently there was a tradition whereby all barristers elected to Parliament were appointed Queen's Counsel as a matter of course. This tradition seems to have died away but at least until quite recently it was still the case that Members of the House of Commons who happened to be barristers stood a better than average chance of becoming Queen's Counsel even if their period in Parliament had meant a substantial break from time spent down at the courts. The traditional explanation for this practice was that there needed to be suitably qualified candidates available within the House of Commons should a government legal office such as the Attorney-Generalship fall vacant. However the practice could also be seen as an exercise in government patronage, a convenient way of rewarding Members of the House who were barristers and who had been loyal to the party leadership and to the government of the day. Still the system has also been used in a more positive way. Lord Mackay of Clashfern, when Lord Chancellor, employed his best efforts to ensure that more coloured candidates were appointed as Queen's Counsel. Lord Irvine, the present Lord Chancellor, has continued this practice. In doing so both men have sought to encourage persons coming from ethnic minorities that there is a place for them within the legal profession and to ensure that there will be a pool of minority group candidates from which to appoint High Court judges in the future.

Although the average Lord of Appeal in Ordinary takes about 16 years to become a Queen's Counsel there are some very wide deviations from this average figure. Thus Lord Steyn managed to become a Queen's Counsel within a mere 6 years of commencing practice at the English Bar. His case of course is somewhat exceptional in that he had already been the equivalent of a Queen's Counsel in South Africa before his arrival in England. The fastest that any other Lord of Appeal in Ordinary has managed to ascend from being an ordinary barrister to being a King's or Queen's Counsel is 9 years. Only two Lords of Appeal have managed this feat.[23] Both these men belong to the select group of Lords of Appeal who have managed to become Queen's Counsel while still in their thirties.[24] Again Lord Steyn falls into an exceptional category of his own. Thus although he became a Queen's Counsel at the age of 47 he was made a Senior Counsel of the South African Supreme

Court at the age of 38. Not all Lords of Appeal enjoy such rapid advancement. Seventeen of them have waited 20 years or more before becoming a Queen's Counsel. And one of them, Lord Gordon, waited 33 years before advancing to this rank. Not surprisingly Lord Gordon is the Lord of Appeal who was oldest when he became a Queen's Counsel. And not surprisingly for someone whom it took a third of a century to progress beyond being an ordinary barrister Lord Gordon did not enjoy much of a reputation as a judge.

By the time they become a Queen's Counsel most Lords of Appeal will have been married for about 10 years. On the whole Lords of Appeal tend to get married for the first time rather later than the rest of the UK population (at an average age of 31), but on the whole their marriages tend to endure. Only 14 Lords of Appeal in Ordinary have ever remarried. And the main reason for this has been the death of a previous spouse. One Lord of Appeal, Lord Jauncey of Tullichettle, has been married three times. In 1948 at the age of 23 he married the daughter of an Admiral. (Lord Jauncey himself is the son of a Royal Navy Captain.) In 1969 this marriage ended in divorce. In 1973 Lord Jauncey married the widow of a Major. In 1977 this marriage too ended in divorce. Later in the same year Lord Jauncey married his third and present wife, the daughter of a Lieutenant-Colonel. Lord Jauncey is one of four Lords of Appeal who got married for the first time at the age of 23, the youngest age at which any Lord of Appeal has got married. The award for oldest Lord of Appeal-to-be when he first got married goes to Lord Wright who was 59 by the time he got round to exchanging vows with his wife, Lady Margery (who was a champion horse-jumper). Of the present Lords of Appeal, the oldest when he married for the first time is Lord Hutton of Bresagh, a Northern Irishman who wed his wife at the age of 44, five years after he became a Queen's Counsel and four years before he became a High Court judge. His colleague, Lord Browne-Wilkinson, was 60 when he got married for the second time in 1990.[25] The youngest of the present Lords of Appeal at the time he got married is Lord Hoffmann who shares with Lord Jauncey the distinction of having been 23 when he 'tied the knot'. Of those Lords of Appeal in Ordinary who have never got married, the last was Lord Morris of Borth-y-Gest who served on the Appellate Committee from 1960 until 1975. No Lord of Appeal has been openly homosexual. Most married Lords of Appeal have had children. On average they have tended to have between 3 and 4 children each with a pretty even spread of sons and daughters. Three Irish Lords of Appeal have had the largest families: Lord Fitzgerald had 13 children, Lord Macnaghten had 11 children and Lord Morris and Killanin had 10 children. Only when one gets to the fourth largest family does an English name appear: Lord Lindley had 9 children. He holds this position jointly with an Irishman, the first Lord Russell of Killowen, who also had 9 children. Of the present Lords of Appeal, Lord Steyn has 4 children and 2 step-children, while Lord Browne-Wilkinson has 5 children. Thus Lord Steyn has the largest family while Lord Browne-Wilkinson has the largest natural family.

Having become a Queen's Counsel the next leap in an aspiring Lord of Appeal's career is to become a judge. The average age upon appointment to the Bench is about 50. The youngest Lord of Appeal to make it into the higher ranks of the judiciary is Lord Morris and Killanin who in 1867 was raised to the Irish High Court bench at the age of 41. Lord Devlin is sometimes claimed to have been the youngest English Lord of Appeal to make it onto the High Court bench (at the age of 43). However he was pipped to the post by his fellow Englishman, Lord Hodson, who in 1937 was made a High Court judge at the age of 42. The youngest of the present Lords of Appeal to be appointed High Court judges (or their equivalent) is Lord Slynn of Hadley who was appointed at the age of 46.

Because all Lords of Appeal begin their legal careers at different ages, the age at which they become High Court judges is not perhaps as helpful in gauging their relative success *vis-à-vis* each other as is a consideration of the length of time it has taken them to progress from being a King's or Queen's Counsel to becoming a judge. Curiously enough Lord Hodson again comes out tops: in 1937 at the age of 42 he was appointed a High Court judge only a few months after becoming a King's Counsel. As it happens neither Lord Hodson nor his fellow barristers were surprised by the speed at which he was appointed to the bench. This is because Lord Hodson only applied to become a King's Counsel after he had been advised to do so by the Lord Chancellor of the day, Lord Maugham, who was badly in need of a divorce judge for the High Court.

Apart from Lord Hodson the Lords of Appeal who have spent the least time as King's or Queen's Counsel before being made judges are Lord Slynn of Hadley and Lord Asquith. Lord Slynn of Hadley is one of the present Lords of Appeal. He spent two years as a Queen's Counsel before his appointment to the High Court bench. So did Lord Asquith. However while Lord Slynn of Hadley's elevation to the judiciary was very much expected – he was after all one of the brightest Queen's Counsel of his day – Lord Asquith's appointment was not quite so well received. Asquith certainly had a very brilliant mind and enjoyed a glittering academic career at Oxford, obtaining a double first in his final degree and winning a string of scholarships before being elected a Fellow of Magdalen College. However he did not shine quite so brightly at the Bar and never had an especially large practice. In fact his promotion into the judiciary was greeted with considerable consternation – his obituary in *The Times* charitably describes it as "surprise" – on the part of Lord Asquith's contemporaries who felt that Asquith was appointed a judge more because his father had been Prime Minister than because of his professional abilities. Lord Hewart, the then Lord Chief Justice and head of the Division of the High Court to which Asquith was appointed, felt particularly aggrieved by the fact that he had not been consulted by the Lord Chancellor before Asquith was appointed to 'his' court. Notwithstanding all of this Asquith went on to put in 16 years as a perfectly competent judge before he died in office as a Lord of Appeal at the age of 64. As a judge he is not remembered for any particularly outstanding judgments. It is something of a reflection on the fate of children of successful men that despite making it to the very apex of the British judiciary the achievement which Lord Asquith is perhaps best remembered for is his co-authorship of the definitive biography of his father.

Until 1998 there was no formal application process whereby one could seek to become a High Court judge. The Lord Chancellor, who is responsible for nearly all judicial appointments in the United Kingdom, took private soundings from the legal great and good as to who might be an appropriate candidate to fill an available position on the High Court bench. Persons consulted by the Lord Chancellor included existing Lords of Appeal, Court of Appeal judges and High Court judges. Taking their advice into account the Lord Chancellor would settle upon a particular candidate who would then be approached and invited to accept a High Court judgeship. If the individual proved amenable to this invitation the Lord Chancellor would then approach the monarch and humbly advise that the person in question be appointed. British monarchs must be singularly affable people as this humble advice has traditionally been accepted. Not everyone asked to become a High Court judge has accepted the Lord Chancellor's invitation. This is scarcely surprising. After all, judges could now be said to be paid worse, respected less, and worked harder than at any other time in recent memory. As a result there is a concern that it is going to prove increasingly difficult to convince a first class Queen's Counsel that out of personal ambition or some sense of public service he (or she) should trade in a lucrative, high-profile, self-managed career for the comparatively ill-paid, hermit-like, routine existence of a High Court judge. This raises the unattractive possibility that in the future many senior judges, including Lords of Appeal in Ordinary (who of course are picked almost exclusively from the ranks of those who have once been superior court judges) will not be premier league material.

The reforms introduced in 1998 to the system of recruiting High Court judges were prompted by problems with the traditional system of selection and appointment. Because of these reforms the problems which occurred in the past may subside in the future. However it is possible to overestimate the likely effect of the 1998 reforms. And it is important to remember that there has been no change to the way in which Court of Appeal judges and Appellate Committee members are chosen. So to a not inconsiderable extent the difficulties with the traditional system of judicial appointment still exist today. Those difficulties have been manifold. Critics have alleged that the Lord Chancellor's practice of taking soundings as to who might make a good judge has tended to restrict the field of possible judges to those known personally or by reputation to the close circle of legal grandees customarily consulted. In consequence it has been suggested that candidates have needed to be 'one of us', part of the old boy, ex-public school, Oxbridge educated, conservative-minded network of white, upper-middle class (or upper class) males which has always dominated the judiciary. Certainly people of colour, women, and openly homosexual people have been notably absent from the bench. Freemasons on the other hand are said to have been warmly received, though given that people of colour, homosexual people, women and a host of other minority groups within the legal profession either may not or tend not to become Freemasons it seems likely that the rate of membership among the judiciary as it is presently structured in terms of gender and class make-up would in any event be rather higher than the general level of membership across society. Because the Freemasons are a secret organization this has prompted concerns among the general public that the impartiality of the judiciary might be compromised. On the other hand it must be remembered that it would be against the judicial oath of office for a judge to unfairly help a brother Mason in court. The number and names of judges who are Freemasons will be apparent in the future as a result of the Lord Chancellor's decision in the autumn of 1998 to make it mandatory for all new appointees to the judiciary to disclose whether or not they are Freemasons. Although he was not caught by this decision Lord Millett, one of the five new Lords of

Appeal who have been appointed since the Blair administration came to power, has never made any secret of the fact that he is a Freemason. The fact that there has never been any suggestion that this has affected Lord Millet in the discharge of his judicial responsibilities or in the conduct of his personal affairs would certainly suggest that in so far as the public is concerned about judges belonging to the Freemasons it is an unfounded concern.

Defenders of the traditional system of appointment and of the judges it produced would assert that in tandem with the Lord Chancellor's consultation process there had always been a natural streaming process in place. After all, the brightest people tend to be educated at Oxford, Cambridge, or equivalent universities in other jurisdictions. So if they entered the legal profession it was likely that they would rise to positions of eminence. And it was likely that the circle of people within which they move would include similarly bright persons who were just as deserving of promotion into the judiciary. If these people tended to fit a certain stereotype this was merely a reflection of who was making it into university and from there into the legal profession. With more people of colour and women entering the profession and the phobia that traditionally surrounded homosexuality on the decline it could be argued that any imbalance inherent in the system should remedy itself in time. And so far as personal grievances might result in an otherwise suitable candidate being blocked from appointment to the High Court surely the Lord Chancellor trawled sufficiently widely in the course of his consultation process to ensure that such a situation could not arise.

However even if one were to accept the rationale which seems to have underpinned the traditional system of appointment the manner in which that system was operated in practice did suffer from serious defects. Not least of these was that rightly or wrongly deserving Queen's Counsel who consistently failed to be offered a High Court judgeship and who happened not to come from the middle class or not to support a mainstream political party, or who happened, say, to be a person of colour, female, or homosexual, were left with the unpleasant suspicion that it was their social antecedents, their politics, their racial origins, their lifestyle, or their gender which precluded them from becoming High Court judges. It was small comfort to such Queen's Counsel to know that at some distant date when they were long dead and gone the system might remedy itself and lawyers who had not been to the right schools, or who had supported the 'wrong' causes, or who were people of colour, homosexual, or female, would be freely appointed to the bench. Making matters worse was the fact that the soundings conducted by the Lord Chancellor regarding prospective judges always took place in secret. As a result there were fears that otherwise suitable candidates could be blackballed by someone who had taken a personal dislike to them. Following his appointment the present Lord Chancellor, Lord Irvine of Lairg sought to assuage such fears but to a great extent the truth as to how adequately the traditional process functioned no longer mattered. The racial, sexual, and political composition of the judiciary which that process produced resulted in a situation whereby no number of pronouncements by the Lord Chancellor that social background, political persuasion, racial origin, sexual orientation, and gender were not relevant factors when it came to selecting judges could dispel the perception that those factors were in fact relevant. In any event there was some evidence to suggest the contrary of what the Lord Chancellor asserted, evidence which indicated that people had been discriminated against in the past for all the wrong reasons. The best known example is that of John Parris, a successful barrister in the 1950s. In the 1980s he discovered that his promotion to the High Court bench had been pretty much blocked by a particular judge who wrote a series of gossipy notes to the Lord Chancellor making a variety of spicy allegations about Parris including one (which was completely untrue) that Parris had slept with some of his clients.

As was mentioned the traditional system of appointing High Court judges has now been altered by the Blair administration – though not perhaps to the extent that some would have considered desirable. To counter the possibility of a John Parris-style situation arising again Lord Irvine of Lairg has introduced a requirement that any allegation of misconduct made in the course of consultation about a prospective judge must be specific and will be subject to disclosure to and correction by the relevant judicial candidate. However it seems that candidates will only be allowed correct mistaken *facts*. It does not appear that they will be allowed access to whatever general *opinions* are given regarding their suitability for judicial office. So it seems that it would still be possible for someone consulted by the Lord Chancellor to secretly blight an individual's chances of becoming a judge by making damaging remarks about intangible characteristics such as an individual's intellectual capacity, skills as an advocate, or demeanour in court.

The new Labour government has shrunk from appointing the independent commission responsible for the recruitment and training of judges which it promised in the run-up to the 1997 General Election. Although the idea seemed to be popular with the electorate it apparently met with strong opposition from senior members of the judiciary who were afraid that the courts might be brought into disrepute if under a more open recruitment procedure prospective judges were obliged to endure a public mauling similar to that which is nowadays afforded nominees to the United States Supreme Court. The compromise solution arrived at has been to commence advertising High Court judgeships publicly. This at least does something to ensure that future appointees will be drawn from a wider pool of candidates than has traditionally been the case. Those eligible to apply are barristers of 10 years' standing, solicitors who have trained as barristers and have enjoyed a right of argument before the High Court for 10 years, and experienced judges from the Circuit Court (the next court down from the High Court in the judicial hierarchy). Significantly the Lord Chancellor retains the right to consider candidates who do not put themselves forward and to reject all of those who do put themselves forward.

Under the new system candidates for the High Court bench are interviewed by a three-person panel composed of an existing High Court judge, a lay person (chosen from a panel of about 30 women and 20 men), and an official from the Lord Chancellor's Department. Ultimately, however, the Lord Chancellor continues to enjoy the last word as to who is to be appointed and his decision continues to be based in part on the results of his own soundings among judges and lawyers about the candidates concerned. In addition there has been no indication as to what criteria the Lord Chancellor will apply when deciding to consider as a possible candidate someone who has not even bothered to make a formal application. One must presume that his decision in this regard will be made on the basis of his own soundings. Lastly it remains the case that Lords of Appeal and Court of Appeal judges (the tier of judges immediately below the Appellate Committee) will continue to be selected behind closed doors. The Lord Chancellor's Department would presumably argue that as Lords of Appeal and Court of Appeal judges tend to be drawn from the High Court bench, any change in the system of appointing judges to the High Court will ultimately have an effect on the composition of the Court of Appeal and the Appellate Committee. However unless there is a concerted effort in the new recruitment process to produce a truly startling change in the composition of the High Court the chances of the higher ranks of the judiciary becoming more representative of society seem pretty slim.

Of course none of these issues are likely to have greatly affected the careers of the present Lords of Appeal or their predecessors in the last century and a quarter, all of whom have been white men, most of whom have been born into the middle or upper classes and an overwhelming number of whom have at some stage in their undergraduate or postgraduate careers attended one of a small selection of the finest universities. Having agreed to become a High Court judge (or the equivalent in Northern Ireland or Scotland) at an average age of about 50 they will have embarked upon a whole new career at a stage in their lives when most people might be slowing things down just a little. As a bonus on their promotion they will have been granted a knighthood sometime soon after their appointment. They will also have been fitted for a new set of work clothes which include a variety of black, red, and purple robes accentuated by a range of ermine, fur, and silk accessories, the particular combination on any given day depending on what type of case they are hearing, what season it is, and whether it is the monarch's official birthday or one of a range of Church of England feast-days. To top it all they will have become entitled to sport a shoulder length bell-bottomed wig (though on normal days they will wear shorter bench-wigs with curly tops, fuzzy sides and a little tail at the back). None of these clothes come cheap. Well over half a million pounds has been spent buying the necessary accoutrements for the present High Court judges, some of whom will also have dipped into their own annual salary for the odd extra item – happily any spending of this nature can be discounted from the relevant judge's income tax returns.

Around 8 years after his appointment to the High Court bench the average Lord of Appeal will be elevated to the Court of Appeal. He will now be in the region of 58 years old. Not all Appellate Committee members are appointed into the Court of Appeal from the High Court bench. Four have been elevated to this position from that of King's or Queen's Counsel. Nonetheless it is very much the norm for a Lord of Appeal to have had several years of judicial experience before he would be considered for appointment to the Court of Appeal. In theory such appointments fall within the gift of the Prime Minister and not the Lord Chancellor. But in fact most of the leg-work is done by the Lord Chancellor and his Department. They draw up a short-list of three candidates, list them in order of merit and give reasons why one appointment would be preferable to another. An explanation may also be offered as to why a particular candidate has not been included. The list is then passed on to the Prime Minister who usually (but not quite invariably) chooses the person ranked first on the list. One former Lord Chancellor, Lord Hailsham of St Marylebone, has stated that it might be a resigning matter for a Lord Chancellor if the Prime Minister chose a candidate who was not included in the Chancellor's list, and it would certainly be a resigning matter if the candidate chosen was entirely unsuitable for high judicial office. Within these parameters, however, the Prime Minister does retain a real discretion as to who will be appointed. Lord Hailsham has recounted how on one occasion someone who was ranked first by him on the list of candidates was rejected by the Prime Minister and the second-named recommended to the Queen instead. Lord Hailsham emphasises in his telling of this story that despite his "disagreement" with the Prime Minister, the judge in question went on to be an "outstanding success". Be that as it may the fact that the ultimate decision as to who should be appointed to the Court of Appeal rests on the personal whim of the Prime Minister is surely a matter for concern. The Prime Minister's role in this regard is nothing less than unnecessary political involvement with the already none too satisfactory judicial appointments process. Whether on a personal level a particular individual is particularly beloved by the Prime Minister does not seem an entirely relevant factor when deciding if they merit appointment to the Court of Appeal. When it is the opinion of the Lord Chancellor and those leading lawyers and judges whom he has consulted, that a particular individual is the best candidate for appointment to the Court of Appeal, it seems strange and wrong that the Prime Minister should be able to pick and choose who will be appointed, with the only real check on their actions being the need not to unduly antagonise the Lord Chancellor.

In any event, with his appointment to the Court of Appeal the prospective Lord of Appeal is only one step away from the very apex of the judiciary. Already as one of the most senior judges in the United Kingdom he wields enormous influence. What he says will be closely scrutinised by legal academics and practitioners in the United Kingdom, by the media of course, and by the many lawyers and judges in the huge number of countries which were once in the British Empire, which have adopted the English legal system (including its unwritten corpus of judicially fashioned laws known as the 'common law'), and which still rely to some extent on decisions of the English superior courts (the more superior the better) when seeking to determine what way the wind is blowing in so far as the development of the common law is concerned.

Membership of the Court of Appeal, like membership of the High Court, carries with it the right to wear a fantastically elaborate set of ceremonial robes: black silk gowns decorated in gold lace and worn over a morning suit, a waistcoat and a fine pair of knee breeches. The breeches are tucked into a pair of white socks or tights depending on the individual judge's preference. The outfit is crowned by the ever popular shoulder-length wig but perhaps most distracting is a fine pair of gold buckled black court shoes. These clothes are so rarely worn, so expensive and presumably so difficult to replace that they are normally passed on from one Court of Appeal judge to another, with a plain black gown and a short bench wig being worn on a normal day in court.

Ordinary judges in the Court of Appeal are known as Lords Justices of Appeal which can be a little confusing as they are not normally members of the House of Lords. That said there is always one member of the Court of Appeal (and often two) with a seat in the House. The Lord Chief Justice, who is head of the Queen's Bench Division of the High Court and an *ex officio* member of the Court of Appeal is always a member of the House of Lords. The present Lord Chief Justice is Lord Woolf. He previously served as Master of the Rolls.[26] Before his appointment as Master of the Rolls he spent four years as a member of the Appellate Committee. In October 2000 Lord Phillips of Worth Matravers will become Master of the Rolls in succession to Lord Woolf. It may seem odd that Lord Woolf and Lord Phillips of Worth Matravers would each agree to cease being a Lord of Appeal in Ordinary in order to assume the office of Master of the Rolls down in the Court of Appeal. However, in the English judicial hierarchy the three most eminent judges have traditionally been perceived as being the Lord Chancellor, the Lord Chief Justice and the Master of the Rolls, so it is considered a promotion for an ordinary member of the Appellate Committee to be appointed Lord Chief Justice or Master of the Rolls. Thus, for example, the first Lord Russell of Killowen quit as a Lord of Appeal in order to become the Lord Chief Justice. And Lord Denning, easily the most famous English judge this century, left the Appellate Committee to become Master of the Rolls. Lord Denning possibly had reasons other than ambition for resigning his tenure as a Lord of Appeal. He is alleged to have said that one of the reasons he agreed to become Master of the Rolls and move down to the Court of Appeal was that the Court of Appeal usually sits in panels of three whereas the Appellate Committee normally sits in panels of five. This meant he only had to persuade a single judge in order to ensure that his opinion prevailed whereas in the House of Lords he always had to get two other judges to agree with him.

Unlike Lords Woolf, Phillips of Worth Matravers, Russell of Killowen, and Denning, most Lords of Appeal tend to stay in the House of Lords after they have been sent there from the Court of Appeal (or the equivalent court in Northern Ireland or Scotland). There is normally one member from Northern Ireland and two from Scotland.[27] Scottish Lords of Appeal are apparently aware for some time before their elevation to the peerage that they are likely to be appointed Lords of Appeal. However any Lord Justice of Appeal (or his Northern Irish or indeed Scottish equivalent) with time to spare between conducting hearings can easily work out whether a vacancy will occur in the House of Lords in their area of specialisation before they reach retirement age. If such a vacancy will not occur there is always a chance that the judge in question will in any event be appointed if he is perceived as being a well-rounded candidate. His chances in this regard may well be improved if he manages to catch the eye of the Lord Chancellor by chairing a government inquiry or commission in addition to performing his ordinary judicial duties. Oftentimes it is pretty clear who is the most likely candidate to succeed a departing Lord of Appeal. But sometimes a couple or more candidates may seem to be appropriate. In these situations it is not entirely clear what selection criteria are applied.

The mechanics of appointing a Lord of Appeal are very similar to those which apply when appointing members of the Court of Appeal. Thus the Prime Minister is presented with a list containing possible candidates for appointment, each of them ranked in order of preference with a brief explanation as to why they might be a desirable choice. Constitutional theory has it that the Prime Minister then decides who is to succeed. It is a moment of absolute power. Or is it? Certainly the opportunity does exist for Prime Ministers to load the Appellate Committee with conservative or radical Lords of Appeal in the same way that American Presidents have traditionally sought to pack the US Supreme Court. However in recent history there has not been a single Lord Chancellor or Lord of Appeal who was appointed in the hope that he would follow a particular voting pattern. One reason why successive Prime Ministers do not seem to have been interested in playing around more with the composition of the Appellate Committee is that the Appellate Committee does not interpret a constitution and so great political issues (as opposed to great legal issues) have tended not to come before it. Of course this is now set to change. As was mentioned in the Introduction, Parliament has in the fairly recent past enacted legislation – the Human Rights Act 1998 – that will make the European Convention on Human Rights a keystone of British justice. The Convention is an international treaty that sets out the basic rights of Europeans in a constitution-like fashion. Once the legislation enacted by Parliament comes into effect in October 2000 the members of the Appellate Committee will be required to ensure that the rights enshrined in the Convention are respected and safeguarded within the United Kingdom. This will fundamentally alter the role of the Appellate Committee. It will become more like the United States Supreme Court. As the most eminent judicial body in the United Kingdom its decisions will have great political ramifications. And in consequence it could be that future Prime Ministers who wish to secure their particular political legacy will for the first time scrutinise the ideological outlook and not merely the professional credentials of those whom they are considering to appoint as Lords of Appeal. That said, the powers which the Appellate Committee will enjoy under the new legislation are so great that an overhaul of the Appellate Committee structure at some stage in the not too distant future is now more of a possibility than it was.[28] Any such overhaul would undoubtedly seek to curtail the potential which presently exists for Prime Ministers to 'pack' the Appellate Committee with Lords of Appeal who could be relied upon to vote in a certain way.

At the moment the only obstacle that might be encountered by a Prime Minister who sought to play around with the political make-up of the Appellate Committee is a run-in with the Lord Chancellor. However for a number of reasons this is not a very great obstacle. The main problem is that it is a matter for the Prime Minister alone to decide who should be appointed a Lord of Appeal. Even if the Lord Chancellor is opposed to a particular candidate the monarch will still be likely to appoint whoever the Prime Minister recommends. The Lord Chancellor might choose to resign but this would not necessarily result in the resignation of the new Lord of Appeal. Indeed short of the new Lord of Appeal being found guilty of some truly heinous crime there would be little or no chance of his being forcibly removed from office as it is thought that Lords of Appeal can only be dismissed following a resolution of both Houses of Parliament – something that is profoundly unlikely to occur. In any event it is probably a pretty futile hope to rely on a Lord Chancellor to resign. The Lord Chancellor is not only a judge. He is also a politician. Because of this it is singularly doubtful that a Prime Minister who appointed Lords of Appeal purely by reference to their politics would ever appoint anyone so thoroughly objectionable to his or her Lord Chancellor – who will after all be from the same end of the political spectrum as the Prime Minister – that the Lord Chancellor would feel compelled to resign. Anyway, for a Lord

Chancellor to quit office on the basis that there was undue political interference in the appointment of judges would blow a hole so big in any administration that only the most skilful of Prime Ministers could survive. So dramatic would the effect of a Lord Chancellor's resignation on this basis be that it is something of a political nuclear weapon: it remains the ultimate threat but it is difficult to envisage a situation in which it would be readily employed. Of greater concern to the Prime Minister would be a very hostile response from the media to the news that a particular individual was to be appointed a Lord of Appeal. However this has never occurred in the past and even were it to occur in the future a popular Prime Minister might well manage to withstand any criticisms were made. In short it seems that the greatest protection for the public would be a more open appointments process in which Lords of Appeal would be interviewed by a Parliamentary committee. This is not a reform which the judiciary wants, it may or may not be a reform that Downing Street wants, but it is possibly a reform that democracy demands.

Although the appointment of a Lord of Appeal is in the gift of the Prime Minister it is usually the Lord Chancellor who is first to pass on the good news. This tends to take the form of a telephone call to whichever judge the Prime Minister has selected. After the usual niceties the Lord Chancellor gets down to business, saying perhaps that Lord 'X' is about to retire, or that it is some time now since Lord 'Y' has died, and the Prime Minister rather wondered if the individual whom the Lord Chancellor is speaking to would be interested in taking the place of Lord 'X' or Lord 'Y' as one of Her Majesty's Lords of Appeal. If the person who receives the telephone call indicates that he would be interested in becoming a Lord of Appeal and most people offered the position are interested, he will be told by the Lord Chancellor that a formal offer will be forthcoming from the Prime Minister either by way of telephone or mail. Once this formal offer is accepted another few days pass before a letter arrives confirming that the Sovereign has been graciously pleased to approve the appointment of a new Lord of Appeal in Ordinary. Thereafter the good news is officially announced by the government. Around 40 years after becoming a barrister, 24 years after becoming a King's or Queen's Counsel, 15 years after becoming a judge, and 7 years after his most recent judicial appointment our new Lord of Appeal in Ordinary will now find himself moving in an exalted world of privilege and power. In the time it has taken him to reach this position he will have shown himself to be a man of learning and a competent judge. However over the same period of time he will have grown rather old. Indeed while Appellate Committee members nowadays tend to be slightly younger than the average figures given above would indicate – in the 1990s Lords of Appeal in Ordinary have been about 61 years of age on their appointment to the Committee – the fact that they are already in their sixties and must retire at 70 (subject to a discretionary power on the part of the Lord Chancellor to retain their services thereafter until they reach the age of 75) means that Lords of Appeal, at least since the introduction of a mandatory retirement age in 1993, have a guaranteed lifespan of less than a decade. This is very different from the situation in, say, the United States where federal Supreme Court judges are appointed for life. Indeed the introduction of mandatory retirement for superior court judges in the United Kingdom proved to be quite controversial when it happened and was the subject of criticism from a number of leading judges (including Lord Ackner, the onetime Lord of Appeal in Ordinary) who were particularly concerned that the Lord Chancellor – a Cabinet Minister – should have the power to select those members of the judiciary whose services he wished to retain once they had gone past the mandatory retirement age of 70. This they considered to be an unwarranted interference by the executive branch of the government with the affairs of the judiciary. However despite these concerns the Judicial Retirement and Pensions Act of 1993 was passed into law. One effect of this Act is that, if Prime Ministers continue to appoint Lords of Appeal in Ordinary who have already entered their sixties some time prior to being raised to the Appellate Committee, then in the future there will never be a Lord of Appeal in Ordinary who will be able over a protracted period of time to have a profound and positive impact on shaping and developing the law as has happened in the United States with such long-serving federal Supreme Court judges as William Brennan, William Douglas, and Felix Frankfurter[29] (or indeed as has happened in the United Kingdom in the past with judges like Lord Denning and Lord Reid whose terms in office preceded the introduction of mandatory retirement). That said the introduction of mandatory retirement may not have been an entirely bad thing. In the United States the fact that federal Supreme Court judges are given lifetime appointments means that they can continue to have an effect on the shaping of US public policy long after the President who appointed them has gone from office. As a result US Presidents have tended to nominate judges whose political ideology is akin to their own. Usually these nominees have been approved by Congress. Sometimes they have not. Either way the whole process has become distinctly partisan and somewhere along the way Supreme Court nominees have become fair game for politicians of all persuasions who are eager to score a point for or against the President of the day. In the United Kingdom things are quite different. The fact that Lords of Appeal in Ordinary are subject to mandatory retirement at seventy means that, even if they are retained for a while after that age, they are unlikely (certainly at the age at which they are presently appointed) to have as great an effect on the law as the average US Supreme Court justice is likely to have by virtue of sheer longevity in office and volume of cases in which an opinion is rendered. This relative lack of influence that any one Appellate Committee member can have may be another reason why British Prime Ministers have not in the past sought to appoint Appellate Committee members by reference to their political ideology. After all at less than ten years the guaranteed term in office of a Lord of Appeal in Ordinary (and hence the timeframe within which he will enjoy the power to shape the law) may well prove to be shorter than the term in office of the Prime Minister who appoints him. Whatever the reason for the traditional ambivalence of British Prime Ministers with regard to the political outlook of prospective Lords of Appeal in Ordinary it will be interesting to see whether this continues from October 2000 onwards when the Human Rights Act 1998 comes into force and the Appellate Committee begins to function, somewhat like the US Supreme Court, as a body charged with determining the compatibility of legislation with a written corpus of human rights.

The Men who have Served as Lords of Appeal in Ordinary[30]

1870s–1880s

Blackburn, Colin, (1813–96), Scotsman. Attended Eton and Cambridge University. Called to English Bar at age 25 (Lincoln's Inn). Never married. Had an unimpressive career as a barrister and was better known for his work as a reporter of cases than as an advocate. Was a surprise appointment to the judiciary. Spent 17 years on the High Court before being made the first Lord of Appeal in Ordinary in 1876. Under the 1876 Act it was intended that Lords of Appeal should only be members of the House of Lords for the period that they worked in that capacity. However this intended practice was thought to result in personal unfairness so when Blackburn resigned as a Lord of Appeal, and so resigned his membership of the House of Lords, he was quickly granted a new peerage.

Fitzgerald, John David, (1816–89), Irishman. Father a merchant. Called to the Irish Bar at age 22 (King's Inns). Married at age 30 and at age 44 after his first wife died. Thirteen children. Became a Queen's Counsel at the astonishingly young age of 31. Entered political life. Was a Liberal Member of Parliament. Served as Irish Solicitor-General and Irish Attorney-General before being appointed to the bench. Spent 22 years on the Irish High Court before being appointed directly into the House of Lords as a Lord of Appeal. As an Irish High Court judge he tried the Irish patriot leader O'Donovan Rossa and the leader of the Irish Home Rule Party, Charles Stewart Parnell. Aged 66 when appointed a Lord of Appeal he worked for 7 years in that capacity before he finally died.

Gordon, Edward Strathearn, (1814–79), Scotsman. Father an Army officer. Attended Edinburgh University and Glasgow University. Called to the Scottish Bar at age 21. Married at age 31. Never had children. Entered political life. Was a Conservative Member of Parliament for a Norfolk constituency. Became a Queen's Counsel at age 54. Spent six years as a superior court judge in Scotland before being appointed to the House of Lords as one of the first two Lords of Appeal to be appointed under the Appellate Jurisdiction Act 1876. Aged 62 when he was appointed a Lord of Appeal. Served for three years in that capacity (1876–9).

Macnaghten, Edward, (1830–1913), Irishman. Father a baronet and landowner. Attended Trinity College Dublin and then Cambridge University. Was elected a Fellow of Trinity College Cambridge. Called to the English Bar at age 27 (Lincoln's Inn). Married at age 28. Had 11 children. Entered political life as Conservative Member of Parliament for Antrim (a Northern Irish constituency) at age 50. Became a Queen's Counsel in the same year. Appointed a Lord of Appeal 7 years later and served in that capacity for a further 26 years.

Morris and Killanin, Michael Morris (took the title of Morris and Killanin), (1826–1901), Irishman. Father the High Sheriff of Galway. Attended Trinity College Dublin. Won a gold medal for his brilliance but was precluded by his religion from receiving a Foundation Scholarship (Morris was a Catholic). Was called to the Irish Bar at age 23 (King's Inn). Married at age 34. Had 10 children. Became a Queen's Counsel at age 37. Entered political life. Was elected Independent Member of Parliament for Galway though subsequently served as Irish Solicitor-General and Irish Attorney-General in two Conservative administrations. Appointed to the High Court at age 41. Served 20 years on that court, 2 years on the Court of Appeal, and went on to serve 11 years as a Lord of Appeal. Notorious among contemporaries for his caustic wit.

Watson, William, (1827–99), Scotsman. Father a clergyman. Attended Glasgow and Edinburgh Universities. Called to the Scottish Bar at age 24. Married at age 41. Was the father of the future Lord Thankerton (who served as a Lord of Appeal from 1929 until 1948). Served as Scottish Solicitor-General and Lord Advocate (essentially the Attorney-General for Scotland) under Disraeli before being appointed straight into the House of Lords as a Lord of Appeal at age 53. Served in this capacity for 19 years (from 1880 until his death in 1899). Was noted for a certain brusqueness of character.

1890s–1900s

Bowen, Charles Synge Christopher, (1835–94), Englishman. Father a Protestant clergyman. Attended school in France when a child. Later attended Rugby and from there progressed to Oxford University. Called to the English Bar at age 26 (Lincoln's Inn). Married at age 27. Had three children. Spent 3 years on the High Court, 11 years on the Court of Appeal, and one year as a Lord of Appeal. Aged 58 on his appointment to the House of Lords his career was cut short by his premature death. A distinguished classical scholar, Bowen managed to produce verse translations of several works of antiquity (including Virgil's *Aeneid*) while working as a Court of Appeal judge.

Collins, Richard Henn, (1842–1911), Irishman. Father a barrister. Attended Trinity College Dublin and (later) Cambridge University. Became a Fellow of Downing College, Cambridge. Called to the English Bar at age 25 (Middle Temple). Married at age 26. Had five children. Became a Queen's Counsel at age 41. Spent 6 years on High Court, 10 years on the Court of Appeal, and 3 years as a Lord of Appeal. Aged 65 when appointed to the House of Lords.

Davey, Horace, (1833–1907), Englishman. Attended Rugby School. Progressed to Oxford University where he initially studied maths and classics before moving on to law. Called to the English Bar at age 28 (Lincoln's Inn). Married at age 29. Six children. Became Queen's Counsel at age 42. Entered political life. Was elected Liberal Member of Parliament for Christchurch. Briefly served as Solicitor-General under Gladstone but lost this position when he lost his seat in Parliament and proved unable to gain and keep another. Appointed to the Court of Appeal at the age of 60 he spent a year on that Court before being elevated to the House of Lords as a Lord of Appeal. Died in office in 1907 after 13 years' service. Was thought to be a rather cold character by his contemporaries.

Hannen, James, (1821–94), Englishman. Father a wine merchant. Attended Heidelberg University. Called to the English Bar at age 27 (Middle Temple). Married at age 26. Became a Queen's Counsel at age 47. Was a government investigator in the Charles Stewart

Parnell case. Appointed straight into the House of Lords at age 70 as a Lord of Appeal. Died three years later.

Lindley, Nathaniel, (1828–1921), Englishman. Father a university professor. Attended University of London. Called to the English Bar at age 22 (Middle Temple). Married at age 30. Nine children. Became Queen's Counsel at age 44. Was appointed to High Court 3 years later, to the Court of Appeal 6 years after that and 19 years on he was appointed a Lord of Appeal, serving in that capacity from 1900 until 1905.

Robertson, James Patrick Bannerman, (1845–1909), Scotsman. Father a clergymen. Attended Edinburgh University. Called to the Scottish Bar at age 22. Married at age 27. Three children. Became a Queen's Counsel at age 40. Became Unionist Member of Parliament for Buteshire – a Scottish constituency. Served as Solicitor-General for Scotland and as Lord Advocate (the chief law officer of Scotland). Became a Lord of Appeal in Ordinary at a youthful 54 years of age. Seemed set for a lengthy career in the House of Lords but died suddenly when he was 64.

Russell of Killowen, Charles Russell, (1832–1900), Irishman. Father a merchant. Attended Trinity College Dublin but did not graduate (a not infrequent practice in the nineteenth century). Married at age 26. Nine children. Called to the English Bar at age 27 (Lincoln's Inn). Acquired a reputation as a rather aggressive advocate. Entered political life. Began campaigning as Liberal Parliamentary candidate for Durham City but withdrew in favour of Farrer Herschell, the future Lord Chancellor, when it became clear that the electorate would not vote for him on account of his being a Catholic. Was ultimately elected Independent Liberal Member of Parliament for the Irish constituency of Dundalk. Later went on to become Member for the London borough of Hackney. Was a prominent supporter of Home Rule for Ireland. Served as Attorney-General under Gladstone. Out of office he acted as defence counsel for the leader of the Irish Home Rule Party, Charles Stewart Parnell, when the latter became embroiled in an adultery scandal. Became a Lord of Appeal in May 1894. Less than a month later he agreed to become Lord Chief Justice. This involved Russell moving down to the Court of Appeal and the Divisional Courts but was considered a step up in the judicial hierarchy. Served as Lord Chief Justice for 6 years. Died in office. Both his son and grandson were also Lords of Appeal.

Shaw, Thomas (later took the title Lord Craigmyle), (1850–1937), Scotsman. Father a baker. Attended Edinburgh University. Taught there for a while before being admitted to the Scottish Bar at age 25. Entered political life. Was elected Liberal Member of Parliament for the Scottish Burghs. Became a Queen's Counsel at age 46. Married at age 49. Never had children. Served as Scottish Solicitor-General and as Lord Advocate before being appointed a Lord of Appeal in 1909. Served in that capacity until his retirement in 1929.

1910s–1920s

Atkin, James Richard, (1867–1944), Australian. A relative of Charles Darwin. Father an Irishman who emigrated to Australia and became member of Queensland Assembly. After father died Atkin was brought up in Wales by his mother. Attended Oxford University. Called to English Bar at age 24 (Gray's Inn). Married at age 26. Seven children. Appointed King's Counsel at age 39. Spent 6 years on the High Court and 9 years on the Court of Appeal before being appointed to the House of Lords. Is remembered among lawyers for his classic account of the law of negligence in *Donoghue* v. *Stevenson* (1932) and his courageous lone dissent in *Liversidge* v. *Anderson* (1941) against what he perceived to be the abuse of the wartime emergency powers conferred on the Home Secretary. Aged 61 when appointed to the House of Lords he remained in office until his death 6 years later.

Atkinson, John, (1844–1932), Irishman. Father a medical doctor. Attended Queen's College Galway (now University College Galway, one of the constituent colleges of the National University of Ireland). Called to Irish Bar at age 21 (King's Inns, Dublin). Married at age 29. Four children. Appointed Queen's Counsel at age 36. Entered political life. Was Conservative Member of Parliament for North Derry. Served as Irish Solicitor-General and Irish Attorney-General. Was appointed Lord of Appeal without having previously served as a judge which prompted some controversy at the time. Spent 23 years as a Lord of Appeal (1905–28). Aged 61 when appointed.

Blanesburgh, Robert Younger, (took the title of Blanesburgh), (1861–1946). Scotsman. Father a brewery-owner. Attended Edinburgh University and later Oxford University. Called to English Bar at age 23 (Inner Temple). Never married. Appointed Queen's Counsel at age 39. Spent 4 years on the High Court, 4 years on the Court of Appeal, and 14 years as a Lord of Appeal (1923–7). Aged 62 when appointed to the House of Lords. Quit the Appellate Committee when his eyesight failed him.

Carson, Edward Henry, (1854–1935) Northern Irishman. Father an engineer. Attended Trinity College Dublin. Called to Irish Bar at age 23 (King's Inns, Dublin). Married at age 25 and re-married at age 60 after his first wife died. Five children. Appointed Queen's Counsel at age 35. Entered political life. Served as Member of Parliament for Trinity College Dublin and as Irish Solicitor-General. While still an MP he moved permanently to England and was called to the English Bar at age 39 (Middle Temple). Became an English Queen's Counsel at age 40. Served as English Solicitor-General. Became leader of the Unionist cause at the age of 56 and remained faithful to this cause for the rest of his political life, to the point of rejecting the chance to become Conservative Party leader. Almost single-handedly managed to ensure that Northern Ireland remained in the United Kingdom. In 1922, the year that the division of Ireland finally occurred, Carson resigned as leader of the Unionist cause and ws appointed a Lord of Appeal in Ordinary. Even as a Lord of Appeal he continued to argue the Unionist cause within the House of Lords. Aged 68 when appointed to the House of Lords he remained a Lord of Appeal for another 7 years and then retired.

Dunedin, Andrew Graham Murray, (took the title of Dunedin), (1849–1942), Scotsman. Father a part-owner of a whisky distillery. Attended Harrow, then proceeded to Cambridge University and later to Edinburgh University. Married at age 25 and at age 74 after his first wife died. Called to Scots Bar at age 25. Became a King's Counsel at age 41. Entered political life. Was a Conservative Member of Parliament for Buteshire (a Scottish constituency). Served as Solicitor-General and as Secretary of State for Scotland. Thereafter he served as a Scottish judge until being made a Lord of Appeal at age 64. Served as a Lord of Appeal from 1913 until 1932.

Moulton, John Fletcher, (1844–1921), Englishman. Father a clergyman. Attended Cambridge University. Elected a Fellow of Christ's College, Cambridge. Awarded a GBE after the First World War for his masterful organisation of the wartime explosives supply department. Called to the English Bar at age 30 (Middle Temple). Married at age 31 and at age 57 (after his first wife died). Two children. Appointed Queen's Counsel at age 41. Entered political life. Was Liberal Member of Parliament for Clapham (a London constituency), for South Hackney (another London constituency) and for a Cornwall constituency. Was appointed straight on to the Court of Appeal at age 62. Was appointed a Lord of Appeal 6 years later. Died in office.

Parker of Waddington, Robert John Parker (took title Parker of Waddington), (1857–1918). Father a clergyman. Attended Westminster School and Eton before advancing to Cambridge University. Called to the Bar at age 27 (Lincoln's Inn). Married at age 27. Five children. Appointed to the High Court at age 49 and 7 years later was created a Lord of Appeal without pausing *en route* to do a stint of judging on the Court of Appeal.

Robson, William Snowdon, (1852–1918), Englishman. Father a Justice of the Peace. Attended Cambridge University. Called to the English Bar at age 28 (Inner Temple). Married at age 35. Four children. Entered political life. Was Liberal Member of Parliament for two London constituencies. Became Queen's Counsel at age 40. Served as Solicitor-General of England and as Attorney-General before being raised directly into the House of Lords as a Lord of Appeal.

Russell of Killowen, Francis Xavier Joseph Russell (assumed title of Russell of Killowen), (1867–1946). Father a Lord of Appeal and Lord Chief Justice of England. Although the younger Russell was born in England and lived all his life in England the fact that his father was a famous Irishman led to the son being viewed by his contemporaries as an Irishman. Attended Oxford University. Called to the

English Bar at age 26 (Lincoln's Inn – like his father before him). Married at age 33. Four children. Became a Queen's Counsel at age 41. Appointed to the High Court at age 52. Chose to refuse the customary knighthood that goes with that position. Spent 9 years as a High Court judge and one year on the Court of Appeal before emulating his father and becoming a Lord of Appeal. On accepting his life peerage he decided to take the same title (Russell of Killowen) that his father, another life peer, had held before him. Served as a Lord of Appeal for 17 years, retiring a few months before he died in 1946. His only son was also to become a Lord of Appeal.

Sumner, John Andrew, (1859–1934), Englishman. Father an iron merchant. Attended Oxford University. Elected a Fellow of Magdalen College, Oxford. Called to the Bar at age 24 (Inner Temple). Married at age 33. Never had children. Became a Queen's Counsel at age 42. Appointed to the High Court at age 50. Spent 3 years as a High Court judge, one year on the Court of Appeal, and 17 years as a Lord of Appeal from 1913 until 1930. Widely considered to have been the premier member of the Appellate Committee in his day. Reputed for the quality of his judgments, for the prose he used in them, and for his acid wit.

Thankerton, William Watson, (1873–1948), Scotsman. Father a Lord of Appeal in Ordinary (Lord Watson). Attended Winchester School and Cambridge University. Called to the Scottish Bar at age 26. Married at age 29. Three children. Entered political life. Elected Unionist Member of Parliament for South Lanarkshire and later for Carlisle (two Scottish constituencies). Became a King's Counsel at age 41. Appointed straight into the House of Lords as a Lord of Appeal at the age of 56. Spent 19 years in this capacity (1929–48).

Tomlin, Thomas James Cheshyre, (1867–1935), Englishman. Attended Harrow School and later went to Oxford University. Called to the Bar at age 24 (Middle Temple). Married at age 29. Three children. Became King's Counsel at age 46. Appointed to the High Court at age 56. Promoted straight into the House of Lords as a Lord of Appeal in 1929 and died in office 6 years later.

1930s–1940s

Du Parcq, Herbert, (1880–1949), Jerseyman. Attended Oxford University. Called to the Bar at age 26 (Middle Temple). Spent 6 years on the High Court, 8 years on the Court of Appeal, and 3 years as a Lord of Appeal (1946–9). Aged 66 when appointed to the House of Lords, he died in office.

Goddard, Rayner, (1877–1971), Englishman. Father a solicitor. Attended Marlborough School and Oxford University. Called to the Bar at age 22 (Inner Temple). Married at age 29. Three children. Became a King's Counsel at age 46. Was a dismally unsuccessful Independent Conservative candidate for Parliament in 1929. Successively spent 6 years on the High Court bench, 6 years on the Court of Appeal, 2 years as a Lord of Appeal in Ordinary (1944–6) and 12 years as Lord Chief Justice of England and Wales. Although he had the reputation of being a very harsh sentencer and a rather gruff judge Goddard was apparently quite convivial in private.

Greene, Wilfrid Arthur, (1883–1952), Englishman. Attended Oxford University. Called to the English Bar at age 25 (Inner Temple). Married at age 26. Never had children. Became a King's Counsel at age 39. Was promoted straight into the Court of Appeal at age 52. Spent 14 years on the Court of Appeal, 12 of them as Master of the Rolls, before being appointed a Lord of Appeal (which was actually a step downwards in the judicial hierarchy). Spent less than a year in the House of Lords before he had to retire as a result of ill-health.

MacDermott, John Clarke, (1896–1979), Northern Irishman. Father a clergyman. Attended Queen's University Belfast and subsequently lectured there. Called to the Irish Bar at age 25 (King's Inns). Married at age 30. Had 4 children. Became King's Counsel at age 40. Entered political life. Was Unionist Member of Parliament for Queen's University Belfast. Served in the Army, as Minister for Public Security and as Attorney General during the Second World War. Appointed to the High Court in 1944. Became a Lord of Appeal 3 years later but quit the House of Lords in 1951 to become Lord

Chief Justice of Northern Ireland. Had the reputation of being an exceedingly stern judge.

Macmillan, Hugh Pattison, (1873–1952), Englishman. Father a clergyman. Attended Edinburgh and Glasgow Universities. Was an examiner at Glasgow University. Called to the Scottish Bar at age 24. Married at age 28. Never had children. Appointed a King's Counsel at age 39. Never had children. Served as Solicitor-General in the Labour administration of Ramsay MacDonald but was never elected to Parliament. Appointed straight into the House of Lords from the Bar at age 57. Served in that capacity until 1947 save for 2 years as Minister for Information during the Second World War. An exceptionally able man, he was not afraid to let others know it.

Morton of Henryton, (1887–1973), Scotsman. Attended Cambridge University. Called to the English Bar at age 25 (Lincoln's Inn). Served in the Army during the First World War and was awarded the Military Cross for Bravery. Married at age 41. One child. Appointed to the High Court at age 51. Spent 6 years on the High Court bench, 3 years on the Court of Appeal and 12 years as a Lord of Appeal. Aged 60 when appointed a Lord of Appeal.

Normand, Wilfrid Guild, (1884–1962), Scotsman. Father a linen merchant. Attended Oxford, Paris, and Edinburgh Universities. Served in the Army during the First World War. Called to the Scottish Bar at age 26. Married at age 29 and at age 43 (after his first wife died). Two children. Became a King's Counsel at age 41. Entered political life. Was Unionist Member of Parliament for West Edinburgh. Served as Solicitor-General for Scotland and as Lord Advocate. Spent 12 years as a superior court judge in Scotland. Appointed Lord of Appeal in Ordinary at age 63 and served for 6 years.

Oaksey, Geoffrey Lawrence Trevethin (took title Trevethin and Oaksey but was known as Lord Oaksey), (1880–1971), Englishman. Father served as Lord Chief Justice of England and was made a peer as a result. Attended Oxford University. Served in the Army during the Second World War and was twice mentioned in despatches.

Called to the English Bar at age 26 (Inner Temple). Married at age 41. Four children. Became a King's Counsel at age 45. Was appointed to the High Court at age 52. Spent 12 years on the High Court bench, 3 years on the Court of Appeal, and 10 years as a Lord of Appeal in Ordinary. In 1945 he served as the British President of the Nuremberg War Crimes Tribunal. Appointed Lord Oaksey when he became a Lord of Appeal he later inherited the peerage that had initially been granted to his father when he became Lord Chief Justice in 1921 and so ended his day as a double peer, Lord Trevethin and Oaksey.

Porter, Samuel Lowry (1877–1956), Englishman. Father a warehouse manager. Attended Cambridge University. Called to the English Bar at age 28 (Inner Temple). Never married. Became a Queen's Counsel at age 47, a High Court judge at age 57, and was appointed straight into the House of Lords as a Lord of Appeal at the age of 61. Enjoyed his fifteen minutes of fame when he dissented from the opinion of his brother Lords of Appeal in the post-war trial of 'Lord Haw-Haw', concluding that the Crown had not done enough to satisfy the burden of proof in a treason trial (the Crown proved that 'Haw-Haw', actually William Joyce, an Irishman, had acquired a British passport in 1939, but did not prove – as Porter felt it ought – that Joyce had in fact kept or used the passport, and so shown sufficient allegiance to the British Crown as to render him liable for treason when he went on to broadcast Nazi propaganda from Berlin to Britain during the Second World War). Retired in 1954 after 16 years service as a Lord of Appeal.

Radcliffe, Cyril John, (1899–1977), Englishman. Father an Army officer. Attended Oxford University. Was elected a Fellow of All Souls College Oxford. Called to the English Bar at age 25 (Inner Temple). Became a King's Counsel at age 36. Married at age 40. Never had children. Was appointed straight into the House of Lords at age 50. Retired 15 years later. Reputed to have preferred government committee work to his judicial duties whilst a Lord of Appeal.

Reid, James Scott Cumberland, (1890–1975), Scotsman. Father a Scots lawyer. Attended Cambridge and Edinburgh Universities. Served in the Army during the First World War. Called to the

Scottish Bar at age 24. Entered political life. Became a Unionist member of Parliament for Stirling (a Scottish constituency) and later for Glasgow. Became a Queen's Counsel at age 42. Married at age 43. Served as Scottish Solicitor-General and as Lord Advocate (essentially the Attorney-General of Scotland) before going on to serve as Lord of Appeal for 26 years (from 1948 to 1974). Is considered to be one of the greatest of the post-Second World War Lords of Appeal.

Roche, Alexander Adair, (1871–1956), Englishman. Father a medical doctor. Attended Oxford University. Called to the English Bar at age 25 (Inner Temple). Married at age 31. Three children. Became a King's Counsel at age 41. Appointed to the High Court at age 46. Spent 17 years as a High Court judge, one year as a Court of Appeal judge and 3 years as a Lord of Appeal (from 1935 to 1938).

Romer, Mark Lemon, (1866–1944), Englishman. Father a Court of Appeal judge. Attended Rugby and then went on to Cambridge University where he studied maths. At college he became a friend of Frederic Maugham who later married Lord Romer's sister and later still went on to become both a Lord of Appeal and Lord Chancellor at roundabout the same time that Lord Romer himself became a Lord of Appeal.[31] Oddly enough Lord Maugham was not the only Lord of Appeal to whom Lord Romer was related – his wife's sister married Lord Russell of Killowen who served as a Lord of Appeal from 1929 to 1946. Lord Romer was called to the English Bar at age 24 (Lincoln's Inn). Married at age 27. Two children. Became Queen's Counsel at age 40. Sixteen years later went on to become a High Court judge. Spent 7 years in that capacity, 9 years on the Court of Appeal, and 6 years as a Lord of Appeal (from 1938 to 1944).

Uthwatt, Augustus Andrewes, (1879–1949), Australian. Father a landowner/lord of a manor. Attended Melbourne and Oxford Universities. Called to the English Bar at age 25 (Gray's Inn). Married at age 48. Never had children. Appointed to the High Court at age 62 and elevated to the House of Lords as a Lord of Appeal at age 67. Died in office 3 years later.

Wright, Robert Alderson, (1869–1964), Englishman. Father a marine superintendent. Attended Cambridge University. Elected a Fellow of Trinity College Cambridge. Was also a part-time teacher of law at Cambridge University. Called to the English Bar at age 31 (Inner Temple). Married at age 59. Never had children. Became a King's Counsel at age 48. Appointed to the High Court at age 58 and put straight onto the Court of Appeal 7 years later. Retired in 1947 after 15 years service. As the first Chairman of the United Nations War Crimes Commission he was the man responsible for assembling the prosecution evidence against the Nazi war criminals tried at Nuremberg.

1950s–1960s

Asquith of Bishopstone, Cyril Asquith, (1890–1954), Englishman. Father was the Liberal Prime Minister who led Britain into the First World War. Attended Oxford University. Called to English Bar at age 30 (Inner Temple). Married at age 28. Four children. Appointed King's Counsel at age 46. Spent 8 years on High Court, 5 years on Court of Appeal and 3 years as a Lord of Appeal (1951–4). Aged 61 when appointed to House of Lords. Died in office.

Cohen, Lionel Leonard, (1888–1973), Englishman. Father a knight. Attended Eton and from there progressed to Oxford University where he studied law. Called to English Bar at age 30 (Inner Temple). Married at age 30. Three children. Appointed King's Counsel at age 41. Spent 3 years on the High Court, 5 years on the Court of Appeal and 9 years as a Lord of Appeal (1951–60). Aged 63 when appointed to the House of Lords.

Denning, Alfred Thompson, (1899–1999), Englishman. Easily the most famous Lord of Appeal of the twentieth century. Father a draper. Oxford graduate – took a first class degree in maths, then lectured in maths before going on to take a first class law degree. Called to the Bar at age 24 (Lincoln's Inn). Married at age 33 and re-married at age 46 after his first wife died (his second wife was herself a widow). Became a King's Counsel at age 39. Was appointed to the High Court at age 45. Moved on to the Court of Appeal four years later and became a Lord of Appeal nine years after that. Quit the Appellate Committee after four years to return to the Court of

Appeal as Master of the Rolls, an office he was to hold for the next two decades. As Lord of Appeal he caught the public eye as the man who headed the investigation into the political scandal that led to the resignation of John Profumo, the Defence Secretary in the Macmillan administration. Was an often controversial judge whose insistence that justice ought to be done in the individual case before him frequently led him into clashes with his brother judges who felt a more uniform approach to deciding cases was preferable. On 23 January 1999 Lord Denning became the first onetime Lord of Appeal to reach the age of 100. Six weeks later he died.

Devlin, Patrick Arthur, (1905–92), Scotsman. Father an architect. Commenced training as a Dominican monk but decided to become a lawyer instead. Attended Oxford University. Called to the English Bar at age 24 (Gray's Inn). Married at age 27. Six children. Became Queen's Counsel at age 40. Spent 12 years on the High Court, one year on the Court of Appeal and in 1961 entered the Appellate Committee as its youngest member (aged 56). Quit the Appellate Committee three years later for reasons that are still unclear. It may have been the personal tension that existed between him and the then Lord Chancellor, Viscount Dilhorne. If so, Lord Devlin left a mite too soon: Viscount Dilhorne lost the Chancellorship a few months after Lord Devlin's resignation and did not sit with the Appeal Committee again until he was appointed a Lord of Appeal in Ordinary in 1969. Another reason that has been suggested is Lord Devlin's frustration at the shoestring manner in which the Appellate Committee was expected to run itself. In his retirement Devlin served as Chairman of the Press Council and on various government committees. In the 1980s he again came before the public eye as an advocate for the release of the 'Guildford Four', four alleged IRA terrorists whom Devlin believed to have been wrongfully imprisoned and who were subsequently released early from prison.

Diplock, William John Kenneth, (1907–85), Englishman. Father a solicitor. Attended Oxford University. Called to the English Bar at age 25 (Middle Temple). Married at age 31. Never had children. Became King's Counsel at age 41. Spent 5 years on the High Court, 7 years on the Court of Appeal and 17 years as a Lord of Appeal (1968–85). Aged 61 when appointed to the House of Lords. One of the most eminent Lords of Appeal this century and perhaps one of the least popular with counsel, towards whom he could sometimes be less than convivial. Among the general public he was best known for helping to bring about the establishment of 'Diplock' courts in Northern Ireland, that is courts in which judges have decided criminal cases without the assistance of jurors (juries being considered by Diplock to be particularly prone to tampering in the abnormal security conditions that have prevailed in Northern Ireland).

Donovan, Terence Norbert, (1898–1971), Englishman. Served in the Army and the Royal Air Force during the First World War. Called to the English Bar at age 26 (Middle Temple). Married at age 27. Became King's Counsel at age 47. Three children. Entered political life. Was a Labour Member of Parliament for Leicester. Was a surprise appointee to the High Court bench at the behest of Earl Jowitt, the Labour Lord Chancellor. Spent 10 years on the High Court, 3 years on the Court of Appeal, and 8 years as a Lord of Appeal (1963–71). Aged 65 when appointed to the House of Lords.

Evershed, Francis Raymond, (1899–1966), Englishman. Father a solicitor. Attended Oxford University. Served in the Army during the First World War. Called to the Bar at age 24 (Lincoln's Inn). Married at age 29. Never had children. Became King's Counsel at age 34. Successively spent two years on the High Court, 15 years on the Court of Appeal (13 of them as Master of the Rolls, the head of the Civil Division of the Court), and 3 years as a Lord of Appeal (1962–5). It was considered a move down in the judicial hierarchy to go from being Master of Rolls to being a regular Lord of Appeal in Ordinary but by the time he made this move at the age of 63 Evershed had begun to feel the stresses of age and was happy to take a job that was of great importance but involved less administrative work. (He was replaced as Master of the Rolls by Lord Denning, who for the previous 5 years had been a Lord of Appeal, and who was to remain as Master of the Rolls until his retirement in 1982 at the age of 83.)

Guest, Christopher William Graham, (1901–84), Englishman. Attended Cambridge University and Edinburgh University. Called to the Scottish Bar at age 26. Married at age 40. Had five children. Became a King's Counsel at age 44. Stood as a Unionist Candidate in the Kircaldy Burghs (a Scottish constituency) in the 1945 General Election. An unlikely prospect from the outset he was roundly trounced by his Labour Party opponent in the Labour Party's landslide victory of that year. His loyalty to the Conservative Party was rewarded when he was appointed a Lord of Appeal at the behest of the Macmillan administration. He was aged 60 at the time of his appointment and retired 10 years later.

Hodson, Francis Charlton, (1895–1984), Englishman. Father a clergyman. Attended Cheltenham College and then advanced to Oxford University. Called to the English Bar at age 26 (Inner Temple). Married at age 23. Three children. Became Queen's Counsel at age 42. Was appointed specifically so that he might be elevated to the High Court bench (a specialist in divorce law, he applied for silk on the recommendation of Lord Maugham, the Lord Chancellor of the day, who was anxious to get a divorce law expert onto the High Court bench). Spent 14 years on the High Court bench, 9 years on the Court of Appeal, and 11 years as a Lord of Appeal (1960–71).

Jenkins, David Llewellyn, (1899–1969), Englishman. Father a surveyor. Attended Charterhouse School before going on to Oxford University. Served with the Army during the First World War. Called to the English Bar at age 24 (Lincoln's Inn). Never married. Became King's Counsel at age 38. Appointed a High Court judge 9 years later. Spent 2 years on the High Court, 10 years on the Court of Appeal, and 4 years in the House of Lords (1959–63).

Keith of Avonholm, James Keith (took the title Keith of Avonholm), (1886–1964), Scotsman. Attended Glasgow University. Studied history first. Later turned to the law. Served in the Army during the First World War. Called to the Scottish Bar at age 25. Married at age 29. Three children (one of them a future Lord of Appeal, Lord Keith of Kinkel). Became Queen's Counsel at age 40. Appointed to the Scottish judiciary at age 51. Sixteen years later was appointed to the House of Lords. Spent 8 years as a Lord of Appeal (1953–61).

Morris of Borth-y-Gest, John William Morris (took the title Morris of Borth-y-Gest), (1896–1979), Welshman. Father a bank manager.

Served in the First World War and was awarded the Military Cross for bravery. Attended Cambridge University and later went to Harvard University for a year. Called to the English Bar at age 25 (Inner Temple). Never married. Twice stood as Liberal Party candidate for the Parliamentary seat of Ilford (in London) but failed each time. Became a King's Counsel at age 39. Appointed to the High Court 10 years later. Spent 6 years as a High Court judge, 9 years as a Court of Appeal judge and 15 years as a Lord of Appeal (1960–75). Aged 64 when appointed a Lord of Appeal.

Pearce, Edward Holroyd, (1901–90), Englishman. Father a headmaster. Attended Charterhouse before proceeding on to Oxford University. Called to the English Bar at age 24 (Lincoln's Inn). Married at age 26. Two children. Became a King's Counsel at age 44. Was appointed to the High Court 3 years later. Spent 9 years as a High Court judge, 5 years on the Court of Appeal, and 7 years as a Lord of Appeal (1962–9). As a young barrister Pearce almost died of tuberculosis. During his recuperation he took up oil-painting. Over the years that followed he became an accomplished landscape artist with several shows to his credit. Indeed the newspaper obituaries that followed his death in 1990 almost invariably describe him as a British lawyer/judge and painter.

Pearson, Colin Hargreaves, (1899–1980), Canadian (but came to England at age 7). Father a Canadian lawyer. Attended Oxford University. Called to the Bar at age 26 (Inner Temple). Married at age 32. Two children. Became a King's Counsel at age 50. Something of a surprise appointment to the High Court 2 years later but quickly established himself as a far more prominent judge than he had been a barrister. Spent 10 years on the High Court, 4 years on the Court of Appeal, and 9 years as a Lord of Appeal in Ordinary (1965–74).

Somervell of Harrow, Donald Bradley Somervell, (1889–1960), Englishman. Father a schoolteacher at Harrow. Attended Harrow before going on to Oxford University. Was elected a Fellow of All Souls College, Oxford. Served in the Army during the First World War. Called to the Bar at age 27 (Inner Temple). Became a King's Counsel at age 40. Entered political life. Was elected Unionist Member of Parliament for Crewe. Served as Solicitor-General,

Attorney-General, and Home Secretary before being appointed straight onto the Court of Appeal at age 57. Married at age 44. Never had children. Spent 8 years on the Court of Appeal before being appointed a Lord of Appeal in 1954. Died shortly after his retirement in 1960.

Tucker, Frederick James, (1888–1975), Englishman. Father a Member of the South African Parliament. Attended Winchester School and then went on to Oxford University. Called to the English Bar at age 26 (Inner Temple). Married at age 30. Never had children. Served in the Army during the First World War. Became a Queen's Counsel at age 45. Appointed to the High Court at age 49. Spent 8 years on the High Court, 5 years on the Court of Appeal, and 11 years as a Lord of Appeal (1950–61).

Ujohn, Gerald Ritchie, (1903–71), Englishman. Father a King's Counsel. Attended Eton and then went on to Cambridge University. Called to the English Bar at age 26 (Lincoln's Inn). Served in the Army during the Second World War. Became a King's Counsel at age 40. Married at age 44. Never had children. Appointed to the High Court at age 48. Spent 9 years as a High Court judge, 3 years on the Court of Appeal, and 8 years as a Lord of Appeal (1963–71).

Wilberforce, Richard Orme, (1907–), Englishman. Attended Winchester School and Oxford University. Was elected a Fellow of All Souls College, Oxford. Called to the Bar at age 25 (Middle Temple). Served in the Army during the Second World War. Married at age 40. Two children. Became a Queen's Counsel at age 47. Appointed to the High Court at age 54. Elevated to the House of Lords as a Lord of Appeal at age 57. Spent 18 years in this capacity from 1964 until 1982 and was considered one of the shining lights of the Appellate Committee in his day.

1970s–1980s

Ackner, Desmond James Conrad, (1920–), Englishman. Father a medical doctor. Attended Cambridge University. Served in the Army during the Second World War. Called to the English Bar at age 25

(Middle Temple). Married at age 26. Three children. Specialised in commercial law. Made a Queen's Counsel at age 41. Spent 9 years on the High Court, 6 years on the Court of Appeal and 6 years as a Lord of Appeal (1986–92). Aged 66 when appointed to House of Lords.

Brandon of Oakbrook, Henry Vivian Brandon, (1920–1999), Englishman. Father an Army officer. Attended Cambridge University. Served in the Army during the Second World War. Called to the English Bar at age 26 (Inner Temple). Married at age 35. Four children. Spent 12 years on the High Court, 3 years on the Court of Appeal, and 10 years as a Lord of Appeal (1981–91). Aged 61 when appointed to the House of Lords.

Bridge of Harwich, Nigel Cyprian Bridge, (1917–), Englishman. Father a Navy officer. Attended Marlborough and Cambridge University. Served in the Army during the Second World War. Called to the English Bar at age 30 (Inner Temple). Married at age 27. Three children. Spent 7 years on the High Court, 5 years on the Court of Appeal, and 12 years as a Lord of Appeal (1980–92). Aged 63 when appointed to the House of Lords.

Brightman, John Anson, (1911–), Englishman. Attended Marlborough and Cambridge University. Served in the Navy during the Second World War. Called to the English Bar at age 21 (Lincoln's Inn). Married at age 34. One child. Spent 9 years on the High Court, 3 years on the Court of Appeal, and 4 years as a Lord of Appeal (1982–6). Aged 71 when appointed to the House of Lords.

Cross of Chelsea, Arthur Geoffrey Neale Cross, (1904–89), Englishman. Attended Cambridge University. Became a Fellow of Trinity College, Cambridge. Called to the English Bar at age 26 (Middle Temple). Married at age 25. Five children. Spent 6 years on the High Court, 10 years on the Court of Appeal and 4 years as a Lord of Appeal (1971–5).

Edmund-Davies, Herbert, (1906–92), Welshman. Attended London University and subsequently studied at Cambridge University. Called to the English Bar at age 23 (Gray's Inn). Married at age 29. Three children. Spent 8 years on the High Court, 8 years on the Court of

Appeal, and 7 years as a Lord of Appeal (1974–81). Aged 68 when appointed to the House of Lords. As a High Court judge he was the man who tried the Great Train Robbers.

Fraser of Tullybelton, (1911–89), Scotsman. Father a stockbroker. Attended Oxford University and Glasgow University. Lectured in constitutional law at Glasgow University and Cambridge University. Served in the Army during the Second World War. Called to the Scottish Bar at age 25. Married at age 32. One child. Became a Queen's Counsel at age 42. Sought to enter political life as a Conservative Member of Parliament for East Edinburgh (though at the time that he ran for Parliament it was not uncommon for Scottish advocates to run for seats that they stood little chance of winning in order that they might become noticed by the political party of their choice and hence likely to receive preference whenever their party triumphed at the polls). Spent 10 years as a superior court judge in Scotland before going on to become a Lord of Appeal. Aged 64 when appointed he spent 10 years as a Lord of Appeal (1975–85). Killed in a car crash at the age of 78.

Goff of Chieveley, Robert Lionel Archibald Goff (assumed the title Goff of Chieveley), (1926–), Englishman. Father an ex-Army officer. Attended Eton and later studied at Oxford University. Served in the Army from 1945 to 1948. Became a Fellow and Tutor at Lincoln College, Oxford. Was called to the Bar at age 25 (Inner Temple). Married at age 27. Four children. Became Queen's Counsel at age 41. Eight years later was appointed to High Court. Spent 7 years on the High Court, 4 on the Court of Appeal. Was a Lord of Appeal for 12 years (1986–98) and senior Lord of Appeal for 2 years. Was called back from retirement to sit on the second Pinochet appeal (ex-Lords of Appeal may sit with the Appellate Committee until they reach the age of 75 at which point they become ineligible to act as judges). Voted to reverse the decision of the Appellate Committee in the first Pinochet appeal.

Griffiths, William Hugh, (1923–), Welshman. Father a medical doctor. Attended Charterhouse School before going on to Cambridge University. Served in the Army during the Second World War. Married immediately after the War at age 26. Four children. Called to the English Bar at age 26 (Inner Temple). Became a Queen's Counsel at age 41. Spent 9 years on the High Court, 5 years on the Court of Appeal and 8 years as a Lord of Appeal (1985–93). Became captain of St Andrews Golf Club in the year after he retired.

Jauncey of Tullichettle, (1925–), Scotsman. Father served as a Royal Navy officer. Attended Oxford University and later went to Glasgow University. Is one of the last Lords of Appeal to have seen service during the Second World War. Called to the Scottish Bar at age 24. Made a Queen's Counsel at age 38. Spent 9 years as a superior court judge in Scotland before being appointed a Lord of Appeal at the age of 63. Served from 1988 to 1996. Is a member of the Royal Company of Archers (the Queen's Body Guard for Scotland).

Keith of Kinkel, Henry Shanks Keith, (took title of Keith of Kinkel), (1922–), Scotsman. Father a Lord of Appeal in Ordinary (Lord Keith of Avonholm). Attended Oxford University and at Edinburgh University. Served in the Second World War and was mentioned in despatches. Called to the Scottish Bar at age 28. Married at age 33. Has 5 children. Became a Queen's Counsel at age 40 (the year after his father died). Spent 6 years as a judge in Scotland before moving on to serve as a Lord of Appeal from 1977 to 1996. Was senior Lord of Appeal in Ordinary for his last 10 years in office. Aged 55 on being appointed a Lord of Appeal.

Kilbrandon, Charles James Dalrymple Shaw (took the title of Kilbrandon), (1906–89), Scotsman. Father a county clerk. Attended Charterhouse School and later Oxford and Edinburgh Universities. Called to the Scottish Bar at age 26. Married at age 31. Had 5 children. Became King's Counsel at age 43. Spent 12 years on the College of Justice (the highest court in Scotland) before being appointed a Lord of Appeal at the age of 65. Served for 5 years from 1971 to 1976.

Lane, Geoffrey Dawson, (1918–), Englishman. Attended Shrewsbury School and then went on to Cambridge University. Served in the RAF during the Second World War. Married at age 26. Has one child. Called to the English Bar at age 28 (Gray's Inn). Became Queen's Counsel at age 44. Appointed to High Court bench 14 years later.

Successively spent 8 years on High Court bench, 5 years on Court of Appeal bench, and barely a year as a Lord of Appeal (1979–80) before leaving to become Lord Chief Justice of England and Wales, an office he held from 1980 until 1992.

Lowry, Robert Lynd Erskine, (1919–99), Northern Irishman. Father was successively a Unionist MP, Attorney-General for Northern Ireland and a judge. Attended Cambridge University. Served in the Army during the Second World War. Called to the Northern Irish Bar at age 28. Married at age 26 and at age 75 (after his first wife died). Three children. Became a Queen's Counsel at age 37. Appointed to the Northern Irish High Court at age 45. Spent 7 years in that capacity before being appointed Lord Chief Justice of Northern Ireland (in succession to Lord MacDermott – oddly enough MacDermott stepped down from being a Lord of Appeal in order to become Lord Chief Justice whereas Lowry moved in the opposite direction). Lowry was the victim of an IRA gun ambush in 1982. His first wife and one of his daughters were the victims of an attempted IRA kidnap in 1983. Was appointed to the House of Lords in 1979 and became a Lord of Appeal in Ordinary in 1988. Served in that capacity until 1984.

Oliver of Aylmerton, Peter Raymond Oliver (assumed title Oliver of Aylmerton), (1921–), Englishman. Father a Cambridge don. Attended Cambridge University. Served in the Army during the Second World War and was mentioned in despatches. Called to the English Bar at age 27 (Lincoln's Inn). Married at age 24 and at age 66 (after his first wife died). Two children. Became a Queen's Counsel at 44. Appointed to the High Court bench at age 53. Spent 6 years on the High Court, 6 years on the Court of Appeal, and 6 years as a Lord of Appeal in Ordinary.

Roskill, Eustace Wentworth, (1911–), Englishman. Father a King's Counsel. Attended Winchester School and Oxford University. Called to the English Bar at age 22 (Middle Temple). Married at age 27. Two children. Became Queen's Counsel at age 42. Appointed to the High Court at age 51. Spent 9 years on the High Court, 9 years on the Court of Appeal, and 6 years as a Lord of Appeal (from 1980 to 1986).

Russell of Killowen, Charles Ritchie Russell (took the title Russell of Killowen), (1908–86). Although he was born in England and lived all his life in England the fact that Russell came from a prominent Irish family meant that he was always viewed as something of an Irishman. Father and grandfather were also Lords of Appeal. Attended Oxford University – went to Oriel College like his father before him. Called to the English Bar at age 23 (Lincoln's Inn – like his father and grandfather before him). Married at age 25. Three children. Served in the Army during the Second World War. Mentioned in despatches and won the French *Croix de Guerre* for bravery. Became a King's Counsel at age forty (like his grandfather before him) and was appointed to the High Court at age 52 (like his father before him). Spent 7 years on the High Court, 13 years on the Court of Appeal, and 7 years as a Lord of Appeal (1975–82). As a Lord of Appeal he chose to assume the same life title that his father and grandfather had held before him. His funeral in 1986 was the occasion of some controversy: a Catholic ceremony, it was attended by Lord Mackay of Clashfern, who later got into trouble with the Elders of the Free Presbyterian church to which he belonged for having attended a Catholic service.

Salmon, Cyril Barnet (1903–91), Englishman. Attended Cambridge University. Called to the Bar at age 22 (Middle Temple). Married at age 26 and at age 43 (after first wife died). Two children. Served in the Army during the Second World War. Became a King's Counsel at age 42. Raised to the High Court bench at age 54. Spent 7 years on the High Court, 8 years on the Court of Appeal, and 8 years as a Lord of Appeal (1972–80). Known among his colleagues for his quite devastating wit.

Scarman, Leslie George, (1911–), Englishman. Attended Oxford University. Called to the English Bar at age 25 (Middle Temple). Served in the Royal Air Force during the Second World War. Was honoured by the Soviets with an Order of Battle Merit for bravery in 1945. Married at age 36. One child. Became a Queen's Counsel at age 46. Appointed to the High Court at age 50. Spent 12 years on the High Court, 4 years on the Court of Appeal, and 9 years as a Lord of Appeal (1977–86). Well known to the public as a champion of law reform.

Simon of Glaisdale, Jocelyn Edward Salis Simon (took the title Simon of Glaisdale), (1911–), Englishman. Attended Cambridge University. Called to the English Bar at age 23 (Middle Temple). Married at age 23 and at age 37 (after his first wife died). Served in the Army during the Second World War. Became a King's Counsel at age 40. Entered political life. Was Conservative Member of Parliament for Middlesborough. Served as Solicitor-General before being appointed to the High Court Bench at age 51. Spent 9 years as a High Court judge before being appointed straight into the House of Lords as a Lord of Appeal. Served as a Lord of Appeal from 1971 until 1977.

Templeman, Sydney William, (1920–), Englishman. Attended Cambridge University. Called to the Bar at age 27 (Middle Temple). Served in the Army during the Second World War and was mentioned in despatches. Became a Queen's Counsel at age 44. Appointed to the High Court at age 52. Spent 6 years as a High Court judge, 4 years on the Court of Appeal, and 12 years as a Lord of Appeal (1982–94).

1990s

Bingham of Cornhill, Thomas Henry Bingham (has assumed the title Bingham of Cornhill), (1933–), Englishman. Attended Sedbergh as a schoolboy before proceeding to Oxford University as a student. Had a distinguished academic career. Called to the Bar at age 26. Married at age 30. Has three children. Succeeded in being made a Queen's Counsel while still in his thirties. Appointed a High Court judge at age 47. Has enjoyed a remarkable judicial career that has included being Master of the Rolls, Lord Chief Justice of England and Wales and, most recently, the senior Lord of Appeal in Oridinary. Has joined the Appellate Committee at a particularly significant moment in its history. With the Human Rights Act 1998 set to come into force in October 2000 the members of the Appellate Committee (like other judges) will from that time forward acquire the power to determine the compatibility of UK legislation with a written constitution-like framework of basic human rights. Of course the Appellate Committee, as the most important judicial body within the United kingdom, will have a particularly significant role to play.

Browne Wilkinson, Nicolas Christopher Henry, (1930–), Englishman. Attended Lancing and Oxford University. Called to the English Bar at age 23 (Lincoln's Inn). Married at age 25 and re-married at age 60 after his first wife died. Five children. Became Queen's Counsel at age 42. Appointed to the High Court at age 47 and to the Court of Appeal six years later. Served as a Lord of Appeal from 1991 and as the senior Lord of Appeal for two years from mid-1998 to mid-2000. His reputation was (and is) of being a pragmatic, middle-of-the-road judge and an affable man. In his free time he is a keen gardener.

Clyde, James John, (1932–), Scotsman. Father a Scottish peer. Attended Oxford University and Edinburgh University. Called to the Scottish Bar at age 27. Married at age 31. Two children. Became Queen's Counsel at age 39. Spent 11 years as a superior court judge in Scotland. Has been a Lord of Appeal since 1996.

Hobhouse of Woodborough, John Stewart Hobhouse (has assumed the title Hobhouse of Woodborough), (1932–), Englishman. Studied at Eton. Then went to Oxford University. Called to the English Bar at age 23. Married at age 27. Related by marriage to Lord Diplock, a Lord of Appeal in Ordinary between 1968 and 1985. Three children. Became a Queen's Counsel at age 41. Appointed to the High Court at age 50. Elevated to the Court of Appeal at age 61. Was among the first two of the new 5 Lords of Appeal appointed by Tony Blair.

Hoffmann, Leonard Hubert, (1934–) Attended Cape Town University and Oxford University (as a Rhodes scholar). Returned to South Africa. Married at age 23. Two children. Called to the South African Bar at age 24. Two years later he returned to England with his family but without a job arranged. Initially found employment with a firm of solicitors. Was later appointed a tutor in law at Oxford University. Called to the English Bar at age 30 (Gray's Inn). Became a Queen's Counsel at age 43. Was appointed to the High Court at age 51. Spent seven years as a High Court judge, three years on the Court of Appeal, and has been a Lord of Appeal in

Ordinary since 1995. Considered to be perhaps the most brilliant of the present Lords of Appeal.

Hope of Craighead, James Arthur David Hope (has assumed the title Hope of Craighead), Scotsman. Father and grandfather were superior court judges in Scotland. Attended Cambridge and Edinburgh Universities. Called to the Scottish Bar at age 27. Married at age 28. Three children. Became a Queen's Counsel at age 40. Served for 7 years as a superior court judge in Scotland. Was granted a peerage in 1995 and made a Lord of Appeal in Ordinary the year after that.

Hutton, James Brian Edward, (1931–), Northern Irishman. Attended Oxford University and Queen's University Belfast. Called to the Northern Irish Bar at age 23. Married at age 28. Two children. Became a Queen's Counsel at age 39. Appointed to the Northern Irish High Court at age 48. Promoted to the Northern Irish Court of Appeal as Lord Chief Justice of Northern Ireland in 1988. Served in this latter capacity for 8 years until his appointment to the House of Lords as a Lord of Appeal in Ordinary.

Lloyd of Berwick, Anthony John Leslie Lloyd (has taken the title Lloyd of Berwick), (1929–), Englishman. Attended Eton. Progressed to Cambridge University. Continued on to Harvard University. Returned to Cambridge as a Fellow of Peterhouse (one of the constituent colleges of Cambridge University). Called to the English Bar at age 26 (Inner Temple). Married at age 31. No children. Became a Queen's Counsel at age 38. Appointed a High Court judge at age 49. Spent 6 years on the High Court bench, nine years on the Court of Appeal and six years as a Lord of Appeal in Ordinary.

Millett, Peter Julian (1932–), Englishman. Was a schoolboy at Harrow. Subsequently studied at Cambridge University. Called to the English Bar at age 23. Married at age 27. Appointed to the High Court in 1986 Millett rapidly established himself as one of the most able and intelligent superior court judges. He also acquired a reputation as being consistently pleasant to counsel who argued before him. Was appointed to the High Court in 1986. Moved to the Court of Appeal in 1994. Was promoted onto the Appellate Committee along with Lord Hobhouse in 1998.

Mustill, Michael John, (1931–), Englishman. Attended Cambridge University. Called to the English Bar at age 24 (Gray's Inn). Twice married (first marriage ended in divorce). Two children. Became a Queen's Counsel at age 37. Appointed to the High Court at age 47. Spent 7 years on the High Court bench, 7 years on the Court of Appeal and 6 years as a Lord of Appeal. Is the author of several legal textbooks including a leading textbook on arbitration law.

Nicholls of Birkenhead, Donald James Nicholls (has taken the title Nicholls of Birkenhead) (1933–), Englishman. Attended Liverpool University and Cambridge University. Called to the English Bar at age 25 (Middle Temple). Married at age 27. Three children. Became a Queen's Counsel at age 41. Appointed to the High Court at age 50. Has been a Lord of Appeal in Ordinary since 1994. Also serves as one of the two British members of the Hong Kong Court of Appeal (the body that replaced the Privy Council as the final court of appeal for Hong Kong when the former Crown Colony was returned to China in July 1997).

Nolan, Michael Patrick, (1928–), Englishman. Attended Oxford University. Called to the English Bar at age 25 (Middle Temple). Married at age 25. Five children. Became a Queen's Counsel at age 40. Appointed to the High Court bench at age 54. Served as a Lord of Appeal from 1994 to 1998. Became well-known publicly when in 1994 he was appointed head of the Committee on Standards in Public Life. Although his involvement with the Committee ended in 1997, Nolan's almost full-time work as its head for over two years meant that he did not have as much time as would otherwise have been the case to devote to being a Lord of Appeal until his work with the Committee was over.

Phillips of Worth Matravers, Nicholas Phillips (has taken the title Phillips of Worth Matravers), (1938–), Englishman. Attended Bryanston School and Cambridge University. Did his national service with the Royal Navy. Called to the English Bar at age 24 (Middle Temple). Became a Queen's Counsel soon after he turned 40. Appointed to the High Court at a comparatively youthful 49. Was elevated to the Court of Appeal eight years later. Appointed a Lord of Appeal in January 1999. Much of his time since becoming a

Lord of Appeal has been occupied with his work as Chairman of the BSE Inquiry established on foot of the 'Mad Cow Disease' crisis. Will become Master of the Rolls in October 2000. Is married with 4 children (2 of whom are step-children).

Saville of Newdigate, Mark Oliver Saville (has assumed the title Saville of Newdigate), (1936–), Englishman. Attended Oxford University. Married at age 25. Called to the English Bar at age 26 (Middle Temple). Two children. Became a Queen's Counsel at age 39. Elevated to the High Court bench at age 49. Spent 8 years as a High Court judge and 3 years on the Court of Appeal before being appointed a Lord of Appeal in 1997. Is known to be something of a fan of computer technology. Has been appointed by the Blair administration to investigate the 'Bloody Sunday' incident in Derry in 1972 when unarmed civilians were shot and killed by members of the Parachute Regiment.

Scott, Sir Richard Rashleigh Folliott, (1934–), Englishman. At the time of writing Sir Richard Scott is not yet a Lord of Appeal in Ordinary. However, it has been announced that he will be appointed to the Appellate Committee in October 2000 following the departure of Lord Phillips of Worth Matravers (who is to become the new Master of the Rolls). Born in India, Scott will be one of three Lords of Appeal in Ordinary who did their primary university degree in South Africa. (The other two are Lord Hoffmann – who, like Scott, studied at Cape Town University – and Lord Steyn, who studied at the University of Stellenbosch). After his time in South Africa Scott proceeded to Cambridge University and after completing his studies there he spent a year at the University of Chicago. Called to the Bar at age 25. Married at age 25. Became a Queen's Counsel at age 41. Eight years after that he was appointed a High Court judge. Since then he has served as a Lord Justice of Appeal and Vice-Chancellor. As a judge Scott is perhaps best known to the general public as the man who conducted the 'Arms to Iraq' inquiry.

Slynn of Hadley, Gordon Slynn (has assumed the title Slynn of Hadley), (1930–), Englishman. Attended the University of London and Cambridge University. Called to the Bar at age 26 (Gray's Inn). Married at age 32. No children. Lectured at the London School of

Economics for 3 years. Became a Queen's Counsel at age 44. Appointed to the High Court bench at age 46. Appointed Advocate-General at the European Court of Justice in Luxembourg at age 51. Appointed a Judge of the European Court of Justice at age 58. Created a Lord of Appeal in Ordinary in 1992 at age 62.

Steyn, Johan, (1932–) Attended the University of Stellenbosch in South Africa and Oxford University (as a Rhodes Scholar). Called to the South African Bar at age 26. Twice married. Has 4 children and 2 step-children. Became a Senior Counsel of the Supreme Court of South Africa at age 38. Moved to England in 1973. Joined Lincoln's Inn and commenced practice at the English Bar. Became a Queen's Counsel in 1979. Appointed to the High Court in 1985, to the Court of Appeal in 1992, and became a Lord of Appeal in 1995.

Woolf, Harold, (1933–), Englishman. Attended London University. Called to the Bar at age 21 (Inner Temple). Married at age 28. Three children. Appointed to the High Court at age 46. Spent 7 years as a High Court judge and 6 years on the Court of Appeal before being appointed a Lord of Appeal in 1992. Quit the Appellate Committee after 4 years to return to the Court of Appeal as Master of the Rolls. A prominent advocate for reform of the legal system and the prisons system. In June 2000 he was appointed Lord Chief Justice of England and Wales in succession to Lord Bingham of Cornhill.

3
The Lord Chancellor

The role of Lord Chancellor – the present Lord Chancellor – the early Lord Chancellors – receiving the Great Seal – the Great Purse – the Lord Chancellor as speaker of the House of Lords – the Lord Chancellor as judge – the problems with having a politician as head of the judiciary – the Lord Chancellor as Government Minister – the Lord Chancellor as Keeper of the Royal Conscience – the Lord Chancellor and religion – the Lord Chancellor as keeper of public records – the future role of the Lord Chancellor

The most eminent person to sit on the Appellate Committee is the Lord Chancellor. But the Lord Chancellor is more than an *ex officio* member of the Appellate Committee. He is the head of the judiciary in England and Wales. He is a senior member of Cabinet. And he is the Speaker of the House of Lords. In short he stands in a unique position at the meeting-point of the judicial, executive and legislative branches of government. The present individual appointed to perform all of these tasks is Lord Irvine of Lairg. He is the 234th person to have been Lord Chancellor since the Norman invasion. At the beginning of 1998 he became a household name to many people in Britain as the member of government who was allegedly spending somewhere in the region of £300 of taxpayers' money on each and every roll of wallpaper that he was using to decorate his official residence inside the Palace of Westminster. It is unfortunate for Lord Irvine that while the great majority of ordinary British people might not be entirely aware of his unique constitutional status as the only public office-holder with a foot in the executive, legislative and judicial branches of government, they are acutely aware of the price of a roll of wallpaper – and at an alleged £300 a go this Lord Chancellor's taste in interior decoration seemed a trifle expensive. It seemed so to journalists as well. Indeed with scurrilous disregard for the dignity of the office of Lord

Chancellor (and with not a lot else to report on the world scene) the mighty British press began rooting around early in 1998 to see exactly how much money Lord Irvine was spending on the Westminster quarters which modern Lord Chancellors are given as their official London home. The figures they came up with did sound like rather a lot: £5,000 for blinds, £5,000 for ceramic tiles, £9,640 for a dinner table, £11,000 for various oddments such as tableware, £16,000 for a couple of beds, £20,000 for curtains, £21,000 for carpets, £56,000 for light fittings, £96,000 for soft furnishings, and somewhere in the region of £350,000 for general renovation work. Indeed Lord Irvine's refurbished flat was soon being portrayed by a bemused press as some sort of latter-day Versailles. Matters were not helped when it was announced that Lord Irvine proposed borrowing more than 90 works of art from galleries including the National Gallery of Scotland, the Imperial War Museum and the Royal Academy to decorate his residence. It is worth noting that these institutions were perfectly happy to lend the works to the Lord Chancellor and that as a result of being exhibited in his residence, part of which can be used for public functions, the works were effectively exhibited to a broader range of people than would otherwise have been the case. Notwithstanding this, however, Members of Parliament were soon demanding that the Lord Chancellor account for his behaviour. At the beginning of March 1998 the matter was raised with the Lord Chancellor in person by members of the Select Committee on Public Administration. They asked why the Lord Chancellor had engaged in such apparently lavish spending on his official residence. But Lord Irvine did not agree that he had been spending lavishly: his effort to preserve the Lord Chancellor's residence was "a noble cause", all the money spent was something for which "future generations will be grateful", he joined with those commentators who were saying "Three cheers that this work has been done". It was a spirited defence from a man who fills an office that is older than Parliament itself and which is in constitutional terms a higher (and in financial terms a better-paid) job than that of Prime Minister.

The office of Lord Chancellor dates from at least the early Middle Ages. It pre-dates the invasion of Britain by William the Conqueror in 1066 and may well have been around for several hundred years before that. The origins of the modern office are generally dated from the reign of Edward the Confessor who became King of England in 1042. Edward was the first King of England to have a standard seal which was attached to all of his formal correspondence and deeds as an indication of their authenticity. The safe-keeping of this seal was entrusted to his secretary. The practice was continued under the Norman kings who referred to this secretary as the *cancellarius*. This was a Latin term which came from the days of the Roman Empire. The Normans took the word and applied it to the King's secretary (who was also the keeper of the King's seal). Over time the word '*cancellarius*' was corrupted into the modern word 'Chancellor'.

Even today the primary task of the Chancellor is to keep safe the 'Great Seal' of Britain or to be more precise the matrix of the Great Seal from which all copies of the Great Seal are made. Indeed the formal commencement in office of a Chancellor begins from the moment he receives the matrix of the Great Seal from the Sovereign. As in the days of Edward the Confessor copies of the Great Seal are attached to the highest documents of state as evidence of their authenticity. To counterfeit the Seal is treason. So important is the Great Seal that when King James II was fleeing England in 1688 he tossed the matrix for the Seal into the River Thames in an attempt to hinder the process of government while he was away. From Saxon times until the 1920s copies of the Seal were made of wax. Unfortunately wax seals are not of great assistance after a few years in determining the authenticity of a state document as they almost invariably crumble and disintegrate. In consequence the Seal is now made of plastic. As environmentalists will unhappily testify plastic never decays. Plastic however is more fun as it means the Seal can be produced in a range of different colours. Thus the seals attached to the letters of appointment of High Court and Court of Appeal judges are red. But the seals attached to the letters of appointment of Lords of Appeal in Ordinary are green.

At one time the matrix of the Great Seal was kept in a special purse. In the thirteenth century the purse was red. In the fifteenth century the purse was white. Then in the sixteenth century Cardinal Wolsey (to whom the present Lord Chancellor has jocularly likened himself) decided to splash out on a magnificent purse of crimson velvet which was glitteringly decorated with the royal coat of arms. Just in case the glitter would lose its sparkle it became the practice to buy a new purse every year. Today new purses are purchased roughly once every three years. However the purse is now only used to hold the speech written by the government and delivered by the Queen at every State Opening of Parliament. These days the matrix of the Great Seal is carried in a box. It is not certain when this practice began but it is a comparatively recent occurrence. Certainly the matrix was carried in a purse in the eighteenth century. One story has it that the change was effected by a Lord Chancellor of that time after the matrix ripped through the Great Purse while he was carrying it and fell and broke his foot. Old purses are given to the serving Lord Chancellor as a little perk on top of his annual salary and in the past have been put to some interesting uses: they have been used as seat covers, cushion covers and have even been stitched together to make sets of curtains.

In the House of Lords the Lord Chancellor normally occupies the 'Woolsack'. This is like a giant bean-bag (supported by a wooden frame and replete with back-rest) which stands in the middle of the floor at the upper end of the House. For generations English schoolboys were taught that the Woolsack was filled with wool to symbolise the traditional importance of the wool trade to the English economy. However generations of English schoolboys have probably been taught wrongly. It seems far more likely that the Woolsack has traditionally been filled with wool in order that the Lord Chancellor might have something soft on which to rest when performing his duties as Speaker of the House of Lords. In any event the term 'Woolsack' is something of a misnomer as horsehair is included in the stuffing in order to maximise comfort. Anyone who has ever owned a bean-bag will know that after people have been sitting on it for a while the beans get a little flat and the bag begins to sag. The Woolsack is no different. As a result of people sitting on it day in, day out the wool inside gradually gets more and more compressed until it eventually turns into felt. At this point the House of Lords authorities do what many bean-bag owners fail to do – they buy a re-fill. This happens once every couple of decades.

Since 1660 the Lord Chancellor has been required "ordinarily to attend the Lords house of Parlyament" and preside over proceedings. Nowadays this responsibility is frequently delegated to Deputy Speakers. On those days that the Lord Chancellor does sit in the Woolsack he dresses in his formal regalia and quits his office for the House of Lords chamber shortly before half past two. His Mace Bearer and Purse-Bearer precede him down the corridor.[33] A train-bearer follows behind. His job is to keep hold of the Lord Chancellor's trailing robes so as to avoid any unseemly incident in which the Chancellor might trip over his ceremonial garb. Bringing up the rear behind the train-bearer are the Gentlemen Usher of the Black Rod and the Serjeant-at-Arms (two House of Lords' functionaries). Together they all troop into the debating chamber of the House of Lords and the Lord Chancellor sits down on the Woolsack with the Mace and Purse beside him. It is a dramatic entry but what follows is not quite so colourful or interesting. This is because while the Lord Chancellor (or his Deputy) is expected to sit in the Woolsack all day, every day when the House is actually sitting – he does not have very much else to do. The House of Lords is not like the House of Commons where the Speaker has the power to control the flow of business and rebuke unruly members. In the House of Lords that power belongs to the House as a whole. In the past this may have sprung from the notion that the House of Lords is a noble body capable of self-regulation. Today the system of collective self-control within the House of Lords continues to operate well. Essentially all the Lord Chancellor gets to do is put various questions to the House. At the start of a debate he states that "The Question is ...". At the end of a debate he says (referring to the original Question): "As many as are of that opinion will say 'Content'. The contrary 'Not-content'". The assembled peers then call out what they think. The Lord Chancellor tries to judge which side has the majority. He then says "I think the Contents have it" or "I think the Not-Contents have it." Some of the peers may disagree with the Lord Chancellor's assessment of what way the House has voted. If so they can shout out their dissent. The Lord Chancellor may then call for a division of the House after which the lords go to the right and the left of the Throne depending on whether they agree or disagree with the motion put to the House. Once the House has divided and the number of peers passing to each side of the Throne has been counted the Lord Chancellor announces whether the relevant motion has been approved or not.

No doubt someone someday will think up a more meaningful role for the Lord Chancellor in his capacity as Speaker of the House of Lords but for the time being putting questions, taking votes, and (when the going gets exciting) asking any peers standing in the area behind the Woolsack to stop talking, represent the full extent of the powers enjoyed by the Lord Chancellor as Speaker. In the century and a quarter since the Appellate Jurisdiction Act 1876 Act came into being Lord Chancellors have tended to be bright, energetic and successful politicians and lawyers. It really does seem a shame to entrust to them a role which any person of moderate skill or intelligence could perform especially as when he is sitting on the Woolsack the Lord Chancellor cannot be doing more worthy tasks like listening to House of Lords appeals with the Lords of Appeal in Ordinary. In the past this was not a problem. The Appellate Committee sat from 2:30 in the afternoon, its hearings ended around four, the Lord Chancellor would then shuffle off for a quick cup of tea, throw on his court suit and wig and dash down to the House of Lords chamber to preside over sittings which started at about 4:15 pm and normally ended about 6:30 pm.

Nowadays the sheer amount of government business means that the political wing of the House of Lords sits through the day while various Lords of Appeal hear appeals in a Committee Room upstairs. While the Lord Chancellor may have three heads he only has one body and so can only be in a single place at the same time. This has tended to be the main chamber of the House. In consequence the Lord Chancellor's connection with the Appellate Committee has tended to become more and more tenuous. Ministerial duties are easier to squeeze in at different times and are generally likely to involve more exciting work than the Lord Chancellor's judicial responsibilities. The present Lord Chancellor manages to combine his duties in the Woolsack with being a very active Cabinet minister and also sitting as a judge, but he is only able to do so because he turns up at his desk at 5:00 or 6:00 in the morning and finishes off late at night – a rather hectic schedule for one rapidly approaching what for most people would be retirement age (in 2000 Lord Irvine will be 60).

As was mentioned in a previous Chapter the Lord Chancellor does not have to be a lord, not even to carry out his duties as Speaker of the House of Lords. Oddly, however, the Chancellor is always styled and addressed as the 'Lord Chancellor' whether he is a peer or not. This is because the term 'Lord' in the title does not flow from the Lord Chancellor being a member of the House of Lords. It is an honorary title used out of respect for the antiquity, the dignity and the seniority of the office – after all in terms of precedence the only person outside the immediate Royal Family who ranks higher than the Lord Chancellor is the Archbishop of Canterbury. Indeed in terms of precedence the Lord Chancellor – whether he is a peer or not – even outranks the Prime Minister (a fact that is reflected in the presently roughly £40,000 difference between the salary earned by Lord Irvine and that earned by Tony Blair). Even if he is not a peer the Lord Chancellor will also rank well above the Lords of Appeal in Ordinary who – if one is to believe the authors of *Debrett's Distinguished People of Today* – come somewhere after the Master of the Horse in terms of precedence. As it happens all Lord Chancellors in the twentieth century have either been peers before they accepted the office or have been made peers very shortly afterwards. Until the 1960s there was also something of a tradition that retired Lord Chancellors were given hereditary peerages. However this practice seems to have died with Lord Manningham-Buller who was made Viscount Dilhorne in 1964 after the Conservative administration in which he had been Lord Chancellor fell from power.

Quitting the office of Lord Chancellor is a decidedly uncomplicated process. The matrix of the Great Seal is surrendered either to the Sovereign personally or to a Royal lackey who calls round to the Lord Chancellor at Westminster and that is it. Although the Lord Chancellor is the head of the Chancery Division of the High Court he does not enjoy the same effective immunity from dismissal that other High Court judges enjoy. He only holds office for as long as the Prime Minister of the day desires it. This makes good practical sense. It would create great difficulty and be a real challenge to the Prime Minister's authority if a Cabinet Minister was not subject to immediate dismissal – after all not even the Prime Minister enjoys security of tenure in his office. None the less it is something of a constitutional oddity that a member of the judiciary can be fired so freely. And sometimes the reason for the dismissal of a Lord Chancellor can be quite trivial: in 1962, for example, Viscount Kilmuir was dismissed by Harold Macmillan for reasons that were so slight they still remain generally unknown.

All Lord Chancellors since the Second World War have had legal qualifications. This is not a prerequisite for the office but it would be unusual to say the least if a non-lawyer were ever to be appointed. As recently as 1987 one commentator was discussing the question whether a lawyer qualified in Scots law but not in English law could be made Lord Chancellor. As the Lord Chancellor is head of a Division of the English High Court and the head of the judiciary in England and Wales one might have thought he ought to be well-versed in English law. Indeed during the 1950s Lord Macmillan of Aberfeldy, a onetime Lord of Appeal from Scotland, suggested that appointing a Scots lawyer to be Lord Chancellor "would be contrary to constitutional convention... incongruous and inconvenient".[34] Enter Lord Mackay of Clashfern. In October 1987 after spending the better part of his lifetime as a Scottish advocate and only two years as a Lord of Appeal he was named by Mrs Thatcher as the man who was to succeed Lord Havers of St Edmundsbury as Lord Chancellor. Mackay was to hold the position for ten years. His successor, Lord Irvine of Lairg is also a Scotsman though he, unlike Lord Mackay, qualified and practised at the English Bar, and even sat as a temporary English High Court judge before being elevated to the Chancellorship.

Once ensconced in office the Lord Chancellor has a fine array of clothes at his disposal for every occasion. At State events he wears a magnificent outfit that is very similar to the formal dress worn by Court of Appeal judges – a black cloth court suit, a gold-embroidered black damask gown, a fine pair of buckled shoes and a full-length bell-bottomed wig. He may also wear a black tricorn hat. The wig and hat are concessions to seventeenth and eighteenth century fashion fads. The other clothes have been worn by Lord Chancellors since the days of the trend-setting fop Sir Christopher Hatton who served Queen Elizabeth I as Lord Chancellor from 1587 to 1591 and was previously a dance instructor at the Royal Court. Full regalia is worn on a variety of formal occasions such as the State Opening of Parliament and has also traditionally been worn at the ceremony of good will between the Lord Chancellor and the Lord Mayor of London that has in the past preceded the Mansion House banquet held to mark the election of a new Lord Mayor. One of the best-known events at which the Lord Chancellor wears his state regalia is the annual ceremony to mark the commencement of the new legal year. This usually takes place in October (in 2000 it will take place in September). It begins with morning service at Westminster Abbey attended by the Lord Chancellor and by members of the judiciary, Queen's Counsel, junior barristers and a sprinkling of foreign dignitaries. After the ceremony there is a procession from the Abbey to the Houses of Parliament where the Lord hancellor treats everyone present to a slap-up 'breakfast'. The term is somewhat misleading. Any of the guests expecting a traditional English breakfast of baked beans and sausage will be sorely disappointed – 'breakfast' is used in its original sense of breaking the fast that traditionally preceded attendance at a religious ceremony and the 'breakfast' is just a regular mid-day reception. The procession from Westminster Abbey to the Houses of Parliament is normally featured in the evening news on television. For many British people it is the only glimpse they will ever catch of the higher echelons of their judiciary.

Naturally no self-respecting twentieth century lawyer would enjoy parading around in sixteenth century *haute couture* all the time but the present Lord Chancellor is the first to do anything about it. In late-1998 he asked the House of Lords to allow him wear a regular pair of black trousers and black shoes under the plain black gown that he wears on ordinary days in the House of Lords. Surprisingly this request actually prompted quite a debate in the Lords. Some peers were opposed to any changes being made in what the Lord Chancellor was required to wear into the House. They seemed to be motivated by a concern that permitting the Lord Chancellor to alter his traditional garb would tear at the very fabric of state. Fortunately, however, good sense prevailed. A majority of the House recognised that the United Kingdom is held together by stronger stuff than breeches, stockings and buckles. They accepted Lord Irvine's contentions that his ceremonial clothes were uncomfortable. They agreed that in future Lord Chancellors may attend the House of Lords wearing a regular pair of trousers and shoes under their gown (though on great state occasions Lord Irvine and his successors will still have to wear traditional attire).[35]

The House's decision was hardly earth-shaking but it did represent a personal and a political victory for Lord Irvine. A personal victory because it means he does not have to wear uncomfortable clothes every time he attends the House of Lords. And a political victory because it showed Lord Irvine to be someone who is more interested in getting on with the business of rebuilding Britain than he is in the ceremony and trappings of high office. It was all a far cry from the beginning of 1998 when the costly refurbishments to Lord Irvine's official residence led to his being publicly derided by the media as some sort of profligate spendthrift. In so far as Committee room hearings of the Appellate Committee are concerned the House's decision means that Lord Chancellors, like Lords of Appeal in Ordinary will always attend proceedings of the Committee dressed in a regular suit and tie.

The responsibilities of Lord Chancellors have changed and expanded over the ages but until the present century judicial duties have been near the top of every Lord Chancellor's agenda. In the 1500s Cardinal Wolsey and Thomas More were Prime Ministers in all but name yet they still squeezed in the time to work as judges too. Indeed More's reputation was very much built on his renown as a judge. He was known to give fair and speedy decisions – so much so that as Lord Chancellor he is alleged on one occasion to have got through every single case that was pending before him in court. By the 1700s Chancellors had become little more than spies for the Sovereign inside Parliament. They kept track of every plot and intrigue, relayed it back to the monarch and took whatever action the monarch directed. They also tended to serve long periods in office: Lord Chancellor Eldon served for a total of 27 years, Lord Chancellor Hardwicke served for a total of 20 years and Lord Chancellor Thurlow served for a total of 16 years.[36] Notwithstanding their Machiavellian machinations Lord Chancellors of the 1700s still managed to squeeze in a few hours of court work (albeit court work that was frequently of a somewhat dubious quality). For much of the 1800s Lord Chancellors – sitting with a couple of peers (possibly with legal qualifications, possibly not) – transacted most of the judicial work which came before the House of Lords. This all changed with the passing of the Appellate Jurisdiction Act in

1876. Once the Lords of Appeal came on the scene the Lord Chancellor was free to do things other than hear cases. And there was a lot to be done. In the 1870s Britain was barely a generation away from its first socialist government and only a couple of generations away from becoming a welfare state. Over this period of transformation the Lord Chancellor's Department was to grow from a sleepy Whitehall backwater staffed only by lawyers into what it is today – the largest of the medium-sized government ministries with some 11,000 staff (both legal and non-legal), 500 buildings, and a yearly budget in excess of £1 billion. With the Lord Chancellor having less cases to hear he was free to take control of the ever-increasing amount of business which started coming the way of his ministry from the 1870s onwards. That business involved and still involves traditional tasks such as appointing judges and administering the courts. It also now includes new responsibilities such as running the free legal aid system and promoting law reform. A possible indication of just how time-consuming the non-judicial responsibilities of Lord Chancellors can be is the fact that Lord Irvine of Lairg did not actually get around to delivering a judgment in a House of Lords case until some eleven months after becoming Lord Chancellor. Lord Irvine's first judgment as Lord Chancellor was given in the case of *Boddington v British Transport Police* (1998). So bad has the situation become in the last half-century that although all Lord Chancellors in the period have managed to sit as judges from time to time probably only one (Viscount Simonds) could be described as being primarily a judge. Not everyone considers that this lack of attention by Lord Chancellors to their judicial responsibilities is necessarily a bad thing. Indeed during the early summer of 1999 one of Lord Irvine's colleagues on the Appellate Committee, Lord Steyn, publicly suggested that the participation by the Lord Chancellor in an Appellate Committee case could present a very real problem were such a case to be appealed to the European Court on Human Rights. This is because the European Court might well decide that participation in a judicial hearing by the Lord Chancellor – who is, after all, a government minister – fatally compromises that independence from the executive branch of government which is generally considered necessary for a fair hearing. A think-tank report published around that time and prepared by an eminent group of individuals which included the former Lord of Appeal in Ordinary, Lord Scarman, reiterated much of what Lord Steyn had to say and indeed went further in terms of the reforms it suggested. The report, prepared under the aegis of the law reform group, JUSTICE, and entitled *Judicial Functions of the House of Lords*, was submitted as written evidence to the Royal Commission on the Reform of the House of Lords in May 1999. In the same month Lord Steyn's comments were made in a paper prepared for the Constitution Unit at University College London and were reported in the media.[37] This was not the first time that Lord Steyn had voiced concern over the role of the Lord Chancellor in the British constitutional framework. In a lecture delivered to the Administrative Law Bar Association in November 1996 he had already expressed concern over retaining the Lord Chancellor, a Cabinet member, as head of the judiciary in England and Wales.[38]

Curiously the calls for Lord Chancellors to confine themselves to their political responsibilities have come at a time when the persons being appointed to the office have less and less real political experience. At first sight the statistics might seem to belie this. Six of the ten Lord Chancellors in the past five decades (Lord Jowitt, Lord Kilmuir, Lord Dilhorne, Lord Hailsham, Lord Elwyn-Jones and Lord Havers) have held elected office. However only three of them (Lord Jowitt, Lord Kilmuir and Lord Hailsham) were ever appointed to a ministerial office which was not also a law office and only two of them (Lord Kilmuir and Lord Hailsham) were ever perceived by their contemporaries as being more politician than lawyer (at least prior to their becoming Lord Chancellor). The two most recent Lord Chancellors (Lord Mackay and Lord Irvine) had limited experience of political life before being raised to the Woolsack and neither of them has ever held elected public office: Lord Mackay was Lord Advocate of Scotland, the chief law officer of Scotland, for five years from 1979 until 1984 and Lord Irvine was the shadow Lord Chancellor in the House of Lords from 1992 until 1997. Mackay and Irvine are slightly different from their predecessors in the post-war period in that as well as their political experience both had experience of high judicial office before becoming Lord Chancellor. By the time Mackay made it to the Woolsack he had been a superior court judge for some years (two of them as a Lord of Appeal). Lord Irvine, for his part, sat as a Deputy High Court judge during the time that he was shadow Lord Chancellor.

Lack of ministerial experience may explain why Lord Irvine of Lairg had such a rough time with the press during his first year in office. Admittedly some of his troubles were self-created. But all the same it was a bumpy ride. In July 1997 Lord Irvine criticised 'fat-cat' lawyers who were earning £1m a year – it then emerged that as a Queen's Counsel he himself had earned a substantial annual income (albeit one that fell well short of £1 million a year). In September 1997 Lord Irvine accepted a salary increase of £1,800 at exactly the same time other government ministers were forgoing the pay increases to which they were entitled. As it happened Lord Irvine was legally obliged to accept the pay increase and in fairness to him he is now reputed to be earning less than what he made while practising at the Bar. That said, it was a curious turn of events that the man who once sought to castigate 'fat cat' lawyers now found his own income to be the subject of criticism. In November 1997 the media frenzy over the expense of the refurbishments to Lord Irvine's official Westminster residence started. In December 1997 Lord Irvine put his foot in it when he referred to himself in an after-dinner comment as a latter-day version of Henry VIII's Lord Chancellor, Cardinal Wolsey. Apparently Lord Irvine was referring to the number of cabinet committees he chairs and comparing them to the labyrinthine network of offices that Wolsey once held. And as it happens Lord Irvine is actually rather similar to Cardinal Wolsey in some ways: both started out from very humble origins and both were good students (though Lord Irvine did rather better at university). Unfortunately for him however the average man in the street (and worse, the average journalist) seems to remember Cardinal Wolsey as the exuberant and extravagant character portrayed by Orson Welles in the 1966 film *A Man for All Seasons*. As a result it was no time at all before Lord Irvine's after-dinner comments were being taken out of context and lampooned by columnists, commentators, and critics up and down the country. There was more to come. In January 1998 the tabloid press ran a story that Lord Irvine had brought his wife on a parliamentary trip of the Caribbean in the midst of the festive season. However the Lord Chancellor quickly retorted that he had not infringed the rules regarding such trips. In February 1998 Lord Irvine was reported as having intimated to the *New Statesman* magazine that he favoured the introduction of some sort of privacy law which would restrain the media from reporting on such stories as the love life of Robin Cook, the Foreign Secretary. This report caused such a furore among the media that even the Prime Minister's Office seemed to back away from the Lord Chancellor. Under such headlines as "Anger over Irvine's 'blunders'" the Prime Minister was reported as having "unleashed the whole of the Downing Street and party machine against ... blunder-prone ... Lord Irvine". A Downing Street spokesman was reported as saying "The Prime Minister's view very strongly is that there will not be a privacy law". And a Labour Party spokesman was reported as saying "We do not have a scheme to gag the press from writing stories that are legitimate. I do not know anyone other than Derry Irvine who thought the Robin Cook story was other than a legitimate one to write." Still February and the Lord Chancellor was back in the news again. This time at the receiving end of a sex discrimination claim. A woman solicitor and longtime Labour Party supporter claimed that she had been discriminated against when Lord Irvine appointed a special adviser without advertising the position and without setting up an objective recruitment procedure. Three weeks later yet another discrimination claim was brought against the Lord Chancellor by a black, female Labour Party activist who claimed that she too had suffered discrimination when the special adviser was appointed. The claims of the two women were vigorously denied by the Lord Chancellor's Department. But by now press attention was focusing on the cost of refurbishing the Lord Chancellor's residence. During March 1998 the newspapers seemed almost to reach fever pitch over the amounts of money being spent on preserving the Lord Chancellor's official Westminster residence. Tongue in cheek one newspaper published a report entitled "It's just like VE Day all over again. The last roll of paper is pasted on Lord Irvine's wall, and a nation rejoices". Judging by the general tenor of the British papers during this period one might almost believe this was a serious piece of news. It was clearly open season on the Lord Chancellor. Alterations by him to his proposed reforms of the free legal aid scheme were billed as "Irvine climbdown on legal aid". The decision by a Cabinet sub-committee, chaired by the Lord Chancellor, that it might be unlawful under European Union law to amend the Sex Discrimination Act and allow political parties practise positive discrimination in favour of women seeking to become election candidates was billed as "Irvine blocks plan for women". In April 1998 the drama regarding the Lord Chancellor's official residence flared up again when his newly renovated quarters were opened up for inspection to a generally unappreciative paparazzi, one of whom described the expensive pineapple-design flock wallpaper as "creating the ambience of a tandoori restaurant".[39]

By this time so much mud was being hurled at the Lord Chancellor by the media that it was inevitable there would be some sort of political backlash. By the end of April 1998 the newspapers were reporting that MPs had been approaching the Prime Minister to complain that Lord Irvine was rapidly becoming a political liability. A Queen's Counsel wrote a newspaper article suggesting that the time had come to transfer the executive responsibilities of the Lord Chancellor to a Minister of Justice. He was but one in a long line of commentators who have argued that not only should a Ministry of Justice be created but that the Minister heading it should be a House of Commons man.[40]

The predicament in which recent Lord Chancellors including the present Lord Chancellor, have found themselves is that they are being asked to act more as ministers than as judges. The problem this creates is that being a minister is no longer (if it ever was) simply a case of running a government department well. It also involves selling the government and its policies to the general public. This is a job for a politician. But in the post-war period Lord Chancellors have tended less and less to be politicians and more and more to be lawyers. The almost inevitable result is the type of media hounding which Lord Irvine suffered from during his first year in office.

Some might say that Chancellor-baiting of the type to which Lord Irvine has been subjected never happened when his predecessor Lord Mackay of Clashfern was Lord Chancellor in the Major administration. However Lord Mackay of Clashfern possibly had something of an edge on his fellow Scotsman in that he spent five years in government office as Lord Advocate of Scotland before being appointed Lord Chancellor. As a result he possibly had rather more experience of the cut and thrust of political fray than Lord Irvine whose only experience of government prior to becoming Lord Chancellor was working as shadow-Lord Chancellor in the relatively sedate environment of the House of Lords. There are, however, other reasons why Lord Irvine may have attracted so much adverse publicity compared to Lord Mackay. Firstly, the present Lord Chancellor is a close political confidante of Tony Blair. Being a Prime Minister's friend is not always easy. Tony Blair's continuing popularity with the general public has made him very much the 'Teflon don' of British politics with the result that the media have had to heap their criticisms on those closest to him – cue Lord Irvine of Lairg. Secondly, it may be that Lord Irvine was the unlucky beneficiary of so much press attention during 1997 and the first half of 1998 simply because in the first year of the Blair administration there was little of real controversy to report about the new men in government.

It must be mentioned that by the end of 1998 things were looking up for Lord Irvine. He seemed more at ease with the media and the media were less critical of him. To counter suggestions that he was mildly distant he had begun to pepper his public speeches with self-deprecating humour. This met with a positive response. In December 1998 he gave a no-holds-barred interview to one of Britain's tabloid newspapers.[41] Regrettably, despite Lord Irvine's charm offensive and despite the fact that he is now proving more popular with the media (though in truth things could hardly get worse than they were at the start of 1998), the media attacks which he has suffered in the past – and which may well reoccur in the future – present a very real problem for the judiciary. It probably does not do much for the morale of judges, or indeed for public confidence in the legal system, when the most eminent judge in the country becomes the butt of jokes, jibes, and jeers from a large section of the press. In 1998 Lord Irvine of Lairg was even featured in a gaudy newspaper advertisement for Channel 5 national television news. Above a full colour head and shoulders picture of the Lord Chancellor in his formal regalia and set against a bright orange background ran the heading "5 facts about Lord Irvine", under which it said:

1 As lord high chancellor of great britain, he earns £142,508 a year, £40,000 more than the prime minister

2 The recent renovations to his official apartments cost £650,000 ...

3 He was brought up in an inverness council house ...

4 He is married to the former wife of scottish secretary, donald dewar

5 Both Tony and Cherie Blair are former pupils of lord irvine

One should not read too much into a single advertisement, but this type of publicity can only have added to any sentiment that exists (both within and outside the judiciary) that it is inappropriate for the judicial branch of government to be headed by a political figure who is privy to party politics and open to political point-scoring. Underpinning such sentiment is the question of judicial independence. Nobody doubts that every one of the post-war Lord Chancellors has acted in a scrupulously impartial fashion when sitting in their judicial capacity. Nobody has ever suggested that Lord Chancellors in reaching their decisions in appeals cases have ever been prompted by raw political considerations. However in the same way that justice must not only be done but must be seen to be done there is a case for the proposition that judicial independence must not only be a reality, it must be seen to be a reality, and surely the best way of ensuring that the public appreciate the reality of an independent judiciary is by severing the connection between the office of Lord Chancellor and the political branches of government or by appointing some other office-holder as head of the Judiciary. Again Lord Steyn, one of the present Lords of Appeal in Ordinary, has suggested publicly that it is the Lord Chief Justice who should be the head of the judiciary in England and Wales, asking: "Why should the public gain the impression that the Lord Chancellor speaks on behalf of the judges? For my part the proposition that a cabinet member must be the head of our judiciary in England is no longer sustainable on either constitutional or pragmatic grounds."[42]

If he is not wanted as Minister of Justice and he is not wanted as head of the judiciary what is there for the Lord Chancellor to do? In addition to being a judge, the Speaker of the House of Lords and a senior Cabinet Minister the Lord Chancellor has a couple of additional responsibilities. One of these is to act as 'Keeper of the Royal Conscience'. This sounds like an important job but for a very long time nobody has known what exactly is meant by the phrase. In the nineteenth century the title was thought to spring from the days when the Lord Chancellor was almost invariably a cleric and so was meant to convey the notion that the Lord Chancellor should function as the monarch's confessor. However this is not very convincing. English monarchs have had confessors who were not Lord Chancellors and, in any event, the first Lord Chancellor to refer to himself as 'Keeper of the Royal Conscience' (Sir Christopher Hatton) was both a lay-man and a former dance instructor, a most unlikely candidate one would have thought for the job of confessor to the Defender of the Faith. An alternative explanation is that the phrase is a reference to the traditional judicial responsibilities of the Lord Chancellor which historically were always rather different to those of other English judges. Those other judges were generally expected to apply the letter of the law when deciding a case. However this could all too easily result in unfairness. The Lord Chancellor was appointed to ensure that whenever the King's justice was dispensed fairness always triumphed. In this way the Lord Chancellor functioned as the 'Keeper of the Royal Conscience': he ensured that whatever the courts did in the monarch's name was both right and fair.

Regardless of which of the explanations one accepts for the origin and meaning of the phrase 'Keeper of the Royal Conscience' it ultimately came to be relied upon as a justification for religious discrimination. It was reasoned that if the monarch was a Protestant (and the British monarch must be a Protestant) then a Catholic could never be appointed 'Keeper of the Royal Conscience'. It was never definitively stated that Catholics could not be Lord Chancellor. However the simple fact of the matter is that for more than four centuries after Thomas More ceased to be Lord Chancellor not a single Catholic was appointed to the Woolsack. And it is almost undoubtedly the case that if the first Lord Russell of Killowen had not been a Catholic he would have been appointed Lord Chancellor and not Lord Chief Justice in the late nineteenth century.[43] Apologists for this system of discrimination explained it away by reference to the fact that the Lord Chancellor was responsible for making a number of ecclesiastical appointments within the Church of England and so he simply had to be a Protestant. This was actually quite a good argument but the solution was very simple – enact legislation making it clear that Catholics could be Lord Chancellor and provide that ecclesiastical appointments were to be made by another government minister whenever a Catholic was Chancellor. This in fact is what was done by the rather cumbersomely titled Lord Chancellor (Tenure of Office and Discharge of Ecclesiastical Functions) Act 1974. This Act was not initiated by a government but by Lord Hailsham of St Marylebone, shortly after he ended his first term in office as Lord Chancellor and became an Opposition spokesman in the House of Lords.

As Catholics can now become Lord Chancellor and so 'Keeper of the Royal Conscience' it would appear that in so far as that phrase has any meaning today it is a reference to the Lord Chancellor's traditional duty of ensuring that the decisions of the courts are conscionable and not to any sort of responsibility on the part of Lord Chancellors to act as moral guardians of the British monarch. Astonishingly it would appear that it is still not completely certain whether a Jewish person could be appointed Lord Chancellor. The definitive encyclopaedia of English law, *Halsbury's Laws of England* suggests that clarifying legislation could be necessary before a Jewish person could be lawfully appointed to the Woolsack.

On the subject of religion there was some speculation in the late 1980s that Lord Hailsham of St Marylebone might be succeeded as Lord Chancellor by Peter Rawlinson, QC, a Roman Catholic who had been Solicitor-General, Attorney-General and Chairman of the Bar. In the end Hailsham was succeeded by Lord Mackay of Clashfern after the very brief Chancellorship of Lord Havers who served for a mere four months.

In addition to being 'Keeper of the Royal Conscience' the Lord Chancellor is also the keeper of government records. In his memoirs Lord Hailsham of St Marylebone has described the scale of the task which being the keeper of these records involves. During his time in office (and indeed for some time before that) the government was getting through so much paper each year that if all the paper involved was piled together the resulting mound would be about 125 miles high. Of this 125-mile pile of government records about 99 per cent were immediately destroyed because they were of no intrinsic or historical value. That left a stack of government records some one and a quarter miles high for which shelf space had to be found in the public archives each year.

Of those government records which were (and are) preserved annually most are kept secret from the public until thirty years after they were originally created. Some may be released sooner. More may be kept secret for up to 50, 75 or even a 100 years. The decision as to when records are to be released is a matter for the discretion of the Lord Chancellor. In January of each year the latest batch of documents to have been certified by the Lord Chancellor for release is made available to the public. To news editors who are usually starved of stories during the Christmas period the release of the papers at this time is like manna from heaven even though the bulk of the material made available tends to be quite bland. The more juicy records are kept in reserve for historians of the future who will be given access to the material when its being made public is no longer deemed detrimental to the national interest. The Lord Chancellor has only been the custodian of public records for the last forty years. Prior to that it came within the remit of the Master of the Rolls. Nowadays the responsibilities of the Master of the Rolls pertain almost exclusively to his role within the Court of Appeal. Historically however the Master of the Rolls was responsible (as his title suggests) for keeping certain public records. One might have thought that it was a good idea to entrust the responsibility for preserving and releasing government papers to a politically neutral superior court judge. However in the 1950s it was decided that the task ought to be entrusted to the Lord Chancellor, a government minister answerable to Parliament. One might ask whether it might not have been preferable if the responsibility for safeguarding, disclosing, and withholding government records had been entrusted to someone other than a Cabinet member who could come under pressure to take partisan political considerations into account when deciding whether or not certain government documents should be released or kept secret. As it happens in the forty years that the responsibility for deciding whether and when to release government records has fallen upon the Lord Chancellor all of the holders of that office up to and including the present Lord Chancellor have been principled and honourable men. However in the future that might not always be the case. It is not difficult to imagine a situation in which an unprincipled or politically motivated Lord Chancellor could decide to withhold or disclose information out of a desire to preserve his own or his party's reputation or to harm the reputation of a political opponent.

Various other responsibilities of the Lord Chancellor include appointing people to the Law Commission (the statutory body charged with promoting law reform), appointing the Official Solicitor (a superior court official whose duties include watching out for the interests of people such as children who may suffer from a slight disadvantage in court actions to which they are party), appointing and making rules for the Public Trustee (who has certain responsibilities in relation to such matters as wills, settlements and pension funds), appointing persons to and making rules for the Land Registry (which is charged with policing the registration of ownership of land) and appointing people to the Court of Protection and various other bodies which look after the interests of people who are insane or otherwise unable to look after their own interests. Prior to the Mental Health Act of 1959 the Lord Chancellor was in fact directly responsible for the interests of the insane. Like many of his responsibilities this sprang from the historically close relationship between the Lord Chancellor and the Sovereign. The latter as the 'fount and source of all justice' was considered to have a moral responsibility to look after people who were unable to look after themselves. However with the notable exception of King George III – who had the misfortune to suffer from bouts of temporary insanity – the plight of the mentally unwell is not something which has tended to feature prominently in the minds of many (if any) other British monarchs. In consequence they have traditionally shuffled off their responsibilities in this regard onto the Lord Chancellor. The insane were entitled to write directly to the Chancellor regarding any grievances they had. Unfortunately rather a large number of them took to writing such letters, some of them several times a day. The Mental Health Act of 1959 partly alleviated this problem. It created a battery of public bodies between the insane and the Lord Chancellor but it apparently has not succeeded in entirely eliminating letters of petition to the Chancellor from the mentally disturbed.

What does the future hold for the office of Lord Chancellor? Some might argue that as one of the oldest offices of state it has stood the test of time pretty well. True, it may not correspond with the Montesquian notion of having split executive, legislative and judicial branches of government but then the office does pre-date Montesquieu by more than half a millennium and has worked perfectly adequately for rather longer than the rigidly tripartite model of government espoused by the famous Frenchman. The phrase 'if it ain't broke, don't fix it' springs to mind. But there are those who would argue that the office of Lord Chancellor is 'broke' and that it is now showing the stresses and strains of age. First of all there seems to be too much for one man to do: what is the point in making the Lord Chancellor head of the judiciary in England and Wales and a member of the Appellate Committee when he next to never sits in a judicial capacity? Secondly, how can any Lord Chancellor meet the dual role of being a government minister subject to Treasury constraints on the one hand and being the head of the judiciary battling for more funding and more judges on the other? Thirdly, it seems the wrong type of man is being asked to do the job of Lord Chancellor: why choose a lawyer without any real political experience to head a government ministry? The answer presumably is that a full-blooded politician could not be head of the judiciary. But the solution surely is to split the responsibilities of the Lord Chancellor between two people, giving the judicial tasks to a lawyer and the ministerial tasks to a politician. Finally, it does rather seem that Lord Chancellors these days are far too well qualified for one of the core duties of Lord Chancellor: why is it that one of the most eminent and best-paid government officials is asked to spend so much of his time in the House of Lords discharging the next to non-existent functions of Speaker of that House?

Perhaps it is time for the powers that be to consider whether something may in fact be going seriously awry and whether changes need to be made if the office of Lord Chancellor is to continue in being for another thousand or more years. With reform and modernisation of the House of Lords a part of the new Labour Government's plans for the future it may also be worthwhile reforming and modernising the office of the person who occupies the Woolsack in that House. At the very least the office of Lord Chancellor needs to be freed from many of the lesser responsibilities it has acquired over the last thousand years. But serious consideration also needs to be given to cleaving the office away from the point of juncture between the three branches of government and re-locating it within one (and only one) of those branches so that in the future the post of Lord Chancellor shall involve being a member of the Appellate Committee and head of the Judiciary in England and Wales *or* as the minister in charge of a government department *or* as speaker of a revamped House of Lords – but not in all three capacities at once.

Biographical Details of the Men who have Served as Lord Chancellor since the Enactment of the Appellate Jurisdiction Act 1876

1870s–1880s

Cairns, Hugh McCalmont, (1819–85), Irishman. Father a landowner and ex-Army officer. Attended Trinity College Dublin. Called to the Bar at age 25 (Middle Temple). Married at age 37. Seven children. Became a Queen's Counsel at age 37. Entered political life. Was Conservative Member of Parliament for Belfast. Served as Solicitor-General. Was appointed directly onto the Court of Appeal and given a peerage. A year later he was appointed Lord Chancellor by Disraeli. Served twice in this capacity (1868–69 and 1874–80). Aged 48 when he was appointed to the House of Lords and 49 when appointed Lord Chancellor. As Lord Chancellor it was Cairns who steered the Appellate Jurisdiction Act 1876 through the House of Lords. Cairns was a religious man who worked as a Sunday school teacher throughout his adult life. On the personal level he was apparently something of a dour dandy who enjoyed snappy dressing but was notorious for not having a sense of humour.

Halsbury, Hardinge Stanley Giffard (took the title of Halsbury), (1823–1921), Englishman. Father a lawyer. Attended Oxford University. Called to the English Bar at age 27 (Inner Temple). Married at age 29 and age 51 (a year after his first wife died). Had three children. Became Queen's Counsel at age 42. Entered political life as Conservative Member of Parliament for Launceston until his elevation to the House of Lords as Lord Chancellor in 1885. Aged 62 on his appointment he initially spent 7 years in that position, then lost office along with his Party before returning to the Woolsack for another 10 years from 1895 to 1905. Famous among lawyers for overseeing the completion of *The Laws of England*, a multi-volume definitive encyclopaedia of English law, now known as *Halsbury's Laws of England*. Halsbury was a Freemason and ultimately became the Senior Grand Warden of English Freemasons.

Herschell, Farrer, (1837–99), Englishman. Father a clergyman. Attended London University and Bonn University. Called to the English Bar at age 23 (Lincoln's Inn). Married at age 39. Became a Queen's Counsel at age 35. Entered political life. Was Liberal Member of Parliament for Durham City. Served as Solicitor-General and Lord Chancellor under Gladstone and Rosebery (1886, 1892–95). His Chancellorship was not at all noteworthy – among his few significant achievements was the legalisation of marriage between a man and his dead wife's sister. In his private life Herschell was an accomplished player of the violin and an enthusiastic Freemason.

Selborne, Roundell Palmer (assumed the title of Selborne), (1812–95), Englishman. Father a clergyman. Attended Rugby and Winchester Schools before proceeding on to Oxford University. Was elected a Fellow of Magdalen College, Oxford. Called to the English Bar at age 25 (Lincoln's Inn). Entered political life. Was elected Member of Parliament for Plymouth and later for Richmond in Yorkshire. Though elected on the Conservative ticket he later went on to serve in two Liberal administrations. Was Attorney-General under Earl Russell and Lord Chancellor under Gladstone. Married at age 36. Five children. Became a Queen's Counsel at age 37. Was appointed to the Lord Chancellorship at age 60. Lost office when Disraeli came to power in 1874. Re-appointed 6 years later when Gladstone returned to power. Was a good friend of the poet Tennyson.

1890s–1900s

Loreburn, Robert Threshie Reid (took the title Loreburn), (1846–1923). Born in Corfu of Scottish parents. Lived and worked the bulk of his life in England (but represented a Scottish constituency in Parliament for ten years). Father a judge (Chief Justice of the Ionian Islands Protectorate). Attended Cheltenham College and Oxford University. Called to the English Bar at age 25 (Inner Temple). As a young barrister he worked under the future Lord James of Hereford who took Loreburn under his patronage and greatly advanced his career. Married at age 25 and at age 61 (after his first wife died). Became Queen's Counsel at age 36, two years after had entered political life as Liberal Member of Parliament for Hereford. Later became Liberal Member for the Scottish constituency of Dumfries. Served as Attorney-General and (from 1906 to 1912) as Lord Chancellor. Is one of the very few British politicians of his day who supported the rights of the Boers in the Boer War. Is the Lord Chancellor who pushed the Parliament Act of 1911 through the House of Lords and thereby established the legislative supremacy of the Commons over the Upper House.

1910s–1920s

Birkenhead, Frederick Edwin Smith, (took the title of Birkenhead), (1872–1930), Englishman. Father an estate agent and also Mayor of Birkenhead. Attended Oxford University. Called to Bar at age 27 (Gray's Inn). Married at age 29. One child. Appointed King's Counsel at age 36. Entered political life. Was Conservative Member of Parliament for Liverpool district. Helped negotiate Irish independence. Served as Solicitor-General, Attorney-General, Lord Chancellor (1919–22), and Secretary of State for India (1924–8). Interestingly Birkenhead commenced hearing appeals as Lord Chancellor before he was actually made a peer. He was aged 47 upon his appointment to the House of Lords. He is remembered more as an outstanding politician than as an outstanding lawyer.

Buckmaster, Stanley Owen, (1861–1934), Englishman. Father started as farm labourer, became a free trade activist, helped out with the organization of the Great Exhibition in 1851, and was befriended by Prince Albert who helped him to become a college inspector. Buckmaster Junior attended Oxford University where he studied maths. Called to English Bar at age 23 (Inner Temple). Entered political life. Was a Liberal Member of Parliament for Cambridge and later for a district of Yorkshire. Appointed a King's Counsel at age 41. Served as Solicitor-General and government Press Spokesman during the First World War before going on to become Lord Chancellor. Spent a year and a half as Lord Chancellor and then 17 years as a Lord of Appeal.

Cave, George, (1856–1928), Englishman. Father a Member of Parliament. Attended school in France as a child. For a while French was his first language. Attended Oxford University. Called to English Bar at age 24 (Inner Temple). Married at age 29. Never had children. Entered political life. Was a Unionist Member of Parliament. Served as Solicitor-General and Home Secretary before being appointed to the Appellate Committee. Served as a Lord of Appeal from 1918 to 1922. Amazingly he continued to act as Home Secretary for several months after he was appointed a Lord of Appeal in Ordinary. Twice served as Lord Chancellor (1922–4 and 1925–8). In 1925 he defeated the Earl of Oxford and Asquith (the onetime Liberal Prime Minister and the father of Lord Asquith of Bishopstone, the future Lord of Appeal) to become Chancellor of Oxford University.

Finlay, Robert Bannatyne, (1842–1929), Scotsman. Father a medical doctor. Attended Edinburgh University from where he graduated as a medical doctor, not a lawyer. Practised briefly as a doctor before being called to the English Bar (Middle Temple). Married at age 32. Had one child. Became a Queen's Counsel at age 40. Entered political life. Was the Liberal (and later the Liberal-Unionist) Member of Parliament for Inverness, Edinburgh University and St Andrews University. Served as Solicitor-General and Attorney-General before going on to be made Lord Chancellor at the ripe old age of 74. Died three years later after underwent operation to have cataracts removed from his eyes.

Hailsham, Douglas McGarel Hogg (took the title of Hailsham), (1872–1950), Englishman. Father a sugar merchant and philanthropist. Attended Eton. Did not go to university. Worked on father's sugar plantations. Fought in the Boer War (narrowly avoided death). Called to the English Bar at age 30 (Lincoln's Inn). Entered political life as a Conservative. Was named Attorney-General before being elected to Parliament. Thereafter elected Member of Parliament for St Marylebone, a London constituency. Ultimately appointed Lord Chancellor (a position he held twice from 1928 to 1929 and 1935 to 1938). Was once considered a possible successor to Neville Chamberlain as Conservative Party leader. Was the father of Lord Hailsham of St Marylebone who also served as Lord Chancellor.

Haldane, Richard Burdon, (1856–1928), Scotsman. Father a Writer to the Signet (a Scottish office akin to that of solicitor in England).

Attended Edinburgh University and Göttingen University. Called to the English Bar at age 23 (Lincoln's Inn). Became Queen's Counsel at age 34. Never married. Entered political life. Was the Liberal Member of Parliament for East Lothian, a Scottish constituency. Served as Secretary of State for War before going to become Lord Chancellor on two occasions (from 1912 to 1915 and in 1924).

Sankey, John, (1866–1948), Englishman. Father a draper/undertaker. Attended Lancing School and advanced from there to Oxford University where he got a third class degree. Called to the English Bar at age 26 (Middle Temple). Never married. Became a King's Counsel at age 43. Raised to the High Court bench five years later. Spent fourteen years as a High Court judge and a year on the Court of Appeal before being invited by Ramsay MacDonald to become Lord Chancellor. Remembered as a Lord Chancellor who concentrated on the political side of his duties.

1930s–1940s

Caldecote, Thomas Walker Hobart Inskip (took the title of Caldecote), (1876–1947), Englishman. Father a solicitor. Educated at Cambridge University. Nearly decided to become a missionary. Called to the Bar at age 23 (Inner Temple). Married at age 38. One child. Appointed King's Counsel at age 38. Entered political life. Was the Conservative Member of Parliament for a district of Bristol. Served as Solicitor-General, Attorney-General, the Minister responsible for re-arming Britain in the late 1930s when the prospect of another European war became likely, Dominions Secretary, Lord Chancellor (for a year), Dominions Secretary again, and finally as Lord Chief Justice.

Maugham, Frederic Herbert, (1866–1958), Englishman. Father a solicitor. Attended Cambridge University. Called to the English Bar at age 24 (Lincoln's Inn). Married at age 30. Four children. Became Queen's Counsel at age 47. Was appointed to the High Court 15 years later. Successively spent 6 years on the High Court, 4 years on the Court of Appeal, 3 years as a Lord of Appeal in Ordinary, one year as a Conservative-appointed Lord Chancellor (from 1938 to 1939), then two further years as a Lord of Appeal until his retirement in 1941. Married the sister of Lord Romer (who served with him as a Lord of Appeal).

Post-war Lord Chancellors

Earl Jowitt of Stevenage (1885–1957)

Lord High Chancellor of Great Britain: 1945–51
Prime Minister with whom served: Attlee (Labour)

Age became Lord Chancellor: 60
Born: Stevenage, Kent
Secondary education: Marlborough
Called to Bar: 1909 (Age 24)
Inn of Court to which belonged: Middle Temple
Age ceased being Lord Chancellor: 66

Father's occupation: Church rector
University education: Oxford University
King's Counsel: 1922 (Age 37)
Married: Once
Age married: 28
Children: 1 daughter

High judicial office other than Lord Chancellorship:
None

Public office other than Lord Chancellorship:
1922–4, MP for Hartlepools (Liberal); 1929, MP for Preston (Liberal); 1929–31, MP for Preston (Labour); 1929–31, Attorney-General; 1939–45, MP for Ashton-under-Lyne (Labour); 1940–2, Solicitor-General; 1942, Paymaster-General; 1943, Minister without Portfolio; 1944, Minister of National Insurance

In the General Election of 1929 Jowitt successfully stood for Parliament as a Liberal Party candidate. Less than a week later he had only just returned to London from his constituency when he was offered the position of Attorney-General by the new Labour Prime Minister Ramsay MacDonald who had been unable to find a suitable candidate from within the ranks of his own MPs. The only condition MacDonald imposed was that if Jowitt accepted the offer he would have to resign from the Liberal Party and join the Labour Party instead. Astonishingly Jowitt accepted MacDonald's offer and did switch party. His decision caused a great stir. Down at the Bar all but one of the members of the chambers from which Jowitt had practised up to that time quit in disgust at his actions. Two years later Jowitt was up to his tricks again. With the United Kingdom facing a massive financial crisis the Labour administration collapsed and a new National government was formed. Jowitt was urged by the Labour Party to resign. But in this hour of need he bravely remained on as Attorney-General. This secured him a few extra months in office. But it also got him expelled from the Labour Party. And it led to him losing his seat in Parliament a few months later. It seemed the voters wanted someone with a little more conviction and a little less ambition. Five years were to go by before Jowitt was welcomed back into the Labour Party fold. Eight years passed before he found himself in Parliament once more. Still Jowitt's years away from Westminster were not wasted – he spent this time working hard down at the Bar making himself one of the richest men to become Lord Chancellor in the twentieth century. But duty called. War was looming in Europe and Jowitt was needed in government. In 1939 he re-entered Parliament. In 1940 he became Solicitor-General. And in 1942 he was appointed Paymaster-General. A year later he was again moving onwards and upwards. In 1943 he was appointed a minister without portfolio. And in 1944 he became minister for national insurance. After the general election of 1945 Churchill lost power, Attlee won office and Jowitt became Lord Chancellor. He entered the House of Lords as Baron Jowitt of Stevenage. There were some wry comments when along with his baronial coat of arms Jowitt took as his motto the Latin for "Tenacious and loyal". Liberal and Labour Party members alike were heard to comment that on more than one occasion in the past Jowitt could have been a little less tenacious and a little more loyal. Even now Jowitt proved himself rather fickle. During a House of Lords debate in 1948 on the suspension of capital punishment he declared himself to be firmly in favour of the death sentence. Then in line with government policy he immediately performed a complete volte-face on what he had just said and proposed that the death sentence should in fact be suspended. As Lord Chancellor Jowitt looked and acted the part. Tall, well-built, handsome, eloquent, witty and sharp he seemed every inch the King's man. There were no great hitches in the despatch of government business during his time. But neither were there resounding achievements which could be attributed to Jowitt. Insofar as the hearing of appeals was concerned only one case in which Jowitt presided (the post-war treason trial of the Nazi broadcaster Lord 'Haw-Haw') is now remembered. In 1951 after his retirement from the office of Lord Chancellor Jowitt was honoured by being made a hereditary viscount.

Viscount Simonds of Sparsholt (1881–1971)

Lord High Chancellor of Great Britain: 1951–4
Prime Minister with whom served: Churchill (Conservative)

Age became Lord Chancellor: 70
Born: Basingstoke, Kent
Secondary education: Winchester
Called to Bar: 1906 (Age 25)
Inn of Court to which belonged: Lincoln's Inn
Age ceased being Lord Chancellor: 73
Father's occupation: Brewer
University education: Oxford University
King's Counsel: 1924 (Age 43)
Married: Once
Age married: 31
Children: None

High judicial office other than Lord Chancellorship:
1937–44 High Court (Age: 56–64); 1940–4 National Arbitration Tribunal (Age: 59–64); 1944–51 Law Lord (Age: 63–70)

Public office other than Lord Chancellorship:
None

Gavin Turnbull Simonds is different from all other Lords of Appeal in Ordinary who have served since the Second World War in that he is the only one to have been promoted straight from the High Court into the House of Lords without stopping en route at the Court of Appeal. He is also one of only two Lord Chancellors in the same period who was already a member of the Appellate Committee when he was made Chancellor. The other is Lord Mackay of Clashfern. The two share another similarity in that neither was ever a Member of the House of Commons nor held elected political office before becoming Lord Chancellor. It is perhaps something of a testament to the general conservatism of the British judiciary that these two men should have been elevated from the judiciary into Cabinet office by Conservative Prime Ministers.

Simonds' politics were considerably to the right of all of his colleagues in the Churchill Cabinet. Indeed it is probably just as well that his purely legal background and training inclined Simonds to confine himself very much to the judicial side of things while he was Lord Chancellor. His natural inclination in this regard was buttressed by the very strong aversion he felt for the inevitable flak which goes with the political side of being Chancellor. In his dislike for the cut and thrust of political fray Simonds was very different from most other post-war Lord Chancellors who seem on the whole to have been more occupied with the political aspects of the job. In fact the extent to which Lord Chancellors have become political rather than judicial animals is something of a growing concern. One former Lord Chancellor, Lord Hailsham of St Marylebone, has opined that the judicial side of the office may well atrophy if Lord Chancellors treat this aspect of their duties as less of a priority than their ministerial chores. That said, the practical reality seems to be that the sheer weight of political responsibility now borne by Lord Chancellors will generally preclude them from devoting a great amount of time to their judicial duties.

Simonds is not only different from most of his successors as Lord Chancellor in terms of the degree of precedence he afforded his judicial responsibilities. He is also a little different in that some of his judgments as Lord Chancellor have become renowned as classic, or at least classic conservative interpretations of the law. In *National Anti-Vivisection Society* v. *Commissioners of Inland Revenue* (1947), Simonds arrived at the conclusion that the Anti-Vivisection Society was not a charity because it had a political purpose and in *Gilmour* v. *Coats* (1949), he decided that an enclosed convent of nuns was not a charity and could not be the legitimate object of a charitable bequest because the work of the nuns could not be demonstrated to be of public benefit. One rather suspects that the Spiritual Lords, those bishops of the Church of England who are members of the House of Lords, might well have had a bone to pick with Viscount Simonds on this particular point.

Simonds was a big man with big eyebrows and a commanding voice. But looks can be deceiving. He was a remarkably reticent individual who strongly disliked any disagreements between himself and his fellow Lords of Appeal over the cases that came before them. He was even known to reconvene hearings in order to clear up lingering dissent between himself and another Appellate Committee member in a case. A gentlemanly trait but hardly one that was conducive to the efficient transaction of judicial business. Given his dislike of political life and his distaste for personal conflict it did not come as a great surprise when in 1954, after only three years in the job, Simonds voluntarily resigned from the office of Lord Chancellor. Shortly afterwards he was awarded a hereditary viscountcy. He served as an ordinary Lord of Appeal for another eight years. Simonds died in 1971. Although he was married he never had any children.

Viscount Kilmuir, Baron Fyfe of Dornoch (1900–67)

Lord High Chancellor of Great Britain: 1954–62
Prime Ministers with whom served: Churchill, Eden and Macmillan (Conservatives)

Age became Lord Chancellor: 54
Born: Edinburgh, Scotland
Secondary education: George Watson's College, Edinburgh
Inn of Court to which belonged: Gray's Inn
Age married: 25
Age ceased being Lord Chancellor: 62

Father's Occupation: Schoolteacher
University education: Oxford University
Called to Bar: 1922 (Age 22)
King's Counsel: 1934 (Age 34)
Married: Once
Children: 3 daughters (one died in childhood)

High judicial office other than Lord Chancellorship:
None

Public office other than Lord Chancellorship:
1935–54, MP for Liverpool (Conservative); 1942–5, Solicitor-General; 1945, Attorney-General; 1945–6, Deputy Chief Prosecutor

at Nuremburg War Tribunal; 1949, Conservative Member of Council of Europe, Strasbourg; 1951–4, Home Secretary and Minister for Welsh Affairs

"He was always a 'beta minus'; the stupidest Lord Chancellor ever…hopeless in Cabinet". That was the considered verdict of Harold Macmillan on the first Lord Chancellor of his administration, Viscount Kilmuir. And "that's", said Macmillan, "why I got rid of him".[44] It was a rather unkind set of remarks to make about a man to whom Macmillan had been less than kind in the past. In July 1962, on Friday the 13th (unlucky for some), Viscount Kilmuir was attending a garden party at Buckingham Palace. It was one of those perks of office which Kilmuir – the son of a Scottish schoolteacher – had come to enjoy as Lord Chancellor. Little did he know that such pleasures were about to be dramatically cut short. Macmillan had paid a morning call on the Queen earlier that day and had arranged for several of his most senior Cabinet Ministers to be replaced. Kilmuir was among the unlucky incumbents who had been dismissed. As he walked around the lawns behind the Palace enjoying his tea and sandwiches a bevy of new Ministers were already coming to the Palace to kiss the hands of Her Majesty the Queen. It was only a short time before Kilmuir would learn of his fate and only a matter of days before he would cease to hold the office of Lord Chancellor. It is still unclear why Kilmuir was dropped from his job. It may be, as Macmillan observed, that Kilmuir was not the brightest of men – he only managed a third class degree at Oxford – but he had proved his political mettle in the course of more than twenty years in the House of Commons and eight years in the House of Lords. Certainly Viscount Dilhorne, the man who replaced Kilmuir on the Woolsack – and who himself had not been the brightest academic achiever while at Oxford (he too got a Third) – was one of Macmillan's less well received appointments. In later years Kilmuir would write of Macmillan's actions at this time: "I got the impression that he was extremely alarmed about his own position, and was determined to eliminate any risk for himself by a massive change of government."[45] In this he was probably right. But whatever the reasons behind Kilmuir's sudden departure it certainly spelled the end of his public career. Kilmuir returned to private life and he never forgave Macmillan. What undoubtedly made matters particularly distressing for Kilmuir was that his personal life at this time was in something of a mess. It was commonly known that Lady Kilmuir had been living with Lord 'Buck' De la Warr whom she eventually married after Kilmuir died. All in all it cannot have been a happy time. Even the hereditary viscountcy which Kilmuir received after his forced retirement can have been of slim comfort especially as Kilmuir had no heir to whom his new title could pass. There was also the problem of money. The pension of a former Lord Chancellor had yet to reach its presently quite generous levels and after years in politics Kilmuir was apparently hard strapped for cash. To make up for this he became a company director with a city firm called Plesseys. This sudden move into the business world – which might be considered rather less remarkable today – attracted considerable criticism at the time with some people suggesting that the Lord Chancellor was cashing in on his political connections. All in all it was a marked turnaround in the circumstances of a man who had once been spoken of as a possible candidate to succeed Churchill and later Eden as Prime Minister. But Kilmuir did not have the glamour of Eden or the mettle of Macmillan. His was a plodding type of success. He worked hard to get into Parliament. He worked hard when he had got into Parliament. He worked hard in junior ministerial office. He worked hard when he finally made it into the Cabinet as Attorney-General. He worked hard when he was sent to Nuremburg for a year as the Deputy Chief Prosecutor at the Nazi War Crimes Tribunal. He worked hard when he was later appointed Home Secretary and Minister for Welsh Affairs. And it was to reward all this hard work that he was ultimately given the plum job of Lord Chancellor by Churchill and continued on in that position by Eden and Macmillan. On a personal level Kilmuir was rather closer to Eden than he was to Macmillan. He was one of the few who knew that Eden was contemplating resigning after the Suez crisis – he advised Eden not to resign – and he was one of the first to learn that Eden would not be acting on Kilmuir's advice and would be stepping down. As Lord Chancellor Kilmuir was popular and effective though he did rather tend to concentrate on the ministerial and not the judicial aspects of the office – he even continued to address party political gatherings despite being the head of the judiciary. He was famous among the counsel who appeared before him for his frightening ability to remember the names of cases and their precise location in the case reports. Still it is perhaps more as a politician than as a lawyer or judge that Kilmuir is now remembered.

Viscount Dilhorne of Green's Norton (1905–80)

Lord High Chancellor of Great Britain: 1962–4
Prime Minister with whom served: Macmillan (Conservative)

Age became Lord Chancellor: 57
Born: Latimer, Buckinghamshire
Secondary education: Eton
University education: Oxford University
King's Counsel: 1946 (Age 41)
Inn of Court to which belonged: Inner Temple

Age ceased being Lord Chancellor: 59
Father's occupation: Lieutenant-colonel; baronet; landowner
Called to Bar: 1927 (Age 22)
Married: Once
Age married: 25
Children: 1 son, 3 daughters

High judicial office other than Lord Chancellorship:
1969–80 Lord of Appeal in Ordinary (Age: 64–75)

Public office other than Lord Chancellorship:
1943–62 MP for Northamptonshire (Conservative); 1945, Solicitor-General; 1954–62, Attorney-General

Viscount Dilhorne was not the most attractive of personalities. Born Reginald Manningham-Buller his bruising way of dealing with others led to his being nicknamed 'Bullying Manners'. Dilhorne was chosen by Harold Macmillan to replace Viscount Kilmuir as Lord Chancellor when Kilmuir was dropped from the Cabinet in 1962. Kilmuir had been a well-known and well-liked figure on the national stage as well as within Parliament and the legal profession. Dilhorne was not publicly known. Nor was he privately liked. And in the 'swinging Sixties' his politics were almost universally perceived among anyone other than the Conservative Party faithful as positively Neanderthal. He was, for example, in favour of the death penalty. And he was something of a fan of 'Big Brother'. Thus Dilhorne considered the good name of government to have been rather sullied and felt the pendulum had swung too far in favour of the individual. He believed, for example, that there was no reason why a suspect should have to be informed of his rights upon his arrest. This is all fine and dandy of course if, like Dilhorne, you are a fully paid-up member of the gentry with an inherited baronetcy, an estate in the countryside, a wife whose father was an Earl, and a father who was a Member of Parliament. The chances of such an individual not knowing their rights (or not having a lawyer who knows them) are pretty slim. Being told of one's rights upon arrest might be rather more necessary if one hails, as most criminal suspects still do, from a financially deprived and less educationally favoured background.

Before becoming Chancellor Dilhorne spent eight years as Attorney-General, the government's chief legal adviser. It was not the first time the office was held by a member of Dilhorne's family. Three centuries earlier his ancestor Sir Edward Coke had served Queen Elizabeth I in the same capacity. In 1957 there was uproar when it was discovered that a barrister whom Dilhorne disliked was being bugged by the government. Dilhorne gave an explanation that a majority in Parliament (which at the time of course had a majority of members from Dilhorne's own party) accepted as satisfactory. But for a time the episode left something of a cloud over Dilhorne's career: when the office of Lord Chief Justice became vacant a year later the job was not offered to Dilhorne. Still the hand of fate favours those who wait and in 1962 Dilhorne became Lord Chancellor. With only a third class degree in law one might have thought there were others more eminently qualified for the position than Dilhorne but presumably Macmillan considered Dilhorne – who like Macmillan was an old Eton boy and an Oxford man – to be an appropriate choice. When Macmillan resigned it was Dilhorne who sounded out the other members of the Cabinet as to whom they thought should become the new party leader. The Earl of Home was the surprise choice – even Home himself was surprised. However he immediately resigned his seat in the House of Lords and as Sir Alec Douglas-Home entered the House of Commons as member for Perthshire and Prime Minister. Five months later he lost the General Election and Dilhorne lost his job as Lord Chancellor, becoming the deputy leader of the opposition. But two years into Opposition Dilhorne was dropped from the front bench by Edward Heath, the new Conservative Party leader. Thereafter Dilhorne dropped from the public stage for a few years until 1969 when he was re-appointed to high office by the Wilson administration, this time as a Lord of Appeal in Ordinary. He was to hold this position until his death in 1980. It is difficult to understand why Dilhorne was appointed a Lord of Appeal. He was not an especially brilliant lawyer. And as Lord Chancellor he had not been an especially brilliant judge. It is not even that Dilhorne's politics resembled those of Wilson or his Lord Chancellor. After all, the Wilson administrations were vaguely liberal in outlook and Lord Gardiner, the Lord Chancellor at the time of Dilhorne's appointment as a Lord of Appeal, was ultra-liberal in outlook. Dilhorne, on the other hand, was no liberal and his time as a Lord of Appeal did nothing to enhance his reputation in this regard.

Baron Gardiner of Kittisford (1900–90)

Lord High Chancellor of Great Britain: 1964–70
Prime Minister with whom served: Wilson (Labour)

Age became Lord Chancellor: 64
Born: London
Secondary education: Harrow
Called to Bar: 1925 (Age 25)
Inn of Court to which belonged: Inner Temple
Age ceased being Lord Chancellor: 70
Father's occupation: Shipping company director
University education: Oxford University
King's Counsel: 1948 (Age 48)
Married: Twice
Age married: 25; 70
Children: 1 daughter

High judicial office other than Lord Chancellorship:
None

Public office other than Lord Chancellorship:
None

Gerald Gardiner surely never thought on being sent down from Oxford that he would one day be made an honorary fellow of his old *alma mater*. Nor can he have thought that he would one day become Lord High Chancellor of Great Britain. But then nothing about Gerald Gardiner was entirely conventional. His father, a wealthy shipping company director who would one day be knighted, came from a well-respected family in the West Country. But his mother was a Prussian princess. At Oxford Gardiner was a member of the smartly-dressed set. But Gardiner was not only worried about the state of his appearance. He was also worried about the state of the nation. And his views were radically progressive for the early twentieth century. Indeed Gardiner got into trouble with Oxford University authorities for his advocacy of women's rights in the university magazine *Isis*. It was this which led to his being sent down. But Gardiner did not give up. His article in *Isis* was the beginning of a life-long association with causes that were unpopular when he took them up but which went on to become more acceptable as the century progressed. At the end of the First World War Gardiner joined the Peace Pledge Union – a pacifist organization. And during the Second World War when he might have had an eye to judicial office he took the courageous step of joining an ambulance unit run by the Quakers and staffed by conscientious objectors. These were not actions likely to endear Gardiner to the ruling classes. Nor was his active participation in the campaign to abolish capital punishment. This was something of a pariah cause when Gardiner joined forces with it in the 1930s but he gave it his all. Indeed it was a mark of the man that when he was first approached by the Lord Chancellor and offered a High Court judgeship he quickly turned it down: at the time of the offer High Court judges still had to pass death sentences on certain criminals and this was something which Gardiner knew he could never bring himself to do. It was fitting that when the death penalty was ultimately abolished it was Gardiner as Lord Chancellor who moved the motion for abolition in the House of Lords.

As a barrister Gardiner was highly successful. He had a large practice and frequently appeared in prominent cases. Perhaps his most famous trial was when he successfully defended Penguin Books in the prosecution brought against them under the Obscene Publications Act 1959 for publishing D. H. Lawrence's *Lady Chatterley's Lover*. In 1963 Gardiner was appointed to the House of Lords on the advice of the Opposition Leader Harold Wilson. One year later when Wilson entered 10 Downing Street as Prime Minister Gardiner became Lord Chancellor, the only post-war Lord Chancellor not to have served as a judge or as an MP prior to his appointment to the Woolsack. As Lord Chancellor Gardiner next to never sat as a judge. Nor did he unduly concern himself with party politics. Instead he concentrated on his ministerial duties almost to the exclusion of everything else. In six years as Lord Chancellor he managed to push through a liberal programme of legislation and establish a rolling programme of law reform. Oddly however despite his legislative achievements Gardiner seems to enjoy a greater reputation among his fellow lawyers than he did among his fellow Cabinet ministers. Lord Hailsham of St Marylebone, who succeeded Gardiner as Lord Chancellor (and who came from a different political party) has written that Gardiner can "claim an important place amongst twentieth-century Chancellors."[46] But Richard Crossman, who sat across from Gardiner in the Wilson Cabinet, wrote in his diaries that Gardiner as Lord Chancellor was "remote from the reality of politics ... ineffective ... Quakerish and high-minded".[47]

Gardiner's time as Lord Chancellor was a lonely one personally. Two years into office his first wife died after forty years of marriage. For the remainder of his term in office Gardiner lived alone in the Lord Chancellor's flat inside the Palace of Westminster being looked after by an elderly Spanish maid. But where there is life there is hope – in 1970 after the Wilson government had lost power and Gardiner had ceased to be Lord Chancellor he re-married at the ripe old age of seventy. In the years that followed he enjoyed life to the full. He continued to champion those libertarian causes he had always supported (along with some new ones too). One of his greatest pleasures came on being appointed Chancellor of the Open University in 1973. The Open University is possibly the premier domestic achievement of the Wilson administrations. It was established by the government to provide distance degree courses for people who had missed out on a regular university education. And it has proved to be a remarkable success. As Chancellor of the University Gardiner did not merely make decisions regarding student life – he became a student himself. He enrolled in the social sciences course and in due time, after doing the prescribed coursework and taking the prescribed exams he was conferred with a bachelors degree in social sciences. Even in old age Gardiner still managed to court controversy just as he had in his student days at Oxford. In 1972 he served on a government committee charged with examining the methods then being used by the British police and defence forces to interrogate terrorists. Gardiner's minority opinion was that the interrogation methods being used were neither legitimate nor appropriate. For his efforts he was later nearly killed by an IRA bomb. In 1975 after serving on another government committee Gardiner arrived at the conclusion that the practice of holding terrorist suspects without trial was not objectionable. It was a surprising conclusion and a curious irregularity in Gardiner's otherwise flawless pedigree of lifelong concern for the protection of personal rights.

Lord Hailsham of St Marylebone (1907–)

Lord High Chancellor of Great Britain: (1970–4; 1979–87)
Prime Ministers with whom served: Heath and Thatcher (Conservative)

Age became Lord Chancellor: 63; 72
Born: London
Secondary education: Eton
Called to Bar: 1932 (Age 25)
Inn of Court to which belonged: Lincoln's Inn
Age ceased being Lord Chancellor: 67; 80
Father's occupation: Barrister; MP; Lord Chancellor
University education: Oxford (Christ Church)
Queen's Counsel: 1953 (Age 46)
Married: Three times
Age married: 25, 37, 79
Children: 2 sons, 3 daughters

High judicial office other than Lord Chancellorship:
None

Public office other than Lord Chancellorship:
1938–50, MP for Oxford (Conservative); 1945, Joint Parliamentary Under-Secretary of State for Air; 1950–63, Hereditary member of House of Lords; 1956–7, First Lord of the Admiralty; 1957, Minister of Education; 1957–9, Lord President of the Privy Council; 1957–60, Deputy Leader of the House of Lords; 1959–60, Lord Privy Seal; 1959–64, Minister for Science and Technology; 1960–3, Leader of the House of Lords; 1960–4, Lord President of the Privy Council; 1962–4, Minister with special responsibility for Sport; 1963–70 (after had disclaimed hereditary peerage for life) MP for St Marylebone; 1963–4 Minister with special responsibility for dealing with unemployment in the North-East; 1963–4 Minister with special

responsibility for higher education; 1964, Secretary of State for Education and Science

Hailsham is the only Lord Chancellor in the post-Second World War period to have held the office of Chancellor twice. He is also the only Lord Chancellor in history whose father was also Lord Chancellor. As it happens Hailsham's father was not the only judge in the family. Hailsham is half-American and his maternal grandfather was a judge in Nashville, Tennessee. Becoming Lord Chancellor could almost be portrayed as having been second-best for Hailsham given that in 1963 he nearly succeeded Harold Macmillan as leader of the Conservative Party and British Prime Minister. There are differing accounts offered as to why he did not. The first is that despite Hailsham's obvious merits there were some doubts as to whether he was necessarily the most desirable candidate to be premier. Even Macmillan himself later claimed that he had doubts. Towards the end of his life he stated that Hailsham was "one of the finest men I knew – a big man, a great churchgoer and idealist. But he didn't always do himself justice; there was an excess of boyishness."[48] History of course is written in hindsight and the views of Home and Macmillan may well have been coloured by what had occurred in the past. What many people seem to forget is that Hailsham did enjoy the support of such Conservative luminaries as former Prime Minister Anthony Eden. Moreover he was popular among the ordinary members of the Conservative Party, he was well-liked in the country and he had the best chance of winning the next general election. In 1963 Hailsham initially believed that he had the backing of Macmillan in the leadership race. Thus he describes in his memoirs how on Monday, 7 October, 1963, Macmillan summoned him to 10 Downing Street and, writes Hailsham, "told me, formally, that he wished me to succeed him". So how was it that little more than a week later Alec Douglas-Home had become Prime Minister? Macmillan, says Hailsham, "had done another of his famous somersaults". He had not supported Hailsham as he could and Hailsham's moment had gone. It was a disappointing and upsetting experience. In his memoirs Hailsham writes "I would have been proud to accept the leadership if the cards had fallen that way. I was sorry that they did not... [T]he whole experience... [was] miserable. I would not have allowed my name to go forward at all had Harold [Macmillan] not pressed me to do so".[49] Seven years later Hailsham accepted the invitation to become Lord Chancellor in the Conservative administration of Edward Heath. It was not perhaps quite the same as being Prime Minister but it was a considerable achievement none the less and one that Hailsham was to repeat in the Thatcher era when he served a further eight years as Lord Chancellor before old age finally forced him to retire. As Lord Chancellor Hailsham had the reputation of being a thoroughly decent man on a personal level. And in so far as being the top judge in England and Wales was concerned he was eminently well qualified for the job having left Oxford with a first class degree before going on to take top place and a Certificate of Honour in the 1932 Bar Finals. Possibly Hailsham's greatest achievement as Lord Chancellor was to firmly re-establish the judicial nature of the office. He was the first Lord Chancellor since Viscount Simonds in the 1950s who made a particularly determined effort to sit in as many Appellate Committee cases as possible and is one of the few Lord Chancellors this century whose claim to fame as Chancellor will perhaps rest as much on his performance as a judge as on his record as a minister. Even so, it is possibly for his early career in politics and most especially his failed attempt to become Premier that Hailsham will be known to a wider readership.

Lord Elwyn-Jones of Llanelli and Newham (1909–89)

Lord High Chancellor of Great Britain: 1974–9
Prime Ministers with whom served: Wilson and Callaghan (Labour)

Age became Lord Chancellor: 65
Born: Llanelli, Wales
Secondary education: Llanelli Grammar School
Called to Bar: 1935 (Age 26)
Inn of Court to which belonged: Gray's Inn
University education: University of Wales, Cambridge University
Queen's Counsel: 1953 (Age 44)
Married: Once
Age married: 28

Age ceased being Lord Chancellor: 70
Father's occupation: Tinplate worker
Children: 1 son, 2 daughters

High judicial office other than Lord Chancellorship:
None

Public office other than Lord Chancellorship:
1945–74, MP for West Ham (Labour); 1974, MP for Newham South; 1964–70, Attorney-General

That Frederick Elwyn-Jones succeeded to the office of Lord Chancellor was a great personal achievement but not an achievement marked by any later successes of particular note. Prior to becoming Lord Chancellor Elwyn-Jones spent six fairly uneventful years as Attorney-General. The only time he really came to the fore was when he was appointed to head a government inquiry into the Aberfan disaster of 1966 in which more than 140 people (mostly children) were killed when a waste-heap of coal subsided and swept into a junior school in Wales. (The inquiry eventually found that the National Coal Board was responsible.)

Elwyn-Jones actually grew up not too far from Aberfan. His father was a tinplate worker by trade. He was also a deacon and Sunday school teacher at the local Congregational church. As a child Elwyn-Jones sang in the church choir and he maintained a love of singing throughout his life. On one occasion as Lord Chancellor he even serenaded the London Lord Mayor's annual banquet with a rendition of the Lord Chancellor's song from Gilbert and Sullivan's *Iolanthe* – something that one could not imagine any of the other Lord Chancellors in the last century and a quarter doing too readily.

As a child Elwyn-Jones attended his local grammar school before moving on to study Arts at the Aberystwyth campus of the University of Wales. He was the first Lord Chancellor in the post-war period not to have received his pre-university schooling at a private institution. After Aberystwyth Elwyn-Jones was awarded a scholarship to study at Cambridge University where he succeeded in getting a Masters in Arts. More impressively perhaps he also succeeded in becoming the President of the Cambridge Union, the principal student society in Cambridge. His time at Cambridge complete Elwyn-Jones went to London to qualify as a barrister. He was called to the Bar in 1935.

While in London Elwyn-Jones became an active member of the Fabian Society, a left-wing think-tank. It was through the Fabians that Elwyn-Jones became involved as a young barrister in defending Austrian socialists who were being persecuted for their beliefs by the Austrian government. Through this political activity Elwyn-Jones came in contact with many socialist luminaries who were to be leading lights in the post-war Labour governments. Elwyn-Jones himself was to play a smaller role in those administrations as a humble back-bencher. In 1945 he was elected Member of Parliament for West Ham (Plaistow Division). Though the name of his constituency was to change more than once Elwyn-Jones would continue to represent the people of West Ham for almost thirty years.

As a politician Elwyn-Jones' career was far from dramatic. His first year as an MP was actually spent in Nuremburg as a prosecuting counsel at the Nazi War Crimes Tribunal. Here he acted under the leadership of David Maxwell-Fyfe who as Viscount Kilmuir was to be Lord Chancellor from 1954 until 1962. After his return to Westminster another eighteen years would pass before Elwyn-Jones was given paid government office as Attorney General. During this time his sole achievement of note, apart from becoming a Queen's Counsel of course, was that he acted as the lead prosecuting counsel in the Moors murder trial, one of the most shocking criminal cases in British legal history and one with which the British public are still familiar today as a result of ongoing but unsuccessful efforts to have Myra Hindley, one of the murderers, released.

In 1974 Elwyn-Jones was asked by Harold Wilson, the Labour Prime Minister, to become Lord Chancellor. Elwyn-Jones jumped at the opportunity and shortly thereafter was promoted into the House of Lords as Baron Elwyn-Jones of Llanelli and Newham, a neat little title whose geographical references combined both his Welsh origins and his longstanding connection with West London. Elwyn-Jones was to remain on the Woolsack for five years, being continued on in office by James Callaghan when the latter took over the reins of the Labour administration from Harold Wilson in 1976. As Lord Chancellor his judgments were solid rather than inspired. On a more mundane level he became known as the Lord

Chancellor who travelled to work each day by Tube. However in this he was perhaps outshone by the man who both preceded and succeeded him as Lord Chancellor, Lord Hailsham of St Marylebone, who was known for sometimes travelling to the House of Lords by bicycle.

After the Conservatives returned to power in 1979 Elwyn-Jones continued on as a Lord of Appeal in Ordinary. In a rather interesting example of the cross-pollination between the judicial and legislative brances of the British government Elwyn-Jones also served from 1983 onwards as the House of Lords spokesperson for the Labour Party on justice and home affairs. Lord Elwyn-Jones died in 1989.

Lord Havers of St Edmundsbury (1923–92)

Lord High Chancellor of Great Britain: 1987
Prime Minister with whom served: Thatcher (Conservative)

Age became Lord Chancellor: 64
Born: 1923
Secondary education: Westminster School
Called to Bar: 1948 (Age 25)
Inn of Court to which belonged: Inner Temple
Age ceased being Lord Chancellor: 64

Father's occupation: Court of Appeal judge
University education: Cambridge University
Queen's Counsel: 1964 (Age 41)
Married: Once
Age married: 26
Children: 2 sons

High judicial office other than Lord Chancellorship:
None

Public office other than Lord Chancellorship:
1970–87, MP for Wimbledon (Conservative); 1972–84, Solicitor-General; 1979–87, Attorney-General

Michael Havers was very much an Establishment figure: the son of a High Court judge, the Solicitor-General in the Conservative administration of Edward Heath, the Attorney-General in all three administrations of Margaret Thatcher. Havers even had that ultimate – though utterly unwelcome – badge of Establishment membership: he was once the target of an IRA bomb.

As Attorney-General Havers did not prove to be entirely uncontroversial. It was he who tried to prevent the publication in Britain of *Spycatcher*, the memoirs of Peter Wright, a onetime British intelligence officer. Havers took this step on the perfectly valid basis that some of what Wright discussed in his memoirs was material which Wright as a onetime Crown employee was actually prohibited from discussing by virtue of the Official Secrets Act. However other authors had long published works containing material covered by the Official Secrets Act and their books had never been suppressed. To make matters worse the media seized on the issue as a matter of press freedom. As a result the British government found itself being criticised by newspapers, radio stations and television networks all around the world. Other controversial legal actions instigated by Havers during his time as Attorney-General were the prosecutions of Sarah Tidsall and Clive Ponting. Tidsall was a Foreign Office official who passed pretty trivial details of Cruise missile deployments to the press. With the level of leaking that goes on in Whitehall one might have expected such a transgression to earn her a stern reprimand or at worst her dismissal. Instead Havers brought a successful prosecution against Tidsall under the Official Secrets Act. Clive Ponting was more lucky. He too was a civil servant. He allegedly leaked documents that were not favourable to the Thatcher administration's version of how an Argentinian ship, the *General Belgrano*, came to be sunk during the Falklands War. The sinking of the *Belgrano* proved very controversial. It caused Mrs Thatcher more than a little difficulty during the 1983 general election campaign. And it occasioned her Attorney-General, Michael Havers, more than a little embarrassment when a jury refused to convict Clive Ponting for what he had allegedly done.

By June 1987 Havers had become the longest-serving Attorney-General in English history. But destiny had marked him out for higher things. Following the retirement of Lord Hailsham of St Marylebone as Lord Chancellor the job was offered to Havers by Margaret Thatcher. It was something of an unusual choice: Havers was known to be a sick man and was not expected to last long in the job. However Geoffrey Howe, who was Foreign Secretary at this time, has suggested in his memoirs that Havers may to some extent have been offered the job precisely because he was sick: "Contrary to some commentary, this could actually work in his favour. Even a few weeks on the Woolsack would qualify him for the generous pension which went with the job."[50] In any event Havers accepted the offer and entered the House of Lords in June 1987 as Lord Havers of St Edmundsbury. Four months later he retired on grounds of ill-health. He had been the shortest-serving Lord Chancellor in English history. Havers died at the age of 69 in 1992. He was survived by his wife and two sons, one of whom is Nigel Havers, the actor.

Baron Mackay of Clashfern (1927–)

Lord High Chancellor of Great Britain: 1987–97
Prime Ministers with whom served: Thatcher (Conservative), Major (Conservative)

Age became Lord Chancellor: 60
Born: Scourie, Scotland
Secondary education: George Heriot's School, Edinburgh
Overall grade of degree: Two first class degrees
Married: Once
Children: 1 son, 2 daughters
Age ceased being Lord Chancellor: 70
Father's occupation: Railway signalman
University education: Edinburgh University; Cambridge University
Became Scots Advocate: 1955 (Age 28)
Queen's Counsel: 1965 (Age 38)
Age married: 31

High judicial office other than Lord Chancellorship:
1979–84, Senator of College of Justice in Scotland; 1985–7, Lord of Appeal in Ordinary

Government office other than Lord Chancellorship:
1975–84, Commissioner of Northern Lighthouses; 1979–84 Lord Advocate; 1990, Elder Brother of Trinity House

James Peters Hymers Mackay was born in 1927 in the Scottish village of Scourie, the son of a railwayman. As a boy he won a scholarship to study at George Heriot's School in Edinburgh. From there he proceeded to Edinburgh University where he earned himself a first class degree in mathematics and physics. After that he lectured for a couple of years at St Andrew's University and even did a spell of research at Cambridge University before deciding that he really wanted to be a lawyer. Back he went to Edinburgh where he took up a job in a solicitor's firm and at the same time began studying law at Edinburgh University. Most people would count themselves lucky just to pass their examinations in these circumstances but in 1955 Mackay managed to graduate with yet another first class degree from Edinburgh University, this time in law. In the same year he was admitted to the Scottish Bar.

As a Scots advocate Mackay's career advanced at a lightning pace. He specialised in tax cases and soon had a flourishing practice. Only ten years after being admitted as an advocate he was appointed a Queen's Counsel at the remarkably young age of 38. What made this achievement all the more remarkable of course is that Mackay had only switched to being a lawyer after several years in an entirely different career. In 1976 he crowned this achievement by being elected Dean of the Faculty of Scots Advocates (the head of the Scottish Bar). Notwithstanding these successes Mackay had never yet evinced such an interest in politics as might lead one to conclude that here was a man on course to becoming a future Lord Chancellor. Fate was now to play a part.

In 1979 Margaret Thatcher became Prime Minister. However her success was largely based on electoral achievements in England. In Scotland the Conservative Party had not done quite so well. Faced with a shortage of talent within the Scottish Conservative Party Mrs Thatcher took the unusual step of inviting a non-Conservative Party member, Lord Mackay to become Lord Advocate for Scotland. Mackay accepted the opportunity, joined the Conservative Party and shortly thereafter leapt for the first time onto the national stage as the newly ennobled Lord Mackay of Clashfern.

Six years on, after a spell as a Scottish superior court judge, and at a younger than average 58 years of age, Mackay was made a Lord of Appeal. Two years later he was invited to become Lord Chancellor by Mrs Thatcher. Geoffrey Howe, who was Foreign Secretary at the time of Mackay's appointment as Lord Chancellor, has written in his memoirs that at the time the Chancellorship could perhaps have been his if he wanted it but Mrs Thatcher preferred him to remain on at the Foreign Office. Looking back it might in one respect have been better for Mrs Thatcher if she had arranged for Howe to become Lord Chancellor. It was Howe's resignation from the office of Foreign Secretary three years later which ultimately triggered Mrs Thatcher's own downfall. Howe resigned partly because of the manner in which Mrs Thatcher interfered with the way in which he conducted the day to day affairs of the Foreign Office. This dispute between the two was already simmering in 1987 but would possibly not have ended quite as it did if Howe had gone to the Woolsack in that year.[51]

Mackay was the first Scots advocate to become Lord Chancellor. This put him in a slightly unusual position. As Lord Chancellor he was head of the English and Welsh judiciary and head of a division of the English High Court even though he had never actually qualified in English law. However this was really no more unusual than is the fact that during his time as a Scottish Lord of Appeal Mackay (like all Scottish Lords of Appeal before and since) was eligible to sit with the Appellate Committee and hear appeals on points of English law from the English courts even though he had trained as a Scottish lawyer.

Despite his contributions to jurisprudence Mackay's time as Lord Chancellor will almost undoubtedly be remembered best for the reforms which he sought to effect within the legal system. These reforms were intended to make the legal system more accessible, more efficient and less expensive.

Baron Irvine of Lairg (1940–)

Lord High Chancellor of Great Britain: 1997–
Prime Minister with whom serves: Blair (Labour)

Age became Lord Chancellor: 58
Secondary education:
Hutcheson's Boys Grammar School

University education:
Glasgow University;
Cambridge University
Age admitted to Bar: 27

Inn of court to which belongs: Inner Temple

Age became Queen's Counsel: 38

Married: Twice

Children: 2 sons

Judicial office other than Lord Chancellorship:
Deputy High Court Judge 1987–97

Public office other than Lord Chancellorship:
None

Lord Irvine of Lairg is a personal friend of Tony Blair. The two first met when Irvine recruited the young Mr Blair, who at that time had yet to enter public life, to work with him at 11 King's Bench Walk, the set of barrister's chambers that Irvine founded in 1981. It was during his time at Lord Irvine's chambers that Blair first met Cherie Booth, the barrister who has since become his wife. Blair and Booth are said to have a great deal of respect for Lord Irvine since the days that they worked under him at the Bar.

Born in 1940, Alexander Andrew Mackay ('Derry') Irvine is the youngest Appellate Committee member. He is one of only three Lord Chancellors since the Second World War to have come from what might be described as an unprivileged background. As a boy Irvine lived with his parents in a rented flat. Money was always tight. So what was it that brought Irvine to the top of the legal profession and the heights of government office? Ambition certainly played its part: Lord Irvine of Lairg is reputed to have told his friends at grammar school and at law school that he intended to become Lord Chancellor one day. Much of it is sheer hard work – Lord Irvine is renowned for getting to his desk around five o'clock in the morning. However there is also a certain brilliance about the man. As a boy he won a scholarship place at his local grammer school. From there he went on to Glasgow University where he succeeded in getting a first class degree in law. From Glasgow he proceeded to Cambridge University where he succeeded in getting another first class degree. From Cambridge, Irvine went on to the London School of Economics where he worked as a lecturer for four years before going on to a successful career as a practising barrister. Of course his life has not been without its disappointments and failures. In 1970 he stood as Labour Party candidate for Parliament in the London constituency

1 Lord Irvine of Lairg. The present Lord Chancellor: Scotsman, lawman, New Labour man. (Born: 1940. Appointed 1997.)

2 Lord Browne-Wilkinson. Retired from the post of senior Lord of Appeal in Ordinary in June 2000. (Born: 1930. Appointed: 1991.)

3 Lord Hoffmann. Perhaps the most brilliant of the present Lords of Appeal. Was the subject of some press attention in late 1998 when his membership of the Appellate Committee panel that reached the original decision in the General Pinochet appeal was a cause of some controversy. (Born: 1934. Appointed 1995.)

4 Lord Denning. Easily the most famous British judge of the 20th century. (Born: 1899. Died: 1999. Served on the Appellate Committee: 1957–62.)

5 Lord Hailsham of St Marylebone. Twice served as Lord Chancellor (1970–74 and 1979–87.) His father also served as Lord Chancellor. One of his grandfathers was a judge in Nashville, Tennessee.

of Hendon but failed to be elected. A few years after that Lord Irvine's first marriage broke up. He subsequently married his second wife, the present Lady Irvine. (As it happens Lady Irvine herself had previously been married. Her first husband was Donald Dewar, who sits with Lord Irvine at the Cabinet table as Secretary of State for Scotland.)

At the Bar Irvine was a tremendous success. He specialised in employment law though he also had an extensive practice in commercial law and public law. In 1978 he became a Queen's Counsel at the comparatively young age of 38. At this stage Irvine was considered to be one of the Bar's high-fliers. So there was a certain astonishment when he took a chance in the middle of his career, quit the chambers where he had previously worked and went off to 11 King's Bench Walk, where he set up a new chambers of his own that took in cases in Lord Irvine's areas of specialisation. This proved to be a very astute move. The 1980s saw an explosion in the number of cases in the employment–public law areas and Irvine's chambers as a specialist set were well placed to capitalise on this sudden growth. It is now one of the most successful chambers in the City.

Despite his flourishing career as a barrister Lord Irvine never lost his connections with the Labour Party. In 1987 he was elevated to the House of Lords as a Labour peer at the behest of Neil Kinnock, the Labour Party leader from 1983 to 1992. In the same year he became a part-time High Court judge. This gave him judicial experience but it did not preclude him from accepting the position of shadow Lord Chancellor in 1992, following the death of Lord Elwyn-Jones, the one-time Lord Chancellor in the Wilson and Callaghan administrations of the 1970s. Irvine was invited to become shadow Lord Chancellor by John Smith, the man who succeeded Neil Kinnock as Labour Party leader. And he would probably have gone on to serve as Lord Chancellor in an administration headed by Smith if it had not been for Smith's sudden death in 1994. As it was Lord Irvine had to wait until Tony Blair swept to victory in the May 1997 General Election before taking office as Lord Chancellor, a position he retains today. As Lord Chancellor, Lord Irvine of Lairg is perhaps the most powerful occupant of that office since the Second World War. Not only is he the head of the judiciary, the head of a government ministry, and the speaker of the House of Lords, Lord Irvine is also the driving force behind the constitutional reforms proposed by the Blair administration and the chairman of a number of Cabinet committees.

4
Life on the Appellate Committee

Inside the House of Lords – the facilities available to the Lords of Appeal – the use of personal researchers – the lay-out at hearings – the conduct of hearings – time limits – recording proceedings – deciding a case – producing a judgment – the everyday strain of being a Lord of Appeal

On his arrival at the Palace of Westminster each new Lord of Appeal in Ordinary is given an office on the second floor overlooking the back end of Westminster Abbey. Oddly enough the offices allocated to the Lords of Appeal are not especially impressive. They have high ceilings and are quite large. But they have a somewhat dilapidated feel to them and are rather noisy – they overlook one of the busiest roads in central London. Inside their offices the Lords of Appeal are free to arrange the furniture according to their own individual taste. However the offices are so sparsely furnished that there is not a great deal of arranging to do. Along with the obligatory desk and two chairs goes a large set of bookshelves. Apart from that there is very little else.

Immediately outside the offices of the various Lords of Appeal is a long, quiet, narrow carpeted corridor from which there is a door exiting onto another brighter, wider, corridor that has been cut off at one end and functions as a sort of reception area for those who have business with the Appellate Committee. Opening onto this reception area is the elevator as well as a couple of offices housing the small administrative, clerical and secretarial support team which serves the Appellate Committee. Despite being some of the most important people in the United Kingdom each of the various Lords of Appeal does not get a secretary of his own. Instead they all have access to a pool of about four secretaries who do any typing that the Appellate Committee requires. On the face of it this means that the 12 Lords of Appeal are allocated roughly one-third of a secretary each. However this is a rather generous estimate as the Lords of Appeal are not the only people with access to the typing pool. The Lord Chancellor may also pray in aid the services of the typing pool on those occasions when he sits with the Committee. Then of course there are the (at the time of writing) 14 other peers who hold or have held high judicial office and who may occasionally be called upon to sit in judgment with the Appellate Committee. Every one of them is free to use the typing pool when he comes to preparing a judgment. Consequently four secretaries may be called upon to serve anything up to 26 people. Such facilities compare badly with those available to members of the European Court of Justice or the United States Supreme Court. Indeed it is doubtful that any other senior figures in government would get by on such a shoestring arrangement. The standard of facilities traditionally afforded Lords of Appeal may have been one of the main reasons why in 1964, after only three years in office, Lord Devlin decided to quit the Appellate Committee at a relatively youthful 59 years of age.

Along with his office and his portion of a secretary the new Lord of Appeal is given very little else by way of administrative help. Unlike members of the United States Supreme Court, members of the Appellate Committee are not given personal researchers (or 'law clerks'). It could be argued that giving personal researchers to the various Lords of Appeal would be a good idea. After all it might be helpful for the Lords of Appeal to have someone intelligent around with whom they could bandy about ideas. That said, there is of course the argument that this – amongst other things – is what the other Lords of Appeal are there for. Indeed the point might also be made that in giving personal researchers to the Lords of Appeal – researchers who would of course be the very best of the most recent graduates from universities such as Oxford, Cambridge and Edinburgh – one would run a serious risk that the Lords of Appeal might be tempted into allowing those researchers to write their opinions for them, or at the very least to prepare drafts which might well bear a striking resemblance to the final opinions of the Lords of Appeal. After all it has long been suspected that to a large extent it is the law clerks in the United States Supreme Court who draft the opinions delivered in that Court. It is very much open to question whether such a practice (if it does exist within the United States Supreme Court) would ever be tolerated in the United Kingdom where there has always been a very strong tradition – indeed it is a cornerstone of the British legal system – that judges give their personal attention to whatever questions are raised before them and that they answer those questions in their own words to the best of their own ability.

Hearings of the Appellate Committee are conducted in a Committee Room inside the Palace of Westminster. Like the personal offices of the various members this room too has a slightly dilapidated feel to it. The desks at which the Lords of Appeal sit are arranged in a semi-circle. Beside them are shelves for books and other materials. The Lords of Appeal do not wear any judicial garb when hearing a case. Instead they dress in ordinary suits. Contrary to what one might expect from those who favour the retention of wigs and gowns this does not in any way diminish their authority or bearing nor does it engender disrespect – though in fairness the mere fact that one is standing inside the Palace of Westminster before some of the most brilliant judges in the United Kingdom endows the hearings with a natural aura of authority which one might not sense in the lower courts where judges wear (and, if surveys are anything to go by, continue to feel it necessary to wear) wigs and gowns in order to convey authority and command respect. In the mouth of the semi-circle is a stand from which counsel address the Appellate Committee. Ranged around and behind him as he speaks are opposing counsel, junior counsel and solicitors. Behind them again sit as many members of the general public as are present.

The Lord Chancellor sits in the centre chair. When the Lord Chancellor is absent – and he frequently is – the senior Lord of Appeal occupies the centre chair. The next two most senior Lords of Appeal take the chairs to the right and left of the centre chair respectively. And on it goes, right, left, in order of declining seniority. Until 1969 seniority was essentially determined by reference to rank in the peerage (whether a Lord of Appeal was a baron or a viscount) along with such factors as whether one had ever served as Lord Chancellor. However delightful such a seating practice may have been to afficionados of *Debrett's Distinguished People of Today* it was found to be unsatisfactory by Appellate Committee members. Hence from 1969 onwards it was decided that seniority would be determined solely by reference to the date of one's appointment to the Appellate Committee. This method seemed to work satisfactorily but in 1984 it was changed again: Lord Hailsham of St Marylebone, who was Lord Chancellor at the time, decided it would be best if it were left to the Sovereign to choose who were the senior and second most senior Lords of Appeal in Ordinary. The power to nominate the senior Lord of Appeal in Ordinary was last exercised in June 2000 when Lord Bingham of Cornhill was brought in from outside the Appellate Committee to become the senior Lord of Appeal following the retirement of Lord Browne-Wilkinson. (If seniority had at that time been determined by reference to longevity of Appellate

Committee membership, Lord Slynn of Hadley would now be the senior Lord of Appeal).

The Appellate Committee gives judgment in somewhere more than seventy cases every year though these cases will have been weeded out by the Appellate Committee from the many cases in which they have been asked to hear an appeal but have refused. Each case is judged by the same criterion: does it involve a point of law which raises an issue of general public importance? If so then it will be heard by the House of Lords. There are of course other factors at play regarding the number and type of appeals coming before the House of Lords. For example, the cost of bringing an appeal the whole way to the House involves a considerable financial burden. This necessarily means that apart from criminal appeals (which will normally be state-funded and of which there are a high number) the type of person who persists in bringing an appeal to the House of Lords will enjoy a certain a degree of affluence.

When a case finally comes before the Appellate Committee for full hearing there are no real restrictions on the length of time for which counsel may speak. This is markedly different from the United States Supreme Court where counsel are limited to speaking for thirty minutes in a case that does not raise constitutional issues and sixty minutes in a case that does. One reason why the Appellate Committee has not seen fit to introduce similar time restraints may stem from the fact that in the United States any attorney – no matter how recently or how poorly qualified he may be – is entitled to argue a case before the Supreme Court. In the United Kingdom, on the other hand, there is a two-tier legal profession. Apart from the very lowest courts cases are almost invariably argued by barristers. Barristers specialise in advocacy, are well used to appearing in court and know exactly how to approach a case in a manner that is satisfying to a judge. And it is of course the better barristers who are entrusted with the privilege of arguing cases before the House of Lords. Such skilled advocates tend to be pretty adept at divining when the Lords of Appeal have heard enough on a particular point or in a given case. Should they fail to discern when the Appellate Committee – or the Judicial Committee of the Privy Council – has heard enough their Lordships will soon make their feelings on the matter clear.

Standards of advocacy aside there may be a further reason why the Appellate Committee does not impose rigid time limits on argument in cases which come before it. The Appellate Committee hears cases almost every week that it is in session. The United States Supreme Court listens to oral argument in only two out of every four weeks during term time. So the simple mathematics of the situation are that in every sense the Lords of Appeal have more time to give to counsel than do the judges of the United States Supreme Court. However all this may be about to change. The sheer volume of cases now coming before the Appellate Committee means that there is ever greater pressure on the Lords of Appeal to get through ever more cases at an ever faster pace. If the Lords of Appeal are to do this and at the same time to afford each case the same unhurried and comprehensive consideration which cases have traditionally been afforded by the Lords of Appeal in the past then logic dictates that it will be necessary for there to be a greater emphasis on the written aspect of the proceedings. In consequence there has been some talk about truncating the time allowed for oral hearings before the Appellate Committee.

The United States Supreme Court tape-records the arguments of counsel who appear before it so that justices hear oral arguments again should they be so inclined. Tape-recordings are not made at Appellate Committee hearings though this is probably just as well – spending taxpayer's money on 60-minute cassette tapes would undoubtedly be considered an unabashed luxury by whoever it was decided that Lords of Appeal in Ordinary should only have between a fraction of a secretary each. Given that the Appellate Committee does not impose time limits at its hearings there is the additional problem that it would no doubt get through rather a lot more audio tape than does the United States Supreme Court. There were moves about a decade ago to begin televising the proceedings of the Appellate Committee but broadcasters would not accept the restrictions on reporting which the Lords of Appeal sought to impose. Had the proposed venture gone ahead the Appellate Committee would have become the first and only judicial body in the United Kingdom to be televised as television and radio broadcasting is presently prohibited in British courtrooms.

Once a case has been argued by counsel what happens next? The first thing to take place is that everybody is sent out of the Committee Room and the Lords of Appeal start discussing the merits of whatever case they have just heard. There is a conference room in which cases can be discussed but it seems that sometimes their Lordships find it just as convenient to conduct their post-case discussion in the committee room where they hear cases. The discussion does not take the form of some sort of coffee-table conversation. Instead it follows a very definite format. The presiding Appellate Committee member calls on the most junior member present to give his concluded views on the case. The latter then gives his views uninterrupted by the other Lords of

Appeal. After him the second most junior member does the same. After him the next most senior Lord of Appeal speaks. And on it goes. Given that the Lords of Appeal will have been discussing the case with each other the whole way through the hearings it is unlikely, though not unheard of, for any of them to come up with any startling or unexpected views at the post-case discussion. It may well be that after the various Lords of Appeal have spoken a majority or near-majority view will have emerged. If not further discussion ensues. This discussion can be any length from very short to very long. There is no set pattern as to how the discussion is conducted. However once a majority view is settled upon then whichever member is deemed appropriate, whether by reason of his particular legal expertise or a particular interest in the case at hand or some other factor thought to be relevant, will be assigned the task of writing a majority judgment. If there is no majority view then any or all of the various Lords of Appeal may choose to write a judgment, each explaining where he agrees with and where he diverges from the views held by his colleagues. Sometimes even at this late stage it will become apparent that there is in fact a majority view. If this happens one or more of the Lords of Appeal may choose to abandon writing individual judgments and subscribe instead to the judgment of another Appellate Committee member. Alternatively they may publish their own individual judgments but indicate that they are actually in agreement with some or all of what another Lord of Appeal has to say.

One might imagine that post-case discussions between the three or five Lords of Appeal who have just completed hearing a case would be the opportune moment for a Lord of Appeal to persuade his brethren to vote in a particular fashion. However in practice this seems not to happen as often as might be expected. There are a couple of reasons why this is so. First, as has been mentioned, the Lords of Appeal take the opportunity when there is a break in hearings to discuss among themselves how a case is proceeding. These opportunities for discussion mean that by the time of post-hearings discussions the views of each of the Lords of Appeal are already coloured or moulded by what their colleagues have had to say to them on their way to lunch or on their way back upstairs to their offices or in the House of Lords library or while waiting at the Peers' Lift or on any other occasion when two or more Lords of Appeal have the opportunity to converse with each other. If there is any persuading to be done then one would have thought that it is during these 'mini-' discussions of a case that the art of persuasion might most effectively be applied. A second reason why post-case discussions do not apparently involve energetic efforts by one or more Lords of Appeal to persuade their brethren to vote in a particular way is the format which those post-case discussions take. A series of contributions from the most junior Lord of Appeal present to the most senior Lord of Appeal present is not perhaps a manner of debating that is likely to facilitate any efforts which a particular Lord of Appeal might make at seeking to persuade his brethren to vote in a particular fashion. A possible third reason why the post-case discussion does not involve the Lords of Appeal engaging in a greater degree of seeking to persuade each other may well stem from a factor mentioned by Lord Macmillan – a pre-war Lord of Appeal – in his memoirs. He wrote that one of the nicest things about becoming a judge is that one no longer has to argue other people's arguments – one gets to resolve them instead. This would lead one to suspect that another reason why the Lords of Appeal do not engage in vigorous efforts to persuade each other to vote in a particular way in cases may simply be that they do not want to and are not expected to act as advocates any more. They just vote whatever way they are each individually inclined.

Of course any consideration of post-discussion hearings and the process whereby the responsibility for writing judgments is allocated is bound to be somewhat contrived – an attempt to rationalise what is a dynamic affair. There are no hard and fast rules as to how the Appellate Committee conducts its business. Thus there have been cases in the past where no real majority view has emerged or where a clear majority view has emerged but it is not certain who is going to write the majority opinion or whether there will be only one opinion from the Appellate Committee members who form the majority. What is certain is that with the continuing rise in the number of appeals coming before the House of Lords there is a real incentive for the Appellate Committee to produce single opinion judgments. In this way the minimum number of Lords of Appeal are caught up in writing a judgment in any one case and the maximum number of Lords of Appeal are free to assume the burden of writing the majority opinion in other cases. Usually when there is only one opinion given in a case it is possible to get a decision out in about six weeks' time. When there are two or more opinions then it can take up to three months to get a judgment out.

Trading of votes as such does not take place. However there is certainly an absorption of other people's opinions. Thus when somebody is assigned the task of writing a majority judgment he necessarily takes on board the views of the majority to make sure that his judgment remains palatable to them. Differences as to wording are dealt with when a draft version of the judgment is circulated among the various members of the majority. Such differences tend to be settled orally rather than by written communications between the Lords of Appeal. If the final version of the judgment does not entirely convey the particular view of one or more of the majority as to the precise position of a particular aspect of the law than he or they are free to write an opinion agreeing with the other but adding a suitable rider or enlarging upon a particular point.

In so far as the mechanics of writing a judgment are concerned it is down to the individual Lord of Appeal whether judgments are handwritten, dictated into a recorder or typed into a computer.

As regards the length of judgments most, if not all Lords of Appeal seem to live by the maxim that they say what they have to say and they say no more. Of course this can be a difficult maxim to adhere to rigidly. The story is told of how one Lord of Appeal in a moment of lightness chided Lord Roskill, a Lord of Appeal in Ordinary from 1980 to 1986, over the length of his judgments, to which Roskill replied: "Well, as Tosca once said 'I'm sorry to write you such a long letter but I didn't have time to write you a shorter one.'" In other words the Lords of Appeal are so busy that they do not often have the time to tweak, tidy and shorten their judgments even though they might like to.

Length of judgments is an issue that might be thought to arise when considering whether to appoint academic lawyers to the Appellate Committee. After all there does seem to be something of an impression abroad that academic lawyers are more prone to long-windedness than their colleagues in practice. Whether this is true or not it seems unlikely that academics will be appointed to the Appellate Committee in the near future, possibly out of a belief within government that the professional route is the best route to the Appellate Committee in that it gives a Lord of Appeal unbeatable experience of preparing, arguing, and adjudicating cases. This may not be such an unreasonable belief. After all the task of a judge is to hone in on the crucial issues in a case and provide the clearest possible answers to those issues. This is a function which it would possibly be difficult for any academic to discharge without having had the benefit of previous courtroom experience.

Finally, is it the case that the Lords of Appeal lead a more serene existence in the sedate atmosphere of the House of Lords than do Queen's Counsel down at the Bar, or indeed fellow superior court judges such as the men and women who sit on the Court of Appeal? Undoubtedly not. Certainly the work pattern of the average Lord of Appeal does not mirror that of the average Queen's Counsel who has to do enormous amounts of work, often at short notice and frequently at times which ordinary people would consider to be leisure hours. Nor are Lords of Appeal subject to exactly the same pressures as Court of Appeal judges who hear many more cases than the average Lord of Appeal in any one year. However Court of Appeal judges know that if they make a mistake there is always the Appellate Committee to correct their mistakes. Moreover it is the Appellate Committee and not the Court of Appeal which to a very great extent has the final responsibility of determining the great legal issues of our time. And that brings with it a pressure and responsibility that neither Queen's Counsel with the number of hours they work nor Court of Appeal judges with the number of cases they hear will ever have to bear – unless of course they eventually make it onto the Appellate Committee.

Lords of Appeal in Ordinary

Lord Bingham of Cornhill of Boughrood in the County of Powys

(Appointed: 2000)

Born: 1933
University education: Oxford University
Number of children: 3
Age became QC: 39
Age became Privy Councillor: 53
Secondary education: Sedbergh
Married: Once
Age married: 30
Age commenced practice: 26
Age became High Court judge: 47
Age became Lord of Appeal: 67

Thomas Henry Bingham has had a particularly distinguished judicial career. He served as a High Court judge for six years, as an ordinary member of the Court of Appeal for six years, as Master of the Rolls for four years and latterly as Lord Chief Justice for four years. In June 2000 he became the senior Lord of Appeal in Ordinary, the natural culmination of a career that has now seen Bingham hold all of the high judicial offices that it is possible for a British judge to hold save for that of Lord Chancellor (which is in any event primarily a political office).

Bingham's appointment to the Appellate Committee prompted a significant reshuffle within the higher echelons of the British judiciary. Bingham was appointed to replace Lord Browne-Wilkinson who was retiring as senior Lord of Appeal. But Bingham's departure from the Court of Appeal meant that a new Lord Chief Justice had to be found. This job was entrusted to Lord Woolf, the incumbent Master of the Rolls. But Lord Woolf's appointment meant that a new Master of the Rolls had to be found. The Prime Minister decided to appoint Lord Phillips of Worth Matravers, a serving Lord of Appeal in Ordinary, to the job. But the imminent departure of Lord Phillips of Worth Matravers meant that there was an additional vacancy to be filled within the Appellate Committee. This went to Sir Richard Scott, the Vice Chancellor of the High Court Chancery Division.

In his 14 years as a superior court judge before joining the Appellate Committee, Lord Bingham of Cornhill naturally encountered a great number of newsworthy and legally significant cases. By way of example, in 1998 Lord Bingham of Cornhill was a member of the three-man court – the Divisional Court – that first heard the challenge by General Pinochet to the validity of his detention in the United Kingdom pending his proposed extradition to Spain. The General's application to the Divisional Court was successful in that the Court quashed the issuing of the two warrants pursuant to which the General had been arrested. However, the Court stayed the quashing of the second warrant pending an appeal to the House of Lords on the issue of to what extent a former head of state should enjoy immunity from arrest and extradition in respect of acts allegedly committed by him whilst a head of state. Thereafter the matter went before the Appellate Committee (which ultimately decided that the General could validly be arrested in the United Kingdom in respect of certain offences). In May 2000 Lord Bingham of Cornhill sat in a rather different case that was of great importance to working parents. In *R v. Secretary of State for Trade and Industry, Ex parte Trades Union Congress* he was one of a 2-man panel of judges asked to determine whether the United Kingdom government had failed to properly implement parental leave legislation agreed at the European level with Britain's fellow EU Member States. The case was brought by the Trades Union Congress (or TUC), the umbrella body to which UK trade unions belong. The significance of the case was that if Lord Bingham of Cornhill and his fellow judge concluded that the UK government had failed to properly implement the EU legislation, then somewhere in the region of 2.7 million workers stood to gain the right to take up to 13 weeks of unpaid parental leave in addition to their existing leave entitlements. As it happened both Lord Bingham of Cornhill and Mr Justice Morison, the High Court judge with whom Lord Bingham sat, decided that before reaching a decision they should refer the issue to the European Court of Justice and obtain that body's interpretation of the relevant EU legislation. That said, both judges considered that the TUC's view of the legislation was "likely to prevail", a prediction which (if it proves true) bodes well for many of the UK's working parents. Although the case was important in and of itself it attracted some extra attention at the time it was heard because counsel for the TUC was Cherie Booth QC, the wife of the Prime Minister.

Before his appointment to the Appellate Committee, Lord Bingham of Cornhill was perhaps best known to some members of the public as the judge to whom the Home Secretary had entrusted the task of determining the appropriate length of sentence for the killers of James Bulger, the Liverpool toddler who was murdered by two children in February 1993.

Lord Slynn of Hadley of Eggington in the County of Bedfordshire

(Appointed: 1992)

Born: 1930
University education: University of London; Cambridge University
Number of children: None
Age became QC: 44
Age became Privy Councillor: 62
Secondary education: Sandbach
Married: Once
Age married: 32
Age commenced practice: 26
Age became High Court judge: 46
Age became Lord of Appeal: 62

For the four years immediately prior to his appointment as an Appellate Committee member Gordon Slynn was a judge on the European Court of Justice in Luxembourg. There he had his own secretary, his own clerks, access to a substantial law library, and a hefty salary. Now, as a Lord of Appeal in Ordinary, he shares the services of a secretary with other Appellate Committee members, must do his own research, is almost obliged to have recourse to libraries other than the House of Lords library, and has to make his own way to work in the morning. One similarity between his old life and his new life as Lord Slynn of Hadley is that he continues to enjoy what for the ordinary man in the street is a substantial salary. The fact that Slynn was happy to become a Lord of Appeal in exchange for his seat in the European Court of Justice would seem to indicate that membership of what is essentially the supreme court of one's own Member State still continues to be more prestigious than 'merely' being a member of the European Court of Justice. His appointment certainly shows the continuing significance of

European Community law on the domestic scene. It has long been traditional to appoint as Lords of Appeal a certain proportion of individuals who have experience in particular fields of the law so that there is a reservoir of expertise on which the Appellate Committee can draw when deciding the various cases that come before it. That it should now be deemed appropriate to have a Lord of Appeal whose particular specialisation is European Community law is perhaps indicative of just how many cases are now coming before the Appellate Committee in which European Community law points are being pleaded.

Lord Slynn of Hadley did not do his primary degree at Oxbridge. Instead he studied at Goldsmith's College in the University of London. However, he did go on to do postgraduate work at Trinity College, Cambridge. In 1958, the year after the European Economic Community was founded, he started lecturing in Air Law at the London School of Economics. Slynn has maintained a certain connection with academic life. Thus over the years he has delivered honorary lectures at many universities in Britain, Europe, the Commonwealth and further afield. He has also held Visiting Professorships at several universities. Indeed while most people of his age would probably be content to settle for being a Lord of Appeal, Lord Slynn of Hadley continues to double as a Visiting Professor at universities in Britain, Australia, and India. After his time at the London School of Economics Slynn took up full-time practice at the Bar.

Twelve years after commencing practice Slynn was made a Queen's Counsel and a mere two years after that he was appointed to the High Court bench. Thereafter his career took a unique twist for a future Lord of Appeal. In 1981, after five years on the High Court bench, at a time when he might have been looking forward to joining the Court of Appeal, Slynn was appointed the British Advocate-General at the European Court of Justice. As Advocate-General, Slynn was now one of the highest-ranking officials in the European Court of Justice, ranking with the individual members of the Court itself in importance and possibly ahead of some of them in terms of influence. His job was to advise the Court of Justice on the appropriate course of action it ought to take in the cases that came before it. It is not a job that has an equivalent in the English legal system. Essentially Slynn would be appointed to various cases which he would hear along with the members of the Court of Justice.

He would give his opinion on the merits of those cases and the Court was then free to follow or to disregard his advice. It was a position that gave Slynn a great deal of influence as he could use his opinion to try and draw the court in whatever direction he himself was leaning. In doing so he had a real part to play in shaping the future of European Community law and indeed the European Community. He did so well at this job that he was eventually nominated by the Thatcher administration to be the British judge on the European Court of Justice. Four years later he was made a Lord of Appeal.

Lord Nicholls of Birkenhead of Stoke D'Abernon in the County of Surrey

(Appointed: 1994)

Born: 1933
University education: Liverpool University; Cambridge University
Number of children: 3
Age became QC: 41
Age became Privy Councillor: 53
Secondary education: Birkenhead School
Married: Once
Age married: 27
Age commenced practice: 25
Age became High Court judge: 50
Age became Lord of Appeal: 61

Lord Nicholls of Birkenhead is one of the few Lords of Appeal who was not educated at one of Britain's leading public schools. Nor did he get his primary law degree at either Oxford or Cambridge University. Instead he attended Birkenhead School and then went on to the University of Liverpool (though he did subsequently study at Cambridge University). His career as a student was highly distinguished. He attained a first class law degree at Liverpool, went on to take a first class qualification from Cambridge, and did so well in the Bar Examinations that he was awarded a Certificate of Honour. Despite his academic successes it would seem that Nicholls did not wish for an academic career. Instead he went into practice as a barrister, becoming a Queen's Counsel at the age of 41 and a High Court judge nine years after that. He rose quickly through the judicial hierarchy. In 1986, after only three years on the High Court, he was appointed to the Court of Appeal. In 1991 he became Vice-Chancellor and in 1994 he was made a Lord of Appeal in Ordinary. He is one of a trio of successive Vice-Chancellors to have been elevated from that position to the Appellate Committee. His predecessor, Lord Browne-Wilkinson, served as Vice-Chancellor from 1985 to 1991, at which point he was made a Lord of Appeal in Ordinary. Lord Nicholls' successor, Sir Richard Scott, has been Vice-Chancellor for the past six years and in October 2000 he too will become a Lord of Appeal in Ordinary. It will be interesting to see whether in time to come the man who is to replace Sir Richard Scott as Vice-Chancellor (Sir Andrew Morritt) will in turn be appointed to the Appellate Committee.

As a judge Nicholls is perceived as being highly intelligent and extremely competent, someone who can take difficult issues of law and express those issues (and his conclusions in relation to them) in a particularly clear fashion. Indeed as a High Court judge he was once commended by the Court of Appeal for the clarity and brevity of a judgment that he gave in a case which arose from the collapse of a bank (the BCCI) and which was of considerable interest to a large number of creditors, many of whom might well have found it difficult to wade through the more complicated or lengthy judgment that another judge might have felt compelled to produce. Of course as a judge it is not always (if ever) possible to please all of the people all of the time: in one case that arose out of the miner's strike in 1984, Nicholls had to order the sequestration of union assets after the union in question (the National Union of Mineworkers) refused to pay a contempt fine. Speaking in court Nicholls criticised the 'folly' of union leaders for having incurred more than £1.5 million of legal expenses. His comments in this regard were not universally well received.

Despite his manifold achievements as a judge it may be that in the public mind Lord Nicholls will be best remembered for his short televised speech following the initial Pinochet appeal, in which he, the third Lord of Appeal to speak, was the first of the five judges in that case to indicate that he did not consider that General Pinochet should enjoy immunity from the British criminal process (and so could be the subject of an extradition application by the Spanish authorities). The immediate effect of his speech at the time it was given was to introduce a real note of tension into how the Pinochet appeal would be decided, a tension that was heightened when Lord Steyn announced that he too considered that General Pinochet's appeal should fail, and which only subsided when Lord Hoffmann, the last of the five Lords of Appeal to speak, indicated that he agreed with the conclusions reached by Lord Nicholls and Lord Steyn.

Lord Steyn of Swafield in the County of Norfolk

(Appointed: 1995)

Born: 1932
University education: University of Stellenbosch, South Africa; Oxford University
Age commenced practice: 26
Age became High Court judge: 53
Age became Lord of Appeal: 63
Secondary education: Jan Van Riebeck School, Cape Town
Married: Twice
Age became QC: 47
Age became Privy Councillor: 60

Johan Steyn is one of only six (the figure will soon rise to seven) Lords of Appeal since 1876 not to have been born in the United Kingdom. It would perhaps be reasonable to assume that, with the exception of Lord Steyn, all of the Lords of Appeal in question served sometime in the late nineteenth/early twentieth century heyday of the British Empire (or at least shortly thereafter), as at that time it would not have been uncommon for the children of men working in the service of the Empire to be born abroad. However, this is not the case. Two of the seven Lords of Appeal in question are contemporaries of Lord Steyn: one is Lord Hoffmann, who joined the Appellate Committee along with Lord Steyn in 1995, and the other is the Indian-born Sir Richard Scott, who will join the Appellate Committee in October 2000. The other non-UK born Lords of Appeal are the Australian-born Lord Atkin, who served as a Lord of Appeal from 1928 to 1934; the Jerseyman, Lord Du Parcq, and Australian-born Lord Uthwatt, both of whom served as Lords of Appeal from 1946 until their respective deaths in 1949; and the Canadian-born Lord Pearson, who served as an Appellate Committee member from 1965 to 1974. (Lords of Appeal who were born in what is now the Republic of Ireland but what was, at the time of their birth, a part of the United Kingdom, are counted for the purposes of this book as having been born in the UK.)

Of all the Lords of Appeal to have been born abroad Lord Steyn is the one who followed the most distinctively 'foreign' career. He started his legal career in South Africa where he attended the University of Stellenbosch, before going on to spend some time as a Rhodes Scholar at Oxford University where he took an MA. Returning to South Africa he began practising as a barrister there in 1958 at the age of 26. He had a successful practice and in 1970, at the age of only 38, he was appointed a Senior Counsel of the Supreme Court of South Africa. Then in 1973, at the age of 41, he moved permanently to the United Kingdom where he became a member of Lincoln's Inn and took up practice as a barrister at the English Bar.

Most advocates would be happy on moving to a new country if they managed to make a living at all, but Lord Steyn quickly established himself as a leading commercial lawyer and succeeded in being appointed a Queen's Counsel a mere 6 years after his arrival in Britain. At 47 years of age he was considerably older than the 'average' age at which Lords of Appeal tend to reach this stage of his career, but given the unusual lateness of age at which Lord Steyn commenced practice in the United Kingdom it is an astonishing achievement that he managed to become a Queen's Counsel at all. As though this were not enough, he was appointed to the High Court only 6 years later. In short, within a 12-year period Lord Steyn transformed himself from newly-arrived barrister to member of the superior court judiciary. A decade later, after 6 years on the High Court and 3 years on the Court of Appeal, Steyn was afforded the ultimate accolade of being appointed a Lord of Appeal.

Lord Hoffmann of Chedworth in the County of Gloucestershire

(Appointed: 1995)

Born: 1934
University of Education:
University of Cape Town;
Oxford University

Secondary education:
South African College School, Cape Town
Married: Once

Age married: 23
Age commenced practice: 23
Age became High Court judge: 51
Number of children: 2
Age became QC: 43
Age became Privy Councillor: 58
Age became Lord of Appeal: 61

When Leonard Hubert Hoffmann arrived in England from South Africa in the early 1960s he had no job waiting for him. However, he managed to get work for a few months with a firm of solicitors before he eventually succeeded in getting a permanent teaching job at Oxford University. At almost the same time Hoffmann also commenced practising at the Bar. Over the next twelve years he continued this dual existence as an academic and a practising lawyer until he became a Queen's Counsel in 1974. Advancement to the High Court bench came eleven years later. Interestingly, the year of Hoffmann's appointment to the High Court bench was also the year that his South African-born colleague, Lord Steyn, became a High Court judge. Both men were also elevated to the Court of Appeal in the same year (1992). And both were appointed to the Appellate Committee in the same year (1995).

Lord Hoffmann has long been considered to be an especially talented judge. However, for a few weeks at the end of 1998 and the beginning of 1999 it looked as though the Appellate Committee might be deprived of his services. This is because Lord Hoffmann came under considerable pressure from the media at that time to resign from the Appellate Committee after he heard an appeal without disclosing in the course of the appeal that there was a connection between him and one of the parties who argued at the appeal. The appeal was the first of what would eventually be 2 appeals and 3 hearings in the case of General Pinochet, the one-time leader of Chile. In what was an international *cause célèbre* featured in newspapers around the world and reported on television stations across the planet, the General and his legal representatives initially came before the Appellate Committee in November 1998, challenging the legality of the General's arrest in London the previous month for offences that he was alleged to have committed during his time as Chilean head of state between 1973 and 1990. In the course of the hearing the Appellate Committee heard argument from lawyers for Amnesty

International, the human rights organization, who argued that General Pinochet's arrest was lawful. As it happened Lord Hoffmann had previously acted as a director of Amnesty International (Charity) Limited, a company that raised funds for Amnesty International. However, Lord Hoffmann did not disclose this fact during the initial Pinochet appeal. When the fact came to light afterwards the Appellate Committee set aside its own decision that the General's arrest had been lawful and ordered a re-hearing of the case. Had it not done so there is every chance that General Pinochet would have gone to the European Court of Human Rights arguing that his right to a fair and impartial hearing of his appeal had been violated.

Inspired perhaps by the controversy over Lord Hoffmann's participation in the hearing of the first appeal brought by General Pinochet to the House of Lords, there did seem to be something of an upturn during 1999 in the number of cases in which it was alleged by litigants that because of the background, characteristics or personal history of the judge before whom they had appeared the decisions in their cases were tainted by the possibility of judicial bias. In November 1999 Lord Bingham of Cornhill (now the senior Lord of Appeal in Ordinary but then the Lord Chief Justice), Lord Woolf (now the Lord Chief Justice but then the Master of the Rolls) and Sir Richard Scott (then the Vice-Chancellor and less than a year away from becoming a Lord of Appeal in Ordinary) considered what factors would disqualify a judge from sitting in a hearing. They did so in the context of no fewer than five applications in which leave to appeal was sought on the basis of alleged judicial bias. In one of the five applications – the *Williams* case – the three appellate court judges rejected the contention that a chairman of an industrial tribunal who had worked in a junior capacity for the Inland Revenue from 1958 to 1961 ought not to have heard an employment-related claim against the Inland Revenue more than 30 years later. In another of the five applications, the *O'Callaghan* case, the three appellate court judges rejected the contention that a High Court judge ought not to have heard a case brought against a company which rented property owned by a family property investment company of which the judge was a non-executive director. Lord Bingham of Cornhill, Lord Woolf and Sir Richard Scott all accepted that the judge in question had not in fact known of the tenancy and that even if he had known there would still be have been no real danger of bias. In a case that combined two applications, the *Locabail* case, the three appellate court judges rejected the contention that a deputy High Court judge ought not to have heard two related sets of proceedings in which the outcome was of indirect interest to a client of a prominent firm of solicitors in which the deputy judge was a partner. But in a fifth application, the *Timmins* case, the three appellate court judges accepted, "not without misgiving", that certain periodical articles written by a Recorder indicated that in a particular personal injuries case he might perhaps have been unconsciously inclined to favour one party over another, and so a retrial was ordered.

Notwithstanding the Court of Appeal's decisions in these five cases, it will be interesting to see what the lasting legacy will be of the setting aside by the Appellate Committee of its own decision in the first Pinochet appeal. It seems fair to suggest that in the future litigants may well pay more attention to the background and personal history of judges than in the past, and that they may well be more alive to the possibility of challenging a judge or upsetting a decision on the basis of some alleged bias to which a judge, by virtue of some factor in his background or personal history, is alleged to be predisposed. What the *Williams, O'Callaghan, Locabail,* and *Timmins* decisions indicate is that any such challenges should not be brought lightly and (of course) will not always succeed.

Lord Hope of Craighead of Barriff in the District of Perth and Kinross

(Appointed: 1996)

Born: 1938
University education: Cambridge University; Edinburgh University
Age married: 28
Age commenced practice: 27
Age became superior court judge: 51
Age became Lord of Appeal: 57
Secondary education: Edinburgh Academy, Rugby
Married: Once
Number of children: 3
Age became QC: 40
Age became Privy Councillor: 51

James Arthur David Hope, the youngest of the present Lords of Appeal in Ordinary, comes from a middle-class background. His father was awarded an OBE and was a Writer to the Signet (a position akin to that of solicitor in England). Hope was educated at Edinburgh Academy before proceeding to Rugby, one of England's premier private schools. Afterwards he studied at Cambridge University and then did his military service with the Seaforth Highlanders before going on to do a law degree at Edinburgh University. He finished his degree and was called to the Scottish Bar in the same year. He is one of the foremost Scottish lawyers of his generation. In the course of his career he has contributed to or edited no fewer than eight books, which places him just after Lord Denning as the most extensively published Lord of Appeal in Ordinary. Lord Hope of Craighead was a relatively young appointee to the Appellate Committee – he turned 58 in the year that he was appointed.

Prior to becoming a Lord of Appeal in Ordinary, Lord Hope of Craighead was the most senior judge in Scotland. It was in this capacity that he took the step of allowing the televising of court proceedings in Scotland. He was able to do this because section 41 of the Criminal Justice Act 1925 – which prohibits the broadcasting of court proceedings – does not apply to Scotland, which has a separate legal system from the rest of the United Kingdom. (Interestingly there were also moves around this time to allow the televising of Appellate Committee hearings. The reason Appellate Committee hearings could be televised without contravening the Criminal Justice Act is because its hearings, though judicial in nature, are a part of the proceedings of the House of Lords and as such can be broadcast.) Although Lord Hope of Craighead was prepared to countenance the televising of Scottish court proceedings, he was careful to put in place a set of guidelines aimed at preserving the dignity of those proceedings and ensuring that such broadcasts as would take place were educational and informational (and not sensational) in nature.

As a Lord of Appeal, Lord Hope of Craighead sat in the re-hearing of the Pinochet appeal following the setting aside of the Appellate Committee's original decision in that case. The thrust of his judgment in the appeal was that General Pinochet, as a former head of state, did not enjoy immunity from arrest in respect of alleged acts of torture and conspiracy to torture that followed the coming into force in 1984 of the international convention on torture.

Lord Hope of Craighead was recently one of a five-man Appellate Committee panel that was asked to adjudicate in an appeal arising from a libel claim brought against the publishers of *The Sunday Times* and certain other individuals by Mr Albert Reynolds, the one-time Taoiseach (or Prime Minister) of the Republic of Ireland. A High Court jury had found that *The Sunday Times* had published an allegation about Mr Reynolds that was untrue. However, the jury considered that the allegation had been made without malice and awarded nil damages. The trial judge substituted an award of 1 pence. Mr Reynolds appealed these findings and a trio of Court of Appeal judges (presided over by the then Lord Chief Justice, Lord Bingham of Cornhill) ordered a new trial. The defendants to the original action then brought an appeal to the House of Lords. The essence of their appeal was that in a modern democratic society it should be possible to engage in good-faith comment about the political lives of public officials without thereby exposing oneself to a successful libel action. The law has long recognised that the public interest does sometimes require that individuals be allowed the privilege of speaking freely without fear of exposure to a successful defamation suit. The guiding principle behind this privilege has been that people acting in good faith should have the right to publish, for the purpose of giving the public information, that which it is proper for the public to know. In the past, once a defendant pleaded this privilege the courts would look to the particular facts of the individual case to see whether it was in fact a case in which the public interest demanded that the privilege of immunity from liability should apply. In the *Reynolds* case the appellants were effectively arguing that when it came to political comment this privilege should always apply unless the person who claimed a statement was defamatory could prove that the maker of the statement had acted maliciously. After hearing the appeal Lord Hope of Craighead joined with the House of Lords in rejecting the notion that the generic privilege advocated by the appellants should apply (though he did consider that the appellants should be allowed to invoke the defence of privilege at the retrial and have the question of whether privilege should apply in the present case adjudicated on by the trial judge).

The original *Reynolds* libel trial and the appeals that followed it naturally attracted a certain degree of media attention, simply because they involved a former Prime Minister of the Republic of Ireland who had acquired a certain prominence in the United Kingdom for his role in seeking to bring about peace in Northern Ireland. However, the appeal to the House of Lords in the *Reynolds* case was also of legal significance in that it required the Appellate Committee to consider the extent to which the public interest should be allowed to prevail over individual rights in a modern Western democracy. Fundamental human rights issues such as this are likely to come before the Appellate Committee more and more frequently following the entry into force of the Human Rights Act 1998 during the autumn of 2000.

Lord Clyde of Briglands

(Appointed: 1996)

Born: 1932
University education: Oxford University, Edinburgh University
Age married: 31
Age became QC: 39
Age became superior court judge: 53
Age became Lord of Appeal: 64
Secondary education: Edinburgh Academy
Married: Once
Number of children: 2
Age commenced practice: 27
Age became judge: 53
Age became Privy Councillor: 53

James John Clyde is one of six Lords of Appeal since the Second World War whose father was a peer before him. He also joins the three Lord Russells of Killowen and Lord Romer in coming from a family that has produced three successive generations of superior court judges. However, Lord Clyde is the first member of his family to have become a Lord of Appeal in Ordinary. Clyde attended Edinburgh Academy as a schoolboy. He then went on to Oxford University after which he proceeded to Edinburgh University. Of the 21 Scottish Lords of Appeal who have served since the office of Lord of Appeal was established he is one of 14 who have spent some time at an English university, one of 7 who have studied at Oxford, and one of 14 who attended Edinburgh University. Called to the Scottish Bar in 1959, Clyde was appointed a Queen's Counsel at the age of 39. Fourteen years after that he was appointed a superior court judge and eleven years after that he was made a Lord of Appeal.

Before his elevation to the Appellate Committee, Lord Clyde was perhaps best known to the general public for his work on the government-commissioned Inquiry into the Removal of Children from Orkney in February 1991, and for his authorship of the Report that followed (the 'Clyde Report'). The Inquiry was established on foot of a highly controversial sequence of events that transpired in Orkney during early 1991. On 27 February of that year nine children from four families residing on one of the Orkney Islands were removed to places of safety by social workers after allegations of abuse were made during interviews with the children of a fifth family residing on the same island. The nine children were detained until early April 1991, and were then returned to their families following a successful legal challenge to the competency of the court proceedings that had followed on their initial removal. Because the court proceedings were successfully challenged on the basis of competency, the allegations which had led to the removal of the children were not the subject of judicial decision – the proceedings were stopped before any evidence was led. However, despite a successful appeal by the authorities against the court decision to halt the original proceedings, it was subsequently decided to abandon the proceedings altogether. Not surprisingly, the removal of nine children from a community which was to a degree isolated, along with all the events that followed thereon, attracted very considerable media attention and prompted a significant degree of public consternation, so much so that in June 1991, Lord Clyde was invited by the Scottish Secretary to conduct an inquiry into all that had transpired. Lord Clyde was not asked to adjudicate on the allegations of abuse that had prompted the whole affair. Rather he was entrusted with the task of inquiring into the original decision to take the children into protective detention, the actual removal of the children from their homes, the detention of the children pending their return home (in particular how they were cared for and interviewed while so detained), and the ultimate decision to abandon the associated court proceedings altogether. Just over a year later, following an extensive inquiry that included oral hearings, Lord Clyde forwarded his completed report on the matter to the Scottish Secretary. Although Lord Clyde was careful to temper his report so as to allow for the fact that he was writing with the benefit of hindsight and in the "calmer setting of a retrospective study", and although he emphasised that (at the very least) all of the staff and officials involved in the case under review had acted in good faith, Lord Clyde did none the less identify a number of improvements that could be made to the child protection process. He also availed of the opportunity which the report offered to make various suggestions for improvement which although not relating specifically to the Orkney case were none the less within the remit of his Inquiry. The contents of the Report produced a swift response from government. In February 1993 a Consultation Paper was published on the emergency protection of children in Scotland. Six months after that a White Paper was published setting out in detail the government's proposals for the reform of child care policy and the law. And in 1995 Parliament enacted the Children (Scotland) Act, a major piece of legislation that gives effect to the proposals contained in the Clyde Report and two other reports on child care in Scotland that were produced round about that time, the Kearney and the Finlayson Reports.

Lord Hutton of Bresagh in the County of Down

(Appointed: 1997)

Born: 1931
University education:
Oxford University;
Queen's University Belfast
Number of children: 2
Age became QC: 39
Age became Privy Councillor: 57

Secondary education: Shrewsbury School
Married: Once
Age married: 44
Age commenced practice: 23
Age became High Court judge: 48
Age became Lord of Appeal: 66

Although he is the Northern Irish member of the Appellate Committee, James Brian Edward Hutton actually had a very English education. As a schoolboy he was sent to Shrewsbury School and then went on to Balliol College, Oxford (where he got a first in jurisprudence). But Hutton's roots were in Northern Ireland and it is to Belfast that Hutton finally returned, putting in a spell at Queen's University Belfast before being called to the Northern Irish Bar in 1954 at the relatively young age of 23. Sixteen years later Hutton went on to become a Queen's Counsel at the age of 39. During his time as a Queen's Counsel, Hutton spent time working as legal adviser to the Northern Irish Minister of Home Affairs. Nine years after taking silk Hutton was appointed to the Northern Irish High Court bench. Nine years after that he was elevated to the Northern Irish Court of Appeal as Lord Chief Justice of Northern Ireland. Every Northern Irish Lord of Appeal appointed since the island of Ireland was split in 1922 has served as Lord Chief Justice of Northern Ireland at some stage in their careers. Both Lord Hutton and his fellow Northern Irishman, Lord Lowry (who served as a Lord of Appeal from 1988 to 1994), were made Lord Chief Justice of Northern Ireland prior to being made Lords of Appeal. But the first Northern Irish Lord of Appeal appointed after the creation of Northern Ireland, Lord MacDermott (who served as a Lord of Appeal from 1947 to 1951), spent 20 years as Lord Chief Justice of Northern Ireland *after* his time as a Lord of Appeal. It is not certain why Lord MacDermott agreed to move back to Northern Ireland following his appointment to the Appellate Committee. It may be that he felt the rank of Lord Chief Justice of Northern Ireland was actually a promotion from being a Lord of Appeal in Ordinary – certainly the Lord Chief Justice of England has traditionally been considered to rank higher than a regular Lord of Appeal. However, Lord Hutton and Lord Lowry have clearly (and, this writer would submit, rightly) viewed their appointment to the Appellate Committee as a promotion. In Lord Hutton's case it undoubtedly was, as he received his peerage following his appointment to the Appellate Committee (Lord Lowry was a peer for 9 years before being made a Lord of Appeal). It will be interesting to see whether, at some future stage, Lord Hutton's successor as Lord Chief Justice of Northern Ireland – Sir Robert Carswell – will be offered the chance to become a Lord of Appeal, an honour which now seems almost automatic for anyone who serves as Northern Ireland's Lord Chief Justice.

Lord Saville of Newdigate in the County of Surrey

(Appointed: 1997)

Born: 1936
University education: Oxford University
Age married: 25
Age commenced practice: 26
Age became High Court judge: 49
Age became Lord of Appeal: 61
Secondary education: Rye Grammar School
Married: Once
Number of children: 2
Age became QC: 39
Age became Privy Councillor: 58

Mark Oliver Saville is one of what seems likely to be an ever-diminishing number of Appellate Committee members with military experience – from 1954 until 1956 Saville did his military service as a second lieutenant in the Royal Sussex Regiment. His tour of duty in the army over, Saville went on to study law at Brasenose College, Oxford, graduating with a first class degree. Saville then went on to become a Queen's Counsel at the age of 39. After this it was really only a matter of time until Saville was offered a judgeship: he became one of the youngest High Court judges of his day at a youthful 49.

In 1992 Saville became the head of the Commercial Division of the High Court and attracted a certain attention when he publicly criticised the under-staffing of the Commercial Division. His criticisms were seconded by leading members of the London financial commercial community, who joined with Saville in voicing aloud their own concerns about the Commercial Division. Criticism by a judge was one thing, but criticism by a judge *and* the City was another – the Commercial Division soon got its extra judges. A year later Saville was appointed to the Court of Appeal and three years after that he became a Lord of Appeal in Ordinary.

After barely a year in office as a Lord of Appeal, Lord Saville was appointed to head the 'Bloody Sunday' Inquiry. This Inquiry was established to investigate the events of Sunday, 30 January 1972, when in the aftermath of a civil rights procession held in Northern Ireland a disturbance occurred that led to shots being fired by the British Army, which in turn resulted in thirteen civilians being killed and a further thirteen being injured (one of whom subsequently died). As it happens 'Bloody Sunday' was the subject of an injury conducted by Lord Widgery, the one-time Lord Chief Justice of England, in the immediate aftermath of the events. However, that initial Inquiry was defective in some respects. Lord Widgery produced his report within eleven weeks of 'Bloody Sunday' and so did not have time to consider all the evidence available: he did not receive evidence from the people who had been wounded on the day, and he did not adequately consider various eye-witness accounts of the events. Because of this the Blair administration decided to establish a further independent injury into what exactly happened on that day. This new inquiry was in part prompted by the perceived defects of the Widgery Inquiry, but it was not an investigation of how Lord Widgery conducted his inquiry. Rather it was an attempt to look afresh at the events of 'Bloody Sunday', to take into account any relevant new information, and to establish, once and for all, the truth as to what happened on that day. The Inquiry formally commenced on 3 April 1998 and at the time of writing is still ongoing. There are three members of the Inquiry, Lord Saville of Newdigate, Sir Edward Somers (who was formerly a member of the New Zealand Court of Appeal) and Mr Justice William Hoyt (the Chief Justice of the Canadian Province of New Brunswick). Lord Saville of Newdigate is not the first and is probably not the last Lord of Appeal who will be asked to head a public inquiry. However, his chairmanship of the 'Bloody Sunday' Inquiry at a time when Northern Ireland appears to be teetering on the verge of peace is a particularly delicate task.

Despite the fact that it is a fairly regular practice to ask Lords of Appeal to head public inquiries, it is possibly open to question whether it is actually a good idea for them to be asked to do so. Given that some, if not all, of these inquiries are concerned with sensitive political matters, there is perhaps a risk that judges might find themselves subject to political criticism. That this has not tended to happen in the past does not mean that it could never happen in the future. In addition there is the practical consideration that if a number of Lords of Appeal are effectively absent from active service as an Appellate Committee member for protracted periods of time, this could impinge adversely on the pace at which the Committee gets through its workload.

Lord Hobhouse of Woodborough in the County of Wiltshire

(Appointed: 1998)

Born: 1932
University education: Oxford University
Number of children: 3
Age commenced practice: 23
Age became Privy Councillor: 61
Secondary education: Eton
Married: Once
Age married: 27
Age became QC: 41
Age became judge: 50
Age became Lord of Appeal: 66

John Stewart Hobhouse was appointed a Lord of Appeal in July 1998. As a boy he attended Eton. He then studied at Oxford before going on to the Bar. Four years after that he was married. Both Lord Hobhouse and his wife come from successful families. Lord Hobhouse's father was knighted and won the Military Cross. His wife's father was a QC. And, at the time of the marriage, her uncle was also a QC (though he would later be elevated to the peerage and, as Lord Diplock, would serve as a Lord of Appeal, indeed one of the most eminent Lords of Appeal since the Second World War, from 1968 to 1985).

Lord Hobhouse became a Queen's Counsel in 1973. He continued practice at the Bar for a further 9 years until being appointed a High Court judge in 1982. Barely a year later he was appointed to the Court of Appeal and five years after that he was made a Lord of Appeal, an appointment that was well received.

As a Lord of Appeal, Lord Hobhouse of Woodborough has sat in a number of the more interesting cases to come before the Lords of Appeal. One of these was *Fitzpatrick v. Sterling Housing Association Ltd*, a case that came before the House of Lords in 1999 and which attracted some media attention. The facts of the case were that from 1976 until 1994 Mr Fitzpatrick, a gay man, had lived together with his partner, Mr Thompson, in a flat of which Mr Thompson was the tenant. Both men had a committed, loving relationship with each other, to the extent that when in 1996 Mr Thompson became seriously unwell, Mr Fitzpatrick quit his job so that he might devote his time to caring for Mr Thompson. He did this until Mr Thompson's death in 1994. Following Mr Thompson's death, Mr Fitzpatrick sought a declaration that he had succeeded to Mr Thompson's tenancy of the flat that the two men had shared for the previous 20 years – under the Rent Act 1977 (as amended) it is possible in certain circumstances for the 'surviving spouse' of a tenant and for 'a member of the original tenant's family' to succeed to a tenancy in this way. Mr Fitzpatrick contended that he should be considered the 'surviving spouse' of Mr Thompson or as 'a member of [Mr Thompson's] family'.

The Appellate Committee unanimously decided that Mr Fitzpatrick did not constitute a 'surviving spouse' of Mr Thompson for the purposes of the legislation under examination, that the phrase as employed in that legislation was restricted to the surviving member of a heterosexual relationship in which a man and a woman – whether married or not – had been living together as man and wife. However, by a 3–2 majority the Committee concluded that Mr Fitzpatrick could succeed to the tenancy as a 'member of [Mr Thompson's] family'. Lord Hobhouse of Woodborough was one of the two dissenters. He was sympathetic to the plight of Mr Fitzpatrick but he did not consider that Parliament, when enacting the legislation which afforded individuals the right to succeed to the tenancy of a deceased family member, had envisaged a situation such as that presented in Mr Fitzpatrick's case. It was Lord Hobhouse's view that "Living together as homosexual lovers is not a familial relationship. It is a different relationship ... no better and no worse – no less or more meritorious, just different." In so far as there was a need for deserving individuals like Mr Fitzpatrick to be protected by the law, Lord Hobhouse of Woodborough considered that this was a matter for Parliament: "It is an improper usurpation of the legislative function, for a court to adopt social policies which have not yet been incorporated into the relevant legislation ... it is a matter for Parliament to consider, not for the courts to ask themselves: 'What would Parliament do now?'"

The fundamental issue that Lord Hobhouse of Woodborough touched upon in his judgment, that of the proper relationship between the courts and the legislature, is an issue that will perhaps prompt further and more general discussion in the future when the Human Rights Act 1998 comes into force and judges are called upon to determine the compatibility or otherwise of legislation with a written corpus of human rights. Another more specific issue that may arise before the Appellate Committee following the coming into force of the 1998 Act, was expressly adverted to by Lord Slynn of Hadley, who also sat in the *Fitzpatrick* case. Lord Slynn was one of the three Appellate Committee members who considered that Mr Fitzpatrick could succeed to the tenancy of Mr Thompson as a 'member of [Mr Thompson's] family', which of course was good news for Mr Fitzpatrick. In so far as the other ground on which Mr Fitzpatrick had based his appeal (the 'surviving spouse' ground) was concerned, although Lord Slynn of Hadley agreed with the finding of the Appellate Committee, that under the legislative provisions that had arisen for consideration Mr Fitzpatrick could not succeed to the tenancy in issue as the surviving spouse of Mr Thompson, he did state that "Whether that result is discriminatory against same-sex couples in light of the fact that non-married different sex couples living together are to be treated as spouses, so as to allow one to succeed to the tenancy of the other, may have to be considered when the Human Rights Act 1998 is in force."

Lord Millett

(Appointed: 1998)

Born: 1932
University education: Cambridge University
Age married: 27
Age became barrister: 23
Age became Privy Councillor: 62

Secondary education: Harrow
Married: Once
Number of children: 3
Age became QC: 41
Age became judge: 54
Age became Lord of Appeal: 66

Lord Millett's appointment as a Lord of Appeal was announced on the same day as that of Lord Hobhouse. The news of his appointment was well received. As a boy Millett was educated at Harrow, one of Britain's premier public schools. He then studied at Cambridge University, one of five of the present Lords of Appeal to have studied at Cambridge before embarking upon his professional studies. Interestingly, the other seven Lords of Appeal attended

Oxford University at some point before going on to study for the Bar. So does this mean that the present Lords of Appeal have exclusively been appointed from the ranks of those who attended Oxford or Cambridge universities? It obviously does, but to stop there is only to give half the picture. A closer look reveals that while all of the present Lords of Appeal have at some point in their careers studied at one or other of Oxford or Cambridge, only five of the present Lords of Appeal (the departure of Lord Phillips of Worth Matravers and the arrival of Sir Richard Scott will reduce this number to four) studied *only* at Oxford or Cambridge. The two Scottish Lords of Appeal (Lord Clyde and Lord Hope of Craighead) also studied at Edinburgh University. The Northern Irish Lord of Appeal, Lord Hutton, also studied at Queen's University Belfast. Two Lords of Appeal (Lord Hoffmann and Lord Steyn – Sir Richard Scott will bring this number to three) also studied in South African Universities. And of the remaining Lords of Appeal Lord Slynn of Hadley also studied at the University of London and Lord Nicholls of Birkenhead also studied at the University of Liverpool. Thus while every one of the present Lords of Appeal bears the *imprimatur* of either Oxford University or Cambridge University, a much wider swathe of academia is currently represented on the Appellate Committee than one might initially imagine.

Lord Millett is one of the five Appellate Committee members who studied exclusively at either Oxford or Cambridge. (Like Lord Phillips of Worth Matravers he studied exclusively at Cambridge University. Lord Bingham of Cornhill, Lord Hobhouse and Lord Saville studied exclusively at Oxford University.) After his time at Cambridge University, Millett went on to become a barrister. Thereafter he became a Queen's Counsel at the age of 41, a High Court judge at the age of 54, and a Lord of Appeal at the age of 66.

In 1999 Lord Millett sat in one of the more widely reported cases to have come before the Appellate Committee since the Pinochet appeals. The case was that of *McFarlane v. Tayside Health Board.* The facts of the case were simple. Mr and Mrs McFarlane had four children. They decided not to have any more. On foot of this decision Mr McFarlane underwent a vasectomy operation. This took place at a health-board controlled hospital. Some months after the operation the consulting surgeon advised the McFarlanes that it was now safe for them to dispense with contraceptive precautions. This the

McFarlanes did. However, the following year Mrs McFarlane became pregnant. The year after that she gave birth to a normal, healthy baby girl. Mr and Mrs McFarlane loved and cared for their new daughter. But they were annoyed with the health board, so much so that they commenced an action against the health board seeking compensation for the financial cost of bringing up their new daughter and for the pain, suffering and distress which had been occasioned to Mrs McFarlane as a result of the pregnancy. The health board admitted the basic facts of the case. However, it argued that the conception and birth of a child are not harms or injuries in respect of which damages can be awarded.

In so far as the costs of rearing the new child were concerned, the Appellate Committee decided that the McFarlanes should not be allowed to recover damages. A number of reasons were offered by their Lordships for this decision. However, the media reports on the case tended in the main to quote some of the words that featured in a particularly eloquent part of Lord Millett's judgment to the effect that. "The law must take the birth of a normal, healthy baby to be a blessing, not a detriment. In truth it is a mixed blessing. It brings joy and sorrow, blessing and responsibility. The advantages and the disadvantages are inseparable. Individuals may choose to regard the balance as unfavourable and take steps to forgo the pleasures as well as the responsibilities of parenthood. They are entitled to decide for themselves where their own interests lie. But society itself must regard the balance as beneficial. It would be repugnant to its own sense of values to do otherwise."

In so far as Mrs McFarlane's claim for damages for the pain, suffering and distress which the pregnancy had occasioned to herself were concerned, a majority of the Appellate Committee considered that if there had been negligence on the part of the defendants (the issue of negligence had yet to be decided by the Scottish courts) then Mrs McFarlane could recover damages for the pain, suffering and distress she had suffered as well as damages for various other matters such as the loss of earnings which resulted from all that had transpired. Lord Millett dissented in part from this aspect of the majority decision. He argued that pregnancy and delivery are just as inseparable a part of parenthood as is the cost of raising a child, and that if the McFarlanes were not to be allowed to recover the cost of rearing their new child, then it logically followed that neither ought they to recover damages in respect of the pregnancy and delivery of that child. However, Lord Millett did consider that the McFarlanes ought to be awarded damages (up to about £5,000) for having lost the freedom to limit the size of their family. And he did agree with the majority that there were certain special damages for which Mrs McFarlane might claim (though Lord Millett confined these special damages to any cost that the McFarlanes might have suffered in having to purchase new baby equipment, where the equipment that they had used for their other children had been thrown out in the belief that they would have no new children).

Lord Phillips of Worth Matravers

(Appointed: 1999)

Born: 1938
University education: Cambridge University
Age commenced practice: 24
Age became QC: 40
Age became Privy Councillor: 57
Age became judge: 49
Age became Lord of Appeal: 60

Secondary education: Bryanston School
Married: Once
Age married: 34
Number of children: 4 (2 step-children)

In December 1997 Lord Phillips of Worth Matravers (then Sir Nicholas Phillips) was appointed Chairman of the Inquiry established by the Blair administration to look at the BSE (or 'Mad Cow Disease') crisis. The job of Lord Phillips and his two fellow Inquiry members was to investigate the cause and history of 'mad cow disease' and its human variant, to look at the adequacy of the response by government to the BSE crisis as it unfolded, and to make suggestions as to what lessons could be learned for the future. At the time that Lord Phillips was appointed it was expected that the Inquiry would produce a report by the end of 1998. However, the sheer volume of evidence presented to the Inquiry meant that this deadline had to be put back on more than one occasion. In all more than 560 witnesses submitted written evidence to the Inquiry, more than 300 witnesses gave oral evidence before the Inquiry, and more than

3,000 lever-arch files of documents were accumulated by the Inquiry in the course of its proceedings. In the end it was not until December 1999 – almost two years after Lord Phillips' appointment as Inquiry Chairman – that oral hearings came to an end and it became possible for Lord Phillips and his fellow Inquiry members to set about writing the Inquiry report. At the conclusion of the oral hearings in December 1999 Lord Phillips indicated in his closing statement that the report would take three months to prepare. However, the scale of the exercise with which the Inquiry team was confronted, as well as the natural desire by Lord Phillips and his fellow Inquiry members to be entirely fair to those people whose actions were to be considered in the report, meant that the target date for producing the report eventually had to be extended to September 2000.

In the midst of all this activity Sir Nicholas Phillips became Lord Phillips of Worth Matravers and a Lord of Appeal in Ordinary. It was a further moment of achievement in a judicial career that had seen Phillips spend eight years as a High Court judge and four years as a member of the Court of Appeal. Within a few weeks of being appointed to the Appellate Committee the newly ennobled Lord Phillips of Worth Matravers and six fellow Lords of Appeal were subject to a blaze of publicity as they commenced the re-hearing of the General Pinochet appeal after the original Appellate Committee decision in that case was set aside. Lord Phillips' eventual decision in the appeal was that in so far as General Pinochet, as a former head of state, enjoyed immunity from prosecution in respect of the performance of his official functions, that immunity did not extend to actions that constituted criminal offences under international law.

Over the months that followed the Pinochet decision Lord Phillips of Worth Matravers was unable to sit in as many cases as would be customary for a Lord of Appeal because of his continuing involvement in the BSE Inquiry. Indeed the level of involvement that the BSE Inquiry demanded of Lord Phillips of Worth Matravers and the similar level of involvement demanded of his colleague, Lord Saville, as Chairman of the Bloody Sunday Inquiry, and the level of involvement that in the fairly recent past was demanded of Lord Nolan as Chairman of the Committee on Standards in Public Life, raises again the question that was touched upon in the account of Lord Saville's career: whether government ministers are right to continue asking Lords of Appeal to chair government inquiries, given that this necessarily involves those Lords of Appeal giving time to those inquiries that would otherwise be spent doing the work of the Appellate Committee. Unfortunately there does not seem to be an easy solution to this predicament. Some Inquiries – such as the three mentioned above – involve issues of such enormous political significance that government ministers might well be criticised for not attaching enough importance to the issues concerned if they did not seek to appoint the most eminent judges available (i.e. Lords of Appeal in Ordinary) to chair the investigation of these matters. One possible solution might be for retired Lords of Appeal in Ordinary to be asked to do this work. These retired Lords of Appeal have had distinguished judicial careers, they are perfectly capable of doing inquiry work, they possibly have more time to spare than sitting Lords of Appeal in Ordinary, and they are sufficiently eminent as individuals for ministers to avoid the suggestion that not enough importance is being attached to the subject of whatever inquiry a retired Lord of Appeal might be asked to chair.

In June 2000 it was announced on foot of Lord Bingham of Cornhill's appointment as senior Lord of Appeal in Ordinary and Lord Woolf's subsequent appointment to the position of Lord Chief Justice, that Lord Phillips of Worth Matravers was to move from being a Lord of Appeal in Ordinary and (like Lord Woolf before him) be promoted into the post of Master of the Rolls in the Court of Appeal. The job of Master of the Rolls has traditionally been considered one of the three top jobs in the judicial hierarchy.

Sir Richard Scott

(To be appointed October 2000)

Born: 1934
University education:
University of Cape Town;
Cambridge University;
University of Chicago
Age became QC: 41
Age became
Privy Councillor: 57

Secondary education:
Michaelhouse College, Natal
Married: Once
Age married: 25
Age commenced practice: 25
Age became
High Court judge: 49
Age will become Law Lord: 65

On 1 October 2000, the day before his 66th birthday, Sir Richard Rashleigh Folliott Scott will succeed Lord Phillips of Worth Matravers as a Lord of Appeal in Ordinary. Born in India, Sir Richard attended secondary school and went to university in South Africa before coming to England to study at Trinity College, Cambridge. On joining the Appellate Committee Scott will bring to eight the number of Lords of Appeal who have studied outside the United Kingdom. He will bring to three the number of Lords of Appeal who have studied at a South African university (the other two are Lord Hoffmann and Lord Steyn). And he will bring to three the number of Lords of Appeal who have attended an American university – Scott was a Bigelow Fellow at the University of Chicago from 1958 to 1959. (Curiously, given the proximity of the United Kingdom to mainland Europe, only two Lords of Appeal have studied on the Continent in their youth: Lord Normand – who was a Lord of Appeal from 1947 to 1953 – studied for a time in Paris. Before him Lord Hannen – who was a Lord of Appeal from 1891 until his death in 1894 – studied at the University of Heidelberg.)

Scott is perhaps best known to the public as the author of the 'Scott Report'. Published in February 1996, the report was the product of a three-year government-commissioned inquiry into the sale of arms to Iran, Iraq, and Jordan between 1984 and 1990. In his report Scott came up with a number of recommendations aimed at the better regulation of arms sales. Whitehall has set about implementing these recommendations. However, aside from the implementation of the recommendations, it is probably fair to say that the mere publication of the Scott Report (coming as it did on foot of a very thorough inquiry) has had, and will continue in and of itself to have, the practical effect of encouraging British governments always to exercise extreme care when it comes to this area of policy.

Of course Scott is not just the author of the 'Scott Report'. On his appointment to the Appellate Committee he will have been a superior court judge for some seventeen years, having spent eight years as a High Court judge, three years as a Lord Justice of Appeal in the Court of Appeal, and six years as Vice-Chancellor (the Vice-Chancellor is deputy-head of the Chancery Division of the High Court – the Lord Chancellor is the head – and an *ex officio* member of the Court of Appeal), a position to which he was appointed following the elevation of Lord Nicholls of Birkenhead to the Appellate Committee in 1994.

One very prominent case that came before Scott during his time as a High Court judge was a case that sprang from the *'Spycatcher'* saga. The case, which attracted international attention, concerned the memoirs of Peter Wright, a former British intelligence officer. Entitled *Spycatcher: The Candid Autobiography of a Senior Intelligence Officer,* the memoirs contained information that, in the opinion of the British government, ought not to be disclosed. The then Attorney-General (and future Lord Chancellor), Sir Michael Havers, instigated proceedings against Mr Wright and his publishers seeking to restrain publication of the memoirs. This naturally excited the attention of the British media. Indeed the Attorney-General was eventually moved to commence High Court proceedings in which (amongst other things) he sought permanent injunctions preventing three major British newspapers, *The Guardian, The Observer, and The Sunday Times,* from publishing certain information pertaining to or derived from Mr Wright's memoirs. However, by the time the case came before the High Court Mr Wright's memoirs had already been published in several countries and could be brought into the United Kingdom without hindrance. It was for this reason that Scott refused the permanent injunctions sought by the Attorney-General against the newspapers when the case came before him in the High Court. Scott considered that the harm which the permanent injunctions would be aimed at preventing – the disclosure of the confidential material – had already taken place, and so granting the injunctions would serve no purpose. Scott also refused to grant a general injunction sought by the Attorney-General which would have prevented the publication of any confidential information ever obtained from Mr Wright or other members of the intelligence services. Scott did conclude, however, that *The Sunday Times* had acted wrongfully when it published a particular extract from the memoirs. Later appeals against these findings failed before both the Court of Appeal and the Appellate Committee.

5
The Judicial Committee of the Privy Council

Membership of the Privy Council – the origins of the Judicial Committee – Lord Brougham's brainchild – the Judicial Committee Act 1833 – becoming a Privy Councillor – No. 1 Downing Street – the conduct of Judicial Committee hearings – appearing before the Privy Council – deciding cases – the practice of giving a single opinion – the shrinking jurisdiction of the Judicial Committee

The Privy Council has long been the principal advisory body to the British sovereign. It is composed of the Prime Minister, other Cabinet ministers, the leaders of the Opposition parties and a number of prominent individuals, most of whom are drawn from the body politic. In the days when the monarch enjoyed real political power the Privy Council was a very important body. However as the monarchy declined in power and Parliament gained its present eminence the role of the Privy Council came to be supplanted by the Cabinet acting under the leadership of the Prime Minister. Today the Privy Council essentially survives as a convenient umbrella body whereby the Sovereign and ministers can be brought together to perform certain government business such as the formal approval by the Sovereign of legislation passed by Parliament. However the Privy Council has another function that is not just a formal process but is of very real significance. Just like the House of Lords, the Privy Council is not only a political body. It is also a judicial body. And just like the House of Lords the judicial business of the Privy Council is not transacted by the main body of the Council but by a committee of the Council which is staffed by professional judges who get through about 70 percent of the volume of business that the Appellate Committee of the House of Lords gets through each year. This committee is known as the Judicial

Committee of the Privy Council. The Lord Chancellor and all the Lords of Appeal in Ordinary are members of this Committee. Their membership of the Committee is regulated by the Judicial Committee Act 1833. They are not the only people entitled to sit on the Judicial Committee but they have dominated its affairs for more than a century and a half through sheer force of numbers. Because the British sovereign is head of the Commonwealth there has been a tradition of appointing Commonwealth judges to the Judicial Committee, just as there has been a tradition of appointing Commonwealth politicians to the main body of the Privy Council. In the case of Commonwealth politicians membership of the Privy Council is an honour of no real significance save that it reaffirms and enhances the ongoing connection between their countries and the United Kingdom. In the case of Commonwealth judges the situation is a little different. Under the terms of the Judicial Committee Act they may be invited to decide appeals along with the rest of the Judicial Committee. Although such invitations now tend to be fairly limited in number there was a time when it was not at all unusual to see a Commonwealth judge regularly sitting with the Judicial Committee. Indeed when India was a colony there was always one or two members from the Indian courts who sat in on the many Indian appeals to the Council. At the time of writing this book there are nine Privy Councillors who have been appointed from the ranks of foreign judges and are eligible to sit on the Judicial Committee. Six of them come from New Zealand, one from Jamaica, one from the Bahamas, and one from the West Indies.

While the Privy Council has been in existence for at least a thousand years the Judicial Committee of the Privy Council is of more recent origin. In fact it has only been in existence since 1833 when the Judicial Committee Act established it as a professionally staffed, London-based court of appeal in which every decision in every foreign place over which the Crown held sway could be reviewed. Even in the early 1830s that meant accepting appeals from a great many places. But by 1900 somewhere in the region of four hundred million people had become subjects of the Crown and any one of them who felt that he had not got satisfaction from the courts of whatever part of the Empire in which he was located could petition for his case to be re-heard and resolved by the British Queen-Empress acting through the medium of the Judicial Committee. The scale of the task involved was phenomenal. In a speech given in the early 1920s to an audience of law students Viscount Haldane of Cloan, the then Lord Chancellor, tried to capture for his listeners a sense of just how vast an undertaking it was to act as the final court of appeal for an Empire which at that time spanned about one-fifth of the world's land surface. He recounted the fictional tale of a British traveller who had been crossing the distant reaches of northern India when he came upon a group of native villagers praying before the statue of a god who had personally intervened to resolve a land dispute between the villagers and their local rajah. Intrigued the traveller asked the villagers the name of this benevolent deity. "His name," they said, "is the Judicial Committee of the Privy Council."[52]

As with House of Lords appeals the practice of appealing to the Sovereign in Council sprang from the Norman notion of the monarch as ultimate arbiter of justice within his dominions. When discharging this responsibility Norman kings tended to pray in aid the assistance of their advisers. The closest of these advisers eventually became known as the Privy Council. Over time the task of hearing cases was left solely to this body – deciding appeals was just too time-consuming and too tedious a task to merit the continuing personal involvement of the Sovereign. Even so the Privy Council continued (as it does today) to conduct its hearings in the name of the Sovereign and to issue its decisions in the form of recommendations to the monarch as to how a particular case ought to be resolved. That said with the collapse of the Empire several newly independent states chose to establish a right of appeal to the Judicial Committee itself and not to the British monarch acting through the medium of the Committee. This means that those states retain the services of the Judicial Committee without making any obeisance to the Crown. It also means that in deciding appeals from such states the Judicial Committee can behave like any court and give effect to its decisions in the form of mandatory orders issued in its own name. However apart from such appeals it still remains the general practice that the Judicial Committee concludes its decisions by stating that in light of its reasoning it will humbly advise the Monarch to act in one way or another. As it happens the Monarch always complies with a recommendation from the Judicial Committee and issues an order directing that the Committee's recommendations be put into effect. Indeed it is now seriously open to question whether the Crown retains any discretion as to whether or not it should implement Judicial Committee decisions. In the recent past only Lord Devlin has openly supported the contention that the monarch could choose to depart from a decision of the Judicial Committee although, in fashioning their decisions as recommendations for the Sovereign, successive generations of Judicial Committee members right up to the present day have, at least in a formal manner, lent their support to the position espoused by Lord Devlin. Whether or not the Sovereign continues to enjoy this freedom may never make any difference in practice as it would be politically unthinkable for the Sovereign to behave in a manner contrary to that suggested by the Judicial Committee in a particular case. Certainly it is likely that some if not all members of the Judicial Committee would feel compelled to resign if any of their decisions were ever to be overridden in this fashion.

The Judicial Committee as it exists today is the brainchild of Lord Brougham. He was Lord Chancellor in the early nineteenth century. As Lord Chancellor he was widely pilloried. It was said of him that it was a pity he had no law for if he had a little of that he would have a smattering of everything. But it was Lord Brougham's reforms that rescued the Privy Council, as a judicial body, from the imminent disaster which had been facing it immediately prior to the enactment of the Judicial Committee Act. These problems with the Privy Council, or at least the 'Appeals Committee' – the name by which the portion of the Privy Council which sat as a judicial body was known prior to 1833 – were essentially twofold. Firstly, a complete lack of planning meant that there had been an increase in the number of jurisdictions from which appeals might be made to the Privy Council without any real thought being given as to how this increased number of cases might best be dispatched with. The problem was suddenly exacerbated in the late 1700s as military triumphs of that time yielded Britain a rich crop of colonies that had hitherto belonged to her enemies. This, and the simultaneous colonisation of ever-larger portions of the Indian subcontinent, soon led to a massively increased number of cases winding their way before the Appeals Committee, most noticeably from India.[53] A second problem which afflicted the Appeals Committee in Lord Brougham's day was the fact that it was a committee which consisted of the entire Privy Council. This meant that any Privy Councillors – regardless of whether or not they had legal qualifications – were entitled to sit and vote in cases. In fact the Appeals Committee could and sometimes did sit in judgment without *any* legally qualified members being present. Just as bad was the fact that each Councillor's vote was equally weighted so there was nothing to stop the lay members from out-voting the legal members. This resulted in the appalling situation that wealthy appellants could seek to swing judgments in their favour by offering to pay lay-Privy Councillors to sit in on their appeal and decide it in a certain way. Capping these difficulties was the added problem that a growing number of colonies being joined to the Empire did not actually have English-law systems. This resulted in a truly absurd situation in which an Appeals Committee principally staffed by amateurs unqualified in English law was being asked to grapple with entirely alien legal issues which only those with a legal background could have any real hope of grasping. Not surprisingly in light of these difficulties the Appeals Committee by Lord Brougham's day was beginning to face something of a credibility problem in the colonies where it was increasingly viewed as being either incompetent or corrupt or both. All in all it was a situation that was crying out for reform and it was Lord Brougham who saved the day.

Brougham decided that the answer to the various problems which were confronting the Appeals Committee was to create a wing of the Privy Council that would be staffed by professional judges and would function independently of the main body of the Council in dealing with appeals. It was very much like the approach that was to be adopted a little over forty years later with regard to the appellate jurisdiction of the House of Lords, namely to hive off responsibility for judicial business and entrust it to a body that was a part of and yet apart from the main body of the ancient institution from which it sprang. The only difference was that in the case of the House of Lords this separation of responsibilities was almost completely effected whereas in the case of the Privy Council the legislative reforms which Lord Brougham originally suggested were only enacted after he accepted a significant degree of compromise. Hence while Brougham initially sought the abolition of political membership of the new 'Judicial Committee' of the Privy Council, by the time his Act entered the statute-books it allowed for an element of political membership: Lord Presidents of the Council and Lord Chancellors were both to retain their membership of the Appeals Committee turned Judicial Committee (as were ex-Lord Presidents and ex-Lord Chancellors). Brougham could at least comfort himself that Lord Chancellors had the saving grace of being lawyers as well as politicians. This was not the case with Lord Presidents of the Council who have never been appointed for their legal abilities even if they have sometimes been lawyers.[54] However in reality this has never posed any difficulty. The 1833 Act effected an immediate and permanent sea-change in the way the Privy Council went about its judicial business. The presence of professional judges became very much the norm and those Lord Presidents of the Council who were appointed in the years immediately after the Act never took a lead role in the conduct of Judicial Committee affairs. Nowadays any suggestion that they might even participate in a hearing would be considered intolerable.

Reducing to a minimum the lay-membership of the Appeals Committee turned Judicial Committee was not the only objective which Brougham sought to achieve by way of the 1833 Act. He also sought to legislate into being four new judges who would each be paid a salary for sitting on the Judicial Committee (previously Appeals Committee members had been unsalaried). However the Cabinet was not inclined to be so generous with public revenues and made it a condition of supporting the Bill that it be altered to provide for the appointment of four retired superior court judges to serve on the Judicial Committee, each of whom was to be paid less than a tenth of what Lord Brougham's full-time judges would have earned. One further reform which Lord Brougham sought to introduce was to give the Privy Council the jurisdiction to grant divorces. Hitherto these had only been available by way of a private Act of Parliament and so were something which only the rich were able to seek. Divorce, however, was a very controversial issue, particularly among the Irish Members of Parliament on whose votes the government to which Lord Brougham belonged depended to get a lot of its legislation enacted. As a result Brougham was prevailed upon to axe the divorce reforms from his Bill.

The end result of all this was that by the time Brougham introduced the Judicial Committee Bill before the House of Lords it had been so watered down that it prompted very little excitement. It may of course have helped that the Bill was brought before the House in the small hours of the morning when most members were absent but there was also the fact that at the start of the nineteenth century colonial business was generally greeted by most peers with the same lack of interest that more recent members of both Houses of Parliament have tended to reserve for Northern Irish, Scottish, and Welsh business. In any event the Bill was approved by the House of Lords a mere three weeks after its first reading and was then sent to the House of Commons. There the Bill was stewarded by Lord Althorp (a distant ancestor of the late Princess Diana). He did not have the same enthusiasm for the measure that Brougham possessed, nor indeed did the House of Commons, but the Bill was none the less passed into law some three and a half months later.[55]

It is a tribute to Brougham's foresight that the legislation which he engineered has stood the test of time without being the subject of great change. Thus although there has been some reform as regards the number of members to be appointed, what their salary and pension rights are to be and when they are to retire the core effect of the Act remains the same. For the last 167 years a professional full-time body appointed from experienced lawyers or judges has heard and decided appeals cases from almost all of the countries which once belonged to the British Empire.

New Privy Councillors are sworn into office by the Sovereign. The swearing-in ceremony is generally preceded by an impromptu lesson at the Privy Council offices in Whitehall on how to kneel on one knee on a cushion, how to get back up again, how to hold a bible in one's right hand, how to take three paces towards the Queen, how to take her hand and kiss it, and how to step ten paces back without falling over anything. Having mastered these skills the prospective Privy Councillor then has to go over to Buckingham Palace and put into practice everything he has just learned. Once he takes the oath of loyalty and kisses the Queen's hand he is a Privy Councillor. Interestingly, while the emphasis is placed on coaching those being initiated into the Privy Council on how to avoid making mistakes it is not unknown for a Sovereign to commit the occasional blunder. In the last century there was one occasion when a person who ought merely to have been appointed to the main body of the Privy Council was accidentally appointed by Queen Victoria to the Judicial Committee as well. The Judicial Committee member concerned was Thomas Pemberton-Leigh (later Lord Kingsdown) who went on to put in a rather successful twenty years as a Judicial Committee member. The mistake arose because Pemberton-Leigh, who was a prominent Queen's Counsel and had been an only slightly less prominent Member of Parliament, accepted the offer of a Privy Councillorship made to him by Lord Lyndhurst, the Lord Chancellor of the day, but declined the offer of Judicial Committee membership which Lord Lyndhurst made to him at the same time. Unfortunately someone forgot to make all of this clear to Queen Victoria or else she simply made a mistake. Either way what would normally be a pleasant experience for most people – being sworn in as a member of the Privy Council – turned into something of a shock for Pemberton-Leigh who when he rose from where he had been kneeling and stepped backwards from the Queen found himself to be not just a Privy Councillor as he had expected but a Judicial Committee member also.

It has sometimes been suggested that because of its status as an adjunct to the Privy Council the Committee is not strictly speaking a court. Certainly Committee members are not like ordinary superior court judges in that they can be removed from office at the Sovereign's pleasure (although this has never happened). Indeed some of the Committee's earlier members did not view themselves as being bound by the normal conventions which apply to judges. Thus even after he was appointed to the Judicial Committee and had started sitting in on appeals Thomas Pemberton-Leigh continued to practice as a barrister before the Court of Appeal and the House of Lords. The Judicial Committee is, and was in Pemberton-Leigh's day, principally an appeals tribunal for overseas cases so technically speaking Pemberton-Leigh was not appearing before brother members of the judiciary when he appeared for appellants in the Court of Appeal and the House of Lords. Even so a similar situation would not be allowed to prevail today and not just because these days it is mainly the same people (the Lords of Appeal) who staff the Appellate Committee and the Judicial Committee. Even in Pemberton-Leigh's day it was a peculiar sight to see a top-level London-based judge arguing cases before fellow top-level London-based judges. In fact no other Judicial Committee member has ever sought to emulate Pemberton-Leigh in this regard though one member, Stephen Lushington, enjoys the equally curious (and again unique) distinction of having been the only Judicial Committee member ever to have simultaneously been a Member of Parliament at the same time that he was listening to and deciding appeals. Pemberton-Leigh and Lushington aside, there is no doubt that the overwhelming view among Judicial Committee members since 1833 has been to see themselves as members of a court and so ineligible to work either as barristers or as public representatives.

As with all British courts the public are generally allowed to attend Judicial Committee hearings. These are heard in the rather magnificent surroundings of No 1 Downing Street, which stands on the site of the house where an aunt of Oliver Cromwell once lived, and is a mere stone's throw away from the British Prime Minister's official residence, which stands further up the same street on the same side of the road. Now that Downing Street has been closed off to the general public for security reasons a visit to see the Judicial Committee in action can be a somewhat dramatic occasion. A quick word in the ear of any of the policemen guarding the entrance to Downing Street and the gates are opened to allow one to enter and stroll up as far as the entrance to the Judicial Committee. Inside one is waved upstairs by a porter. Having passed the porter one climbs a winding set of stairs as far as the first floor. The oil portraits of long gone legal *eminenti* line the walls of the staircase. At the top of the stairs one can turn right to gain access to the Privy Council Offices (which are not open to the public) or left for the Judicial Committee chamber. Having turned left one walks straight down the landing past yet another porter to a small panelled room with a large marble fireplace. This is the ante-chamber to the rooms where Judicial Committee hearings are conducted. It is normally very quiet and the sound of voices can be heard from the room beyond. Tossed untidily on the table are several sheets of paper. These list the name (or names) of whatever hearings are being conducted in the room beyond. Hanging on the walls around the room are pictures of various Lord Chancellors. On the left-hand side over by the windows are a couple of coat-racks as well as an untidy pile of boxes and papers from past cases. The windows overlook Downing Street. At each end of the wall behind the table are two small doors through which access is gained to the chamber beyond. A small sign indicates that the door to the right is for Appellant's Counsel and the door to the left is for Defendant's Counsel. The public can enter by either door.

The chamber in which the hearings are conducted dates from the start of the nineteenth century. It is a long, wide room with a high ceiling. On the left hand side a row of windows overlooks Downing Street. On the right hand side a similar row of windows overlooks a garden to the rear of Downing Street. In each corner of the room there is a door. In the centre of each wall in which the doors are set are two matching fireplaces that face each other across the room. Between each door and each fireplace hang oil portraits of famous judges. The walls themselves are painted in a sickly sea-green colour. Close to the centre of the room is what looks like a very large dinner table. On one side of this table sit the members of the Judicial Committee. They do not wear any gowns or regalia though in the nineteenth century the chamber was so cold that one member took to wearing a wig in order to keep warm. Since the end of the Second World War the room has been provided with heating.

At the table the presiding member of the Judicial Committee sits in the centre chair with the various other members sitting in chairs to his right and left depending on their seniority. At those hearings where the Judicial Committee decides what cases it will proceed to hear in full there are normally three members present. At full hearings there are normally five members present. There is a microphone in front of each member and all the materials with which they have been provided are spread across the table in front of them. On the right-hand side of the Judicial Committee members at a smaller table a small distance away from them is a porter who re-fills the water-glasses of the various members when necessary and provides them with the relevant materials pertaining to each case when the Judicial Committee finishes one hearing and moves on to the next. Directly across from the Judicial Committee members but seated at a smaller table perpendicular to them is a case reporter who in turn is wedged up against a podium from which counsel address the Judicial Committee. Counsel when standing at this podium are actually higher than the members of the Judicial Committee at the table across from them. Thus in common with the Appellate Committee, but unlike every other court in the United Kingdom where judges look down on counsel, in the Judicial Committee the Lords of Appeal look up to them. As there is only slightly more than the width of a dining table between them, both judges and counsel also come within rather closer proximity of each other at Judicial Committee hearings than is the general norm in British courts. This has in the past enabled certain judges who have had to retire from other courts because of increasing deafness to live out a meaningful retirement in the Judicial Committee chamber where they can actually hear counsel because they are situated right across from the judges. It has also led to argument assuming a more subdued form in the Judicial Committee chamber than would be norm in other British courtrooms, except again the Appellate Committee chamber over at the House of Lords.

Opposing counsel when sitting are placed directly across from each other at two tables that stand on either side of the podium and perpendicular to the table at which the Judicial Committee members are seated. Behind this front row there is a second table and a second row of chairs which may be taken by junior counsel or by the solicitors in a case or even by counsel who will be appearing in the next case. Behind this second row of chairs there is a knee-high wooden bookshelf which contains several sets of law-books which look to be incomplete. Jammed in behind these bookshelves is a double row of leather-upholstered chairs for ordinary members of the public and anyone else who might need them. There is a similar row of chairs against the back wall though these normally seem to be occupied by counsel who are waiting to argue a case. While members of the Judicial Committee dress in normal, everyday suits, counsel appear in whatever court-wear is normal for the jurisdiction from which they come. Because the Privy Council sits in London most cases are argued by practitioners at the English Bar. The proximity of the Channel Islands to the British mainland means that one sometimes gets Channel Island counsel appearing personally in cases and wearing rather interesting court-wear which owes more to French influence than to English tradition and would not look amiss on a Catholic monsignor.

Judicial Committee hearings are conducted in a similar manner to that in which hearings by the Appellate Committee of the House of Lords are conducted. A slight difference is that there tends to be a smaller turnover of counsel appearing before the Privy Council so Lords of Appeal get to see familiar faces rather more often when sitting on the Judicial Committee of the Privy Council than when sitting on the Appellate Committee of the House of Lords. In those cases where it is only permission to bring an appeal before the Judicial Committee that is being sought (rather than the main body of an appeal being heard) an immediate answer is usually given by the Committee. Before giving their opinion as to whether leave ought to be granted the members of the Judicial Committee may confer privately with each other. Such conferences take place in the room where the hearings are held. A buzzer is sounded and everyone present is told to wait in the antechamber outside. This can be an interesting experience. The ante-chamber is so small that opposing parties are thrust rather closer together than they might otherwise choose to be. Almost invariably they move to opposite ends of the room and have low-key conversations with their lawyers. The middle of the room seems to become a neutral space that is either left vacant or is occupied by any journalists or members of the public who happen to be present. After a few minutes the buzzer is sounded once more and everyone returns inside to the hearings room. The presiding member of the Appellate Committee then says whether or not the Judicial Committee will be advising the Queen to grant leave to appeal.

As well as hearing these overseas appeals the Judicial Committee has in the last century and a half enjoyed something of a hodge-podge of additional responsibilities on the domestic front. For example the Committee is the tribunal of last recourse for disputes within the Church of England. This might be thought to be – and indeed it is – a rather strange responsibility for a body of lay-men notwithstanding the fact that when the Committee sits in this capacity (which it very rarely does) its members can be joined by the Archbishop of Canterbury, the Archbishop of York and up to four other bishops who sit with the Committee as expert advisers or 'assessors'. Along with its jurisdiction in ecclesiastical cases the Judicial Committee also functions as the ultimate court of appeal for any dentists, doctors and opticians who wish to appeal against their having been 'struck off' the register of their respective professional bodies. A further duty which falls on Judicial Committee members is to hear appeals from Prize Courts (which are courts established to determine questions arising from the wartime capture of enemy ships). Happily this particular jurisdiction has not of late been an especially fruitful source of appeals, nor has there been a great number of cases forthcoming from the Court of Admiralty of the *Cinque Ports*, an ancient body responsible for deciding certain maritime disputes, or indeed from disgruntled MPs who have fallen foul of the House of Commons Disqualification Act 1957, who consequently stand to lose their Parliamentary seats, and whose right of remedy under the 1957 Act lies with the Privy Council, a non-Parliamentary body, and not, as one might have expected, with Parliament itself.

One further duty of the Judicial Committee is to consider 'special references'. These are questions referred directly to the Judicial Committee by the Sovereign on behalf of the government and normally involve political (or near-political) issues which are so sensitive it is thought best to entrust their scrutiny to an impartial body. This aspect of the Judicial Committee's responsibilities is actually a throwback to pre-Brougham days when the Appeals Committee was an integral part of the main body of the Privy Council. Thus curiously when the Lords of Appeal in Ordinary consider special references they do so as an esteemed group of Privy Councillors. It is of course open to question whether the Lords of Appeal should be called upon to exercise this function. It does seem somewhat unusual that senior members of the judiciary should occasionally advise governments on live political issues such as the legitimacy of state-authorised telephone-tapping and the propriety of government behaviour in the run-up to the Falkland Islands invasion, two very controversial areas of public concern which have in the past been the subject of special references. That said, the Judicial Committee is now set to assume an additional responsibility that will in the future involve it resolving legal issues that have a distinctly political flavour: under the legislation establishing the new national assemblies for Scotland and Wales it is the Judicial Committee which will be responsible for deciding disputes that arise between each of the two new assemblies and the Westminster Parliament regarding their respective responsibilities.

When Judicial Committee decisions are given they are printed as an opinion with an indication of how it is proposed that the Queen be advised in light of that opinion – i.e., whether she should allow or refuse the appeal that has been made. Until 1966 only a single opinion was ever given in a Judicial Committee case. Dissenting opinions were never published though a record of who voted what way has long been maintained by Privy Council officials and may be consulted by Judicial Committee members when they are considering whether a previous Committee decision ought to be revised or set aside – presumably members would be less likely to modify or reverse a previous decision that had been decided unanimously than one which had been adopted by a bare majority of votes. Unfortunately a complete set of these records or 'Judgment Books' is only available back to 1940. Previous volumes were destroyed when the Privy Council offices suffered a near-direct hit by a bomb in the course of the Second World War. The policy of giving one collective judgment and not giving dissenting judgments stemmed from a rule of practice adopted by the Privy Council some two years into the reign of Charles II in 1627 and from the terms of the oath of secrecy still taken by every Privy Councillor on appointment into office. Although both the rule of practice and the oath of office were designed with political business in mind there was no rigid distinction between the judicial and political work of the Privy Council at the time that they were introduced so the one-judgment rule came to be applied to the Privy Council in its conduct of appeals cases also. This did not prove controversial in pre-Brougham days when the Appeals Committee was primarily staffed by lay Privy Councillors untrained in the law – such men were unlikely to betray their ignorance of the law by issuing a dissenting opinion. However the requirement that only one judgment be given made rather less sense when in the years following the enactment of the Judicial Committee Act 1833 prominent lawyers and judges began to be appointed to the Judicial Committee. These were men who each had something to say about the legal points that came before them and judicial tradition demanded that they be allowed the right to say it. At first they were denied this right. There were a variety of reasons why this was so. To begin with a single judgment was thought to lend authority and certainty to Judicial Committee decisions. These were important attributes when one was seeking to adjudicate on matters which affected the lives of millions of subjects within a vast and diverse Empire. Limiting the number of appeals to the Committee was also a consideration. In the absence of dissenting judgments there was reduced scope for litigation that sought to exploit any differences of opinion which existed between Appellate Committee members on the various legal questions brought before them. There were also constitutional implications. It was thought inappropriate that the Sovereign should be provided with conflicting advice by the various members of the Committee.[56] Lastly, there was the matter of ecclesiastical cases: to avoid fuelling the disputes that existed within the Church of England it was considered best to issue single judgment decisions and so minimise the potential of Judicial Committee rulings to further excite controversy.

As time went by the persuasive force of each of the reasons for single judgment decisions slowly waned. The Empire withered away. The number of cases coming before the Committee dropped. The notion that the monarch held the reins of government was seen for the constitutional formality it has become. And the role of the Church of England in society declined. With each of these developments the cause for issuing single judgment decisions grew steadily weaker. There were additional factors too. Enforced unanimity was perceived to result in a certain blandness in judgments. Dissenting opinions were increasingly viewed as a means whereby the law could be enriched and improved. They provided a means whereby judges could give their particular insights into areas of jurisprudence where they did not subscribe to what happened for the moment to be the majority view. Moreover dissenting judgments came to be seen as a way of assuring litigants and the general public that justice was being exercised in a free and fair fashion which did not crush dissent but allowed freedom of expression. Finally in 1966 the Privy Council changed its rules so as to allow members of the Judicial Committee to issue dissenting opinions. At the same time the Committee abandoned its longstanding policy of holding itself bound by its own previous decisions. However while this latter freedom has been exercised it is still very much the practice for the Judicial Committee to print a single collective opinion in the cases that come before it. In consequence the standard of its jurisprudence has never quite matched that of the Appellate Committee of the House of Lords. Still public dissent is now possible and in the long-run that is likely to have a beneficial effect on the quality of the judgments emanating from the Judicial Committee.

Today New Zealand is the only sizeable jurisdiction that continues to allow appeals from the decisions of its domestic courts to the Judicial Committee. Efforts have been made in New Zealand to cut this umbilical cord with the United Kingdom but so far these have not proved successful. Among the various other countries, dependencies and territories which allow or enjoy a right of appeal to the Privy Council are Anguilla, Antigua and Barbuda, Barbados, Belize, Bermuda, the British Antarctic Territory, the British Indian Ocean territory, the Cayman Islands, the Channel Islands, Dominica, the Falkland Islands, Gibraltar, Grenada, the Isle of Man, Jamaica, Kiribati, Mauritius, Montserrat, the Pitcairn, Henderson, Ducie and Oeno Islands, St Christopher and Nevis, St Helena and its Dependencies, St Lucia, St Vincent and the Grenadines, South Georgia and the Sandwich Islands, the Sovereign Base Areas of Akrotiri and Dhekelia (on Cyprus), The Bahamas, The Gambia, Trinidad and Tobago, the Turks and Caicos Islands, Tuvalu, and the Virgin Islands. Some of these places are so small that many people have probably never heard of them and those who have heard of them might well not be able to locate all of them on a map. As it happens their smallness may actually be the reason why the bulk of these places continue the practice of bringing appeals before the Judicial Committee. They may enjoy the lustre of having a body of international renown as their final court of appeal. Moreover some of these jurisdictions are so small that their standards of advocacy (and sometimes the quality of their judges) may not always be the best. Having the benefits of a reasonably well-funded, well-managed, and (in so far as its judicial make-up is concerned) outstandingly well-staffed court of final appeal is therefore desirable for many of them.[57] One might ask whether the fact that the Judicial Committee still conducts hearings for so many poor jurisdictions or jurisdictions in which the majority of the population is of colour betrays an unspoken presumption on someone's part that the justice meted out by a rich man's tribunal or by a white man's tribunal is rather better than that obtainable elsewhere. However there is no such presumption: retaining the right of appeal is a voluntary action on the part of the jurisdictions which have chosen to do so. They are free to end the right of appeal whenever they desire and the simple fact of the matter is that they have chosen not to do so. They most certainly would not retain the right of appeal if they thought the Judicial Committee to be in any sense or fashion a tribunal tainted by notions of suprematism.

One jurisdiction which did produce a lot of cases for the Judicial Committee but which recently ended the right of appeal is Hong Kong. However there is not to be a complete severance of Hong Kong's connection with the United Kingdom. It was agreed as part of the handover agreement with the United Kingdom that the Hong Kong Court of Appeal – the new court of ultimate jurisdiction in the former Crown colony – is to include two non-permanent English members who will be seconded from the English judiciary for a period of about one month each year. The first two judges to have been seconded in this fashion are Lord Nicholls of Birkenhead and Lord Hoffmann. That the new Hong Kong authorities have been happy to retain the services of the Lords of Appeal is testament to the esteem in which top British judges have generally been held.

Given that the jurisdiction of the Judicial Committee in overseas appeals cases is something of a relic from the hey-day of Empire it is sometimes asked whether – and if so for how long – its appellate jurisdiction can continue in a post-Imperial age. Gone are the days when there was talk of merging the Judicial Committee with the Appellate Committee and creating an Imperial Court of Final Appeal. Nowadays one encounters suggestions that those countries that have retained their right of appeal to the Judicial Committee should sever this connection with their colonial past. Whether or not to do so is, of course, ultimately a matter for politicians in those jurisdictions that have thus far retained the right of appeal, but the simple fact of the matter is that politicians in those jurisdictions seem happy for the present state of affairs to continue.

In the recent past there seems to have been an increase in the amount of time that Lords of Appeal in Ordinary have spent on Judicial Committee business. In an interview published in 1999, Lord Browne-Wilkinson, then the senior Lord of Appeal in Ordinary, expressed concern over the amount of time that was being taken up by death penalty cases coming before the Judicial Committee. One reason why death penalty cases may have been taking so much time is the fact that various City firms of solicitors have been agreeing to bring appeals before the Judicial Committee on behalf of death row prisoners in Caribbean countries. Appeals brought by such firms are well-prepared, well-argued and, well, quite time-consuming – though even the best-prepared appeals are not always successful: on 29 May 1999 the Judicial Committee unanimously rejected appeals against death sentences brought by nine convicted murderers from Trinidad and Tobago. This decision cleared the way for Trinidad and Tobago to carry out its first executions in more than 4 years (previously the last man to be executed by the Trinidad and Tobago authorities was actually hanged while the Judicial Committee was in the course of hearing an appeal brought on his behalf). Death sentence appeals are obviously cases in which the Judicial Committee as a court of last resort has a singularly important role to play. However the manner in which such appeals are decided might not only determine the fate of the unfortunate individuals in whose name those appeals are brought. They may yet play an important role in determining the future of the Judicial Committee itself. This is because while every case in which the Judicial Committee allows death sentences to go ahead is perhaps likely to buttress support for the Committee in the Caribbean region (where the death penalty is said to enjoy a certain popularity) it is surely equally likely to engender a certain clamour within the United Kingdom for the right of appeal to the Judicial Committee to be ended on the basis that more than 30 years after Parliament abolished the death penalty it is inappropriate for the most senior judges in the British judiciary to be deciding death penalty cases. Whenever the British public or indeed Members of Parliament do rouse themselves sufficiently to do something about this state of affairs one suspects that the Lords of Appeal in Ordinary will welcome any lightening of their workload that might follow.

Afterword

...For those not intimately connected with the Pinochet appeal an early indication that something might be amiss with the original decision of the Appellate Committee in the case came only a few hours after the decision was approved at a full meeting of the House of Lords. *Newsnight*, a popular current affairs programme on BBC television, decided to devote some air-time to the Pinochet appeal. Guests were invited into the studio and there was a live satellite link with Chile. All in all the programme went as might be expected. Some people were delighted with what the Lords of Appeal had decided, hailing it as a triumph for human rights and British justice. Others were not so convinced. One speaker in Chile mentioned that Lord Hoffmann's wife was a member of Amnesty International. He clearly believed that this could have affected the fairness of the General's trial. After all, Amnesty International had argued before the Lords of Appeal and through his wife Lord Hoffmann had a connection with the organisation.

Initially this notion that Lord Hoffmann had somehow acted inadvisedly in the Pinochet appeal by hearing argument from a party with whom his wife had a connection did not excite much attention, even when the General's lawyers later included it in their formal submissions to the Home Secretary as a reason why he should exercise his statutory discretion not to allow Pinochet's extradition to go ahead. The reason for the general lack of interest in the story is probably that people outside the Pinochet camp sensed that Lady Hoffmann's membership of Amnesty International simply did not impinge on Lord Hoffmann's actions as a judge. For this story to go anywhere it really had to be shown that Lord Hoffmann himself enjoyed some sort of connection, however tenuous, with Amnesty International.

On the morning of 7 December General Pinochet's lawyers were in their London offices when they received an anonymous telephone call. The caller told them that Lord Hoffmann was a director of a company linked to Amnesty International. It is not known who the caller was or what motive he had for making the call but one thing is certain – what he had to say was significant. If it was true then the General and his lawyers had a fairly good ground for arguing that Lord Hoffmann ought not to have sat in the Pinochet appeal and that consequently the decision in that appeal ought to be set aside.

By the morning of 8 December this dramatic twist in the Pinochet affair had surfaced in the press. A national newspaper, *The Guardian*, ran the story as a lead article on its front page. There was even an accompanying picture of Lord Hoffmann. On the same morning a letter from the lawyers acting for Amnesty International arrived on at the offices of the General's lawyers. This letter was dated 7 December. By way of introduction it explained that

> Amnesty International have instructed us that after contacting Lord Hoffmann over the weekend both he and they believe that the following informationa about his connection with Amnesty International's charitable work should be given to you.

The letter went on to say that since 1990 Hoffmann had been working as an unpaid director of a company which is in effect the fund-raising arm of Amnesty International. The letter explained that the company had never played any part in any of Amnesty International's political activities but the letter did create an impression that Lord Hoffmann might perhaps have been better advised not to sit as a judge in the Pinochet appeal. Even so, the letter was no guarantee that the decision of the House of Lords in that appeal would be set aside and General Pinochet allowed go free.

An early indication of the task that still lay ahead of the General's lawyers came only one day later – on 9 December – when the Home Secretary announced that he had concluded there was no reason for him to halt the extradition of General Pinochet. The Home Secretary did this after being formally notified by the General's lawyers of the letter they had received regarding Lord Hoffmann's link to Amnesty International. So it was clear that the Home Secretary did not attach any great significance to the allegations of apparent bias being made by the General's lawyers.

The Home Secretary's decision was greeted with widespread jubilation by the press and by opponents of General Pinochet. But it met with a rather different response from the General's lawyers. They had already made plans to bring a new appeal to the House of Lords asking the House to set aside the decision it had made in the original Pinochet appeal a mere two weeks previously. On 10 December the General's lawyers formally instigated this appeal. As with all cases brought to the House of Lords it fell to be heard by the Appellate Committee. Very soon the excitement about the Home Secretary's decision was replaced with a certain apprehension on all sides as to what the decision of the Appellate Committee would be.

Hearings began on 15 December. They were presided over by five Lords of Appeal, none of whom had been previously involved in the case. Counsel for General Pinochet argued that the decision to which Lord Hoffmann had been party ought to be set aside because as a result of his connection to one of the parties who argued in the original appeal Lord Hoffmann might be perceived as having been biased. Opposing counsel argued that there had been no real danger of bias on the part of Lord Hoffmann, and that in any event the question of bias had already been raised with (and rejected by) the Home Secretary so there was no reason why the General should be allowed to raise the issue yet again, this time with the Appellate Committee – there had to be some sort of end to the number of times the General could seek relief on this ground and having tried but failed to persuade the Home Secretary on the point that really ought to have been the end of the matter.

The issues raised by counsel were not especially complex and after only two days of hearings the Appellate Committee members retired to consider their decision. On 17 December they entered the main chamber of the House of Lords and, in a short speech, Lord Browne Wilkinson, the then senior Lord of Appeal in Ordinary – announced what the Committee had decided: that in light of everything which had occurred the original decision in the Pinochet appeal would be set aside and the case re-heard. Full reasons for this decision were to be given to the House following the Christmas vacation.

His speech over Lord Browne-Wilkinson and the other Lords of Appeal left the House. In all the announcement of their decision had taken less than twenty minutes but it had been an occasion of enormous legal and political importance. It was the first time that it had ever been agreed to set aside a decision of the House of Lords because of a possible perception of bias on the part of a Lord of Appeal. It is worth emphasising that it was merely a possible *perception* of bias that was at issue. By sitting in the Pinochet appeal without declaring his link to one of the parties who argued in that appeal, Lord Hoffmann unintentionally created a situation in which it could be *suggested*, no more, that his judgment in that case had been tainted by bias. However, the mere fact that the suggestion could be made was sufficient for Lord Hoffmann's colleagues on the Appellate Committee to conclude that the original decision in the Pinochet case had to be set aside. They did not for a moment doubt Lord Hoffmann's integrity. Their sole concern was that justice should not only be done, it should be *perceived* as having been done. And in the present case there could be a possible perception that justice had not been done. For the Appellate Committee to set aside a decision of its own would have been bad enough in any case, but it was particularly awkward that it should happen in a case which had attracted so much international attention. That a situation such as this could and did happen prompted some commentators to question whether Lord Hoffmann should continue as a Lord of Appeal and whether the Appellate Committee was performing satisfactorily as a court of appeal. Neither of these questions was particularly fair. Anyone – even a Lord of Appeal in Ordinary – is capable of a mistake. And to judge the Appellate Committee's performance within the context of or in the immediate aftermath of a particularly controversial case was unlikely to result in a measured conclusion. At least Christmas was to provide something of a break from all the excitement and controversy of the previous two months. But in January the full judgments of the Appellate Committee in the second Pinochet appeal were due to be given and the re-hearing of General Pinochet's original case was expected to begin. As the Lords of Appeal went their separate ways for the Christmas vacation they must have known that it was only a matter of time before Lord Hoffmann's future and the role of the Appellate Committee were to become the subject of popular discussion once again.

On 15 January 1999, Lord Browne-Wilkinson, Lord Goff of Chieveley, Lord Nolan, Lord Hope of Craighead and Lord Hutton issued the full text of their judgments concerning Lord Hoffmann's actions in the original Pinochet appeal. Their comments tended to concentrate on the importance of the principle that justice must not only be done, it must be seen to be done. They certainly did not engage in the scathing criticism of their fellow Appellate Committee member which the public had possibly expected. Notwithstanding this the media still raised the possibility that Lord Hoffmann might feel compelled to resign – indeed some journalists went even further and openly called on Lord Hoffmann to step down from office. Lord Hoffmann did not yield to the pressure that was brought upon him to quit. A mere three weeks later his refusal to go was being defended by the Lord Chancellor, Lord Irvine, who stated during a briefing for press correspondents on another matter that Lord Hoffmann had simply been guilty of an "error of judgment", and that "a lawyer of the highest ability... should not be lost to the system because of a single error."[58] Of all the judges who sit on the Appellate Committee Lord Irvine is perhaps the one who could most empathise with Lord Hoffmann for withstanding the taunts of a harshly critical press. After all, barely a year had passed since the Lord Chancellor himself had withered such a barrage of criticism from the media that there had been talk of him being prevailed upon to resign. But that was yesterday's news and slowly but surely Lord Hoffmann's error was becoming yesterday's news too. Instead by the time the Lord Chancellor made his public defence of Lord Hoffmann the re-hearing of the Pinochet appeal (this time by seven Lords of Appeal in Ordinary) was complete and the world was again awaiting to see what the fate of General Pinochet would be.

As it happened the world was kept waiting for rather a longer period of time than might have been expected. Judgment in the appeal was delayed as a result of overwork and understaffing on the Appellate Committee. The end result was that the judgments in the Pinochet rehearing were not given until the end of March, some two months after oral argument in the re-hearing had been completed, and some five and a half months after the General's original arrest in London. Although the Lords of Appeal are not themselves responsible for the resourcing of the British appellate courts system, and indeed the over-working of British superior court judges which led to this delay, it is perhaps regrettable that such a delay occurred in so prominent a case as the Pinochet appeal. Certainly some elements of the British media seemed convinced that the delay, on top of everything else which had occurred since the original House of Lords decision in the Pinochet case, added weight to the contention that it was time consideration be given to implementing reforms within the highest tier of the British judiciary.

In any event, on 24 March 1999 the seven Lords of Appeal who had sat in the re-hearing of the Pinochet appeal produced seven extremely fine (and exhaustively argued) judgments in which by an overwhelming (6–1) majority they rejected the contention that General Pinochet, as a former head of state, enjoys blanket immunity for all of the humanitarian offences alleged to have been perpetrated by him during his time as Chilean head of state, though a smaller majority decided that the range of offences for which the General could be extradited were limited in time to any offences that occurred in the period after the internationally agreed Torture Convention of 1984 became law – it is the Torture Convention which now outlaws torture in signatory countries such as Chile, Spain, and the United Kingdom and allows any one of those countries to prosecute an individual within its own boundaries for torture committed by that individual within the territory of another signatory country.

Thus Lord Browne-Wilkinson, the senior Lord of Appeal, wrote that

> [I]f, as alleged ... [General] Pinochet organised and authorised torture after [the operative date of the Torture Convention] he was not acting in any capacity which gives rise to immunity ...

Lord Hope of Craighead, the youngest Lord of Appeal, wrote that:

> [W]hile ... [General] Pinochet has immunity ... from prosecution for [amongst other crimes] ... such conspiracies ... to commit acts of torture ... as could be shown to precede [the operative date of the Torture Convention] ... he has no immunity from prosecution for the charges of torture and of conspiracy to torture which relate to the period after that date ...

Lord Hutton, the Northern Irish Lord of Appeal, wrote that

> I am of opinion that ... [General] Pinochet is not entitled to claim immunity in the extradition proceedings in respect of conspiracy to torture and acts of torture alleged to have been committed by him after [the Torture Convention was incorporated into English law] ...

Lord Saville of Newdigate, making what was to become a somewhat less frequent appearance on the Appellate Committee as a result of his chairmanship of the 'Bloody Sunday' Inquiry, wrote that:

> The words ... [of the Torture Convention] are wide enough to cover not only ... public officials or persons acting in an official capacity who themselves inflict torture but also ... [to] those who order others to torture or conspire with others to torture ... To my mind it must follow ... that a head of state, who for state purposes resorts to torture, would be a person acting in an official capacity [and so a criminal] within the meaning of this Convention. He would indeed to my mind be a prime example of an official torturer.

Lord Millett, one of Tony Blair's first appointees to the Appellate Committee, agreed that General Pinochet did not enjoy absolute immunity from prosecution for humanitarian offences committed during the time that the General was head of state in Chile. Indeed Lord Millet did not consider that the General's liability should even be restricted in time to a period after the coming into being of the Torture Convention. He wrote:

> It is important to emphasise that... [General] Pinochet is not alleged to be criminally liable because he was head of state when other responsible officials employed torture to maintain him in power. He is not alleged to be vicariously liable for the wrongdoing of his subordinates. He is alleged to have incurred direct criminal responsibility for his own acts in ordering and directing a campaign of terror involving the use of torture. Chile insists on the exclusive right to prosecute him. The Torture Convention, however, gives it only the primary right. If it does not seek his extradition (and it does not) then the United Kingdom is obliged [under the terms of the Torture Convention] to extradite him to another requesting state or prosecute him itself.

Finally, Lord Phillips of Worth Matravers, the newest appointee to the Appellate Committee and, like Lord Saville of Newdigate, an Appellate Committee member whose chairmanship of a government inquiry (the BSE Inquiry) meant that he too was to make a somewhat less frequent appearance at Appellate Committee hearings, wrote:

> Insofar as [Britain's State Immunity Act of 1978] entitles a former head of state to immunity in respect of the performance of his official functions I do not believe that those functions can... extend to actions that are prohibited as criminal under international law.

Only Lord Goff of Chieveley, the onetime senior Lord of Appeal in Ordinary who had been called back from retirement to buttress numbers on the Appellate Committee, considered that General Pinochet, as a former head of state, did enjoy immunity for all the crimes alleged against him in the extradition case made by the Spanish authorities. Out of a total of twelve Appellate Committee members who sat in the two appeals brought by General Pinochet before the House of Lords, Lord Goff was one of only three members who reached this conclusion (the other two being Lord Slynn of Hadley and Lord Lloyd of Berwick).

As the majority of Lords of Appeal in both of the Pinochet appeals gave (and gave in such overwhelming numbers) the green light to the continuation of extradition proceedings against General Pinochet – the result that humanitarian organisations and human rights activists had been baying for – one might have thought that their actions would meet with a certain applause from the media. However on the whole this did not happen. One of the reasons for this was that by the time the Appellate Committee got round to delivering judgment in the Pinochet case, the attention of the press and public had to a very great extent switched from the alleged human rights abuses committed by the former President of Chile to the alleged human rights abuses being committed by Slobodan Milosevic, the incumbent President of Yugoslavia. There was, however, another reason. Since the publication in December 1998 of a government White Paper on House of Lords reform and the subsequent enactment of legislation that has seen most (though not quite all) of the hereditary peers evicted from the House – some 92 hereditary peers have been granted a temporary reprieve until government reforms of the Upper Chamber are complete – and with the (at the time of writing) forthcoming implementation of the Human Rights Act 1998, much of the media comment about the Appellate Committee since the beginning of 1999 has tended to be concerned with what role the Lords of Appeal should play in this revamped constitutional framework. It has been suggested that Lords of Appeal ought to lose their right to vote in House of Lords debates. After all, the reasoning goes, there is no other country in which senior judges are given the right to sit and vote in the legislature. The reason the Lords of Appeal enjoy this right is of course a result of the fact that back in 1876 when the office of Lord of Appeal was created, the government of Benjamin Disraeli would have been unable to get the necessary legislation through Parliament if it had sought (as it initially wanted) to divorce the legislative and judicial functions of the House of Lords from each other and establish a completely separate Supreme Court. Instead Disraeli and his Lord Chancellor, Lord Cairns, adopted a compromise solution whereby the full House of Lords would continue to be the body that acts as the court of final appeal for most cases decided in the United Kingdom (even though it was to be the Lords of Appeal who would enjoy the real power to decide cases). As a result of this compromise Lords of Appeal have had to be members of the House of Lords and as members of the House they have been (and are) entitled to participate in its debates. The reverse of course does not hold true. Ordinary members of the House of Lords, though ostensibly entitled to vote in appeals cases, have not actually done so since the trial of Daniel O'Connell in 1843.

With the Blair government bent on House of Lords reform there seems no reason why these nineteenth century arrangements and accommodations should necessarily continue in place. In fact as the House of Lords becomes a more party-political body in which one's ancestry will count for less and one's political allegiance will count for more, the case for such a body acting as – or even containing – the United Kingdom's final court of appeal becomes ever less convincing (if indeed there has ever been a convincing case, at least in recent times, for having a legislative chamber that doubles as a court of appeal).

Not surprisingly the present talk of House of Lords reform has led to suggestions that the Appellate Committee should be cut free from the House of Lords, both legally and physically (i.e., moved away from Westminster and down to the Royal Courts of Justice on the Strand), so that in law and in fact the Committee is, and it is seen to be entirely separate from Parliament and the government of the day. In one sense Parliament might be the poorer if this separation were to occur: some Lords of Appeal have in the past made valuable contributions to House of Lords proceedings though this has usually been in debates which have touched on their area of expertise as lawyers and judges.[59] Still, just as it seems inappropriate for a political body like the House of Lords to double as a court it seems equally inappropriate that judges who work full-time in an impartial court of justice should also work part-time in a political body.

Advocates for sweeping reform of the House of Lords contend that the Appellate Committee is especially in need of modernisation given that it is soon to assume the role of a constitutional court interpreting and applying the provisions of the Human Rights Act 1998 rather like the United States Supreme Court interprets the American Constitution. It has been suggested that if Lords of Appeal are to assume the crucially important role of watchdogs over the rights of British citizens and the actions of Parliament then their appointment to the Appellate Committee should in the future be publicly scrutinised so as to ensure that individuals nominated by the Prime Minister to become Lords of Appeal continue to be desirable candidates for high office and not judges who might be expected to vote in a particular way and so preserve the legislative achievements of the Prime Minister who arranges for their appointment.[60] The point might also be made that in a multiracial, multi-cultural and multi-denominational United Kingdom the idea that the basic rights and freedoms of ordinary British citizens should to a very great extent be defined and protected by twelve moderately wealthy, upper middle-class white men is untenable (no matter how well-intentioned or well educated such men may be, and no matter how well they may have proved that they are capable of deciding controversial appeals cases in a manner that conforms with the popular notion of justice).[61]

It might be argued that it would be a backward step if the appointment of Appellate Committee members was to become a more politically charged affair, that it would be a mistake if prospective Appellate Committee members were to be subjected to public grillings by Members of Parliament (who might well be more intent on scoring a hit for or against the government of the day than in deciding whether the individual before them would make a competent Lord of Appeal), and that it would damage the present reasonably high standing of the judiciary with the public if it were to be perceived that top judges were not always being chosen because of their intellect or ability but were sometimes selected in part because they happened to come from a particular minority group or be representative of a particular section of society. However one could respond that the United States Supreme Court enjoys a very high standing with the American public even though prospective members of that court are subjected to a rigorous appointments process that can involve an indepth public examination of every facet of their lives, including their political views (if known). Indeed one could argue that the candidates who survive this appointments process and become members of the United States Supreme Court (which like the Appellate Committee and the Judicial Committee of the Privy Council is an unelected body) enjoy an enhanced reputation and legitimacy as judges as a result of their appointment having received the imprimatur of the democratically elected Congress following what is clearly a thorough consideration of their abilities and failings. Moreover the United States Supreme Court does not seem to have suffered any great loss of credibility by virtue of the fact that successive American Presidents have sought to appoint men and women with whom they share a common political outlook as Supreme Court judges. Nor does the Court seem to have suffered any loss of credibility by virtue of the fact that more recent United States Presidents have sought to ensure that the Court does not remain what it long was – and what the Appellate Committee still is – an all-white, all-male tribunal. Each of these practices would be objectionable if Presidents were to begin nominating Supreme Court candidates solely because they had a particular political viewpoint or were representative of a particular group within society, and regardless of whether they were otherwise suitable persons to be Supreme Court judges. However this has never yet happened. Instead the system of appointing Supreme Court judges, as it presently functions, seems to reflect a realisation by American politicians, and perhaps even the American public, that judges are people, that people are political beings, that a system of appointment which takes account of the inately political nature of judges is therefore merited, and that any pretence that a system of appointing judges could or should be apolitical, or that judges in their actions can ever cease to be political, would be quite false. This honesty of approach seems eminently more healthy than the mindframe which seems to underly the appointment of Lords of Appeal, namely that the British legal system and the British public are best served if the best candidate is appointed (even if no indication is ever given as to why an individual is thought to be the 'best' candidate for office), and that a good judge of any background or colour will always be able to act in an entirely impartial fashion and render impartial judgment. In fairness to the exclusively middle to senior-aged, middle to upper-income, and middle to upper-middle class white men who have been appointed as Lords of Appeal since 1876 they have done a good job at dispensing impartial justice in the cases that have come before them. However the truth of the matter is that if a court is to retain the confidence of those whom it serves then it must not only do justice, it must be seen to do justice. In short, even if the Appellate Committee continues to have an excellent record for impartiality the fact of the matter is that it will possibly never be perceived by women or ethnic minorities or indeed by other minority groups as being a body that can fully take their interests into account and do them justice until it becomes a little less representative of the white, male dominated, relatively homogeneous United Kingdom of a century and a quarter ago, and a little more representative of the culturally, ethnically and socially diverse United Kingdom of today. The fact that the Appellate Committee has not been the subject of significant reform since 1876, and, more especially, that it has not been modernised to reflect the massive transformations which have taken place in society since the end of the Second World War, is possibly attributable to the exceptionally high quality – both in terms of intellect and character – of all of the men who have served on the Appellate Committee to date and the fine job that they have done at dispensing justice. However, if the future of the Appellate Committee of the House of Lords or the Judicial Committee of the Privy Council is not to be called into question any time a particularly controversial decision is made or a Lord of Appeal makes a mistake, whether large or small, it seems to this writer that the reputation of those Committees cannot be allowed to rest solely on the undoubted personal intelligence and integrity of the Lords of Appeal, without regard to institutional characteristics such as the democratic legitimacy of the system whereby Lords of Appeal are appointed and the degree to which Lords of Appeal are representative of the people whom they serve.

Notes

1 The Lord Chancellor has never had to be a peer. Historically the title 'Lord' has tended to be an honorary title traditionally afforded to Chancellors out of respect for the office they hold. The two most famous Chancellors in British history, Cardinal Wolsey and Thomas More, both of whom served King Henry VIII, were not peers. Nowadays the Lord Chancellor is always a peer but this is very much a twentieth-century phenomenon.

2 Three peers constitute a quorum of the House of Lords.

3 Curiously, the last Lord of Appeal in Ordinary to hold a hereditary title served as a Lord of Appeal quite recently – from 1969 to 1980. This was Viscount Dilhorne. However he was something of an exception in that he was given his hereditary title in the early-1960s after he served as Lord Chancellor in the administrations of Harold Macmillan and Sir Alec Douglas-Home.

4 Only 13 barristers have ever been appointed directly into the House of Lords as Lords of Appeal in Ordinary. All other Lords of Appeal in Ordinary appointed pursuant to the 1876 Act have previously been superior court judges.

5 In practice judicial members of the House have tended to confine their appearances before the House in its legislative capacity to those debates which are somehow concerned with the legal system.

6 As it happens even the very early Lords of Appeal were invariably granted life peerages on their retirement from office (if not before). The practice appears to have arisen from a feeling that it was ungrateful to drop someone from membership of the House merely because he had elected to retire. Granting life peerages to Lords of Appeal has of course weakened the distinction which the 1876 Act originally sought to establish between a legislative wing of the House of Lords staffed by peers who were politicians and a judicial wing of the House of Lords staffed by judges who were also peers, but who owed their peerages to the fact that they were judges and who lost their peerages (just as any judge would lose his title of office) upon retiring from active service as a judge.

7 *Bradlaugh* v. *Clarke* (1883) 8 App. Cas. 354.

8 Lord Thankerton's father was Lord Watson and Lord Keith of Kinkel's father was Lord Keith of Avonholm.

9 All three members of the Russell family who became Lords of Appeal in Ordinary chose to be known as Lord Russell of Killowen. The name Killowen was taken from the place in Northern Ireland to which the Russells, a Catholic family, trace their roots. The first Lord Russell of Killowen was Charles Russell. He is the only one of the three Lords Russell of Killowen who was actually born in Northern Ireland. He became a Lord of Appeal in Ordinary at the beginning of May 1894 but quit after a month in order to become the Lord Chief Justice of England, a position he held until his death in 1900. The second Lord Russell of Killowen, Francis Xavier Joseph Russell, was a Lord of

Appeal from 1929 to 1946. The third Lord Russell of Killowen was Charles Ritchie Russell who spent seven years as a Lord of Appeal in Ordinary between 1975 and 1982.

10 The average figures quoted in this chapter have been calculated on the basis of extensive research into the backgrounds of each of the Lords of Appeal in Ordinary and Lord Chancellors who have served since the enactment of the Appellate Jurisdiction Act 1876. In a few circumstances it has not proven possible to unearth the details about every aspect of a particular individual's career. When this has happened the average figures have been calculated by reference to those Lords of Appeal (and, where relevant, those Lord Chancellors) in respect of whom the relevant details are known. Unless otherwise indicated in the text, the age of a Law Lord upon the occurrence of a specific event or the attainment of a particular achievement in his life is taken as being the age that he would have or will become in the year of the relevant event or achievement. Average ages have been calculated on a similar basis.

11 Lord Mackay's father was a railway worker. Lord Mackay also served as Lord Chancellor but only after he had served as a Lord of Appeal.

12 These figures include those Lords of Appeal in Ordinary who have also served as Lord Chancellor at some stage during their careers. The figures also include Sir Richard Scott who, at the time of writing, has not yet joined the Appellate Committee but has been nominated to take the place of Lord Phillips of Worth Matravers when the latter quits the Appellate Committee to become Master of the Rolls in October 2000.

13 Lord Moulton taught at Cambridge University. Lord Denning taught at Oxford University. Lord Mackay of Clashfern taught at St Andrews University.

14 Lord Devlin was not the only member of his family to embark upon a career in the Catholic church. One of his brothers became a Jesuit priest and two of his sisters became nuns. Devlin's departure from the seminary where he studied was the beginning of a prolonged estrangement from the Catholic Church. Indeed he openly disavowed Catholicism at university though he did receive the sacraments shortly before his death.

15 Although he did not attend university Lord Fitzgerald had a brilliant career as an advocate. He was appointed a Queen's Counsel at the incredibly young age of 31 which easily makes him the youngest person to have reached this rank and then gone on to become a Lord of Appeal. However, in common with all other Lords of Appeal who have managed spectacular achievements at a relatively young age Lord Fitzgerald's early success did not accelerate his promotion onto the bench. Thus he had to wait until the perfectly respectable (albeit younger than average) age of 43 before being appointed a judge. In the meantime Fitzgerald served as a Liberal Member of Parliament and very nearly lost his chances of becoming a judge when he became embroiled in a corruption scandal. However he managed in the course of a single speech before the House of Commons to completely defuse the controversy which had threatened to bring him down without quite establishing that he was entirely innocent of the charges which had been made against him. During the course of his 22 years on the Irish bench Fitzgerald presided over several of the most prominent trials of Irish patriot leaders including Charles Stewart Parnell. This won Fitzgerald few friends among the ordinary

Irish but his loyalty to the Crown was rewarded when at the age of 66 he was appointed a Lord of Appeal. He was to hold this office until his death 7 years later. By one of those odd twists of history Lord Fitzgerald is buried in Glasnevin Cemetery in Dublin where he still lies today in a grave that is a stone's throw away from the more frequently visited and better maintained burial plots of many of the Irish patriots whose fate once rested in his hands.

16 Three Lords of Appeal from Scotland studied at both Edinburgh and Glasgow Universities: Lord Gordon, Lord Macmillan, and Lord Watson.

17 Obviously southern Ireland is not now part of the United Kingdom but it was when the Lords of Appeal who have studied in Ireland were students there so for present purposes those Lords of Appeal are counted as having studied inside the United Kingdom.

18 At the time of writing two Appellate Committee members (Lord Hoffmann and Lord Steyn) and one incoming member (Sir Richard Scott) were born abroad and commenced their university studies in South Africa.

19 The 5 Lords of Appeal who trained as barristers in southern Ireland are Lord Atkinson, Lord Carson, Lord Fitzgerald, Lord MacDermott, and Lord Morris and Killanin. The 2 who trained as barristers in Northern Ireland are Lord Hutton and Lord Lowry. Although Lord MacDermott trained in southern Ireland and was called to the Bar there in 1921 he was actually a Northern Irishman by birth and practised almost exclusively at the Northern Irish Bar following the establishment of Northern Ireland in 1922.

20 One of the four is Lord Hoffmann who is of course a serving Lord of Appeal.

21 Lord Wright was also the oldest of his colleagues when he started at university at the age of 24. The oldest Scottish Appellate Committee member to embark upon his professional career as a Scots advocate is Lord Mackay of Clashfern, the last Lord Chancellor. He only became an advocate at the age of 28 after abandoning an illustrious career in mathematics which saw him take a first class degree in mathematics and physics at the University of Edinburgh, spend two years teaching mathematics at the University of St Andrews in Scotland, and commence a postgraduate degree in maths at Cambridge University (which was funded by way of a scholarship) before he finally decided that mathematics was not for him and what he really wanted to do was become a lawyer.

22 When the monarch is a Queen the highest-ranking barristers are known as 'Queen's Counsel' and when the monarch is a King the highest-ranking barristers are known as King's Counsel. Unless the context requires otherwise the term 'Queen's Counsel' is used here as a generic term for 'King's or Queen's Counsel'.

23 Lord Fitzgerald and Lord Lowry.

24 So far over one-fifth of all Lords of Appeal have managed this achievement.

25 Lord Browne-Wilkinson's first wife whom he married at the age of 25 died three years previously after 32 years of marriage.

26 It is worth noting that unlike Chief Justices in other jurisdictions, Lord Woolf, despite being Lord Chief Justice of England and Wales is not the head of the judiciary in England and Wales. That responsibility falls to the Lord Chancellor. The Lord Chief Justice spends most of his judicial time presiding in the Court of Appeal, Criminal Division, and in the Divisional Courts of the Queen's Bench Division of the High Court.

27 Lord Hutton is the present member from Northern Ireland. The two incumbents from Scotland are Lord Clyde and Lord Hope of Craighead.

28 Some Lords of Appeal have been 'political' appointees but 'political' in the sense that they have supported a particular party in government, not in the sense that they have espoused views which they have been expected to reflect in their judgments. Twenty-one Lords of Appeal in Ordinary have been Members of Parliament at some stage in their careers. Six of them have been Conservatives, 5 of them have been Liberals, 5 of them have been Unionists, 3 of them have been Labour representatives, and 2 of them were Independents. There have been 4 Lords of Appeal who were unsuccessful candidates for Parliament, 3 of them for the Unionist Party and one of them for the Labour Party. There has also been 3 Lords of Appeal who have not been Members of Parliament but who have spent a portion of their careers in political office, 2 of them as wartime government Ministers and 2 of them as the Lord Advocate of Scotland. The judicial function of the House of Lords was the subject of consideration in the final report published in January 2000 by the Royal Commission on the Reform of the House of Lords. (See *A House for the Future*, Cm 4534, (HMSO, 2000), ch. 9). Some of the submissions to the Royal Commission are also worth reading in this regard, most notably the written submission made by JUSTICE, the law reform group, entitled *Judicial Functions of the House of Lords* (JUSTICE, May 1999).

29 Justice William Douglas spent 36 years on the United States Supreme Court, retiring in 1975 at the age of 77. Justice William Brennan spent 33 years on the United States Supreme Court, retiring in 1990 at the age of 84. And Justice Felix Frankfurter spent 23 years on the United States Supreme Court, retiring in 1962 a few months before he turned 80. Lengthy terms in office such as these – though notable – are not hugely unusual for United States Supreme Court judges.

30 The details of any Lords of Appeal in Ordinary who have also served as Lord Chancellor are set out in Chapter 4.

31 The biographical details of Lord Maugham and his fellow Lord Chancellors are set out in Chapter 4.

32 For the text of the Lord Chancellor's evidence before the Select Committee on Public Administration see http://www.parliament.the-stationery-office.co.uk/pa/cm199798/cmselect/cmpubadm/398-v/398v06.htm at Question No 349 *et seq*.

33 The Purse has already been mentioned. The mace is a hang-over from the days when it was sometimes necessary to strike people who got in the way of an important dignitary. With the present mace weighing in at around twenty pounds it had could still pack quite a wallop if it ever had to be used. However maces have on the whole become more ornamental than functional. Presumably any striking that needs to be done would nowadays be effected by the police assigned to protect the Lord Chancellor. The result of all this is that the end of the mace which in the past would have been used to hit someone is nowadays a mere rounded knob while the end that would once have been the handgrip is a beautiful piece of Crown-shaped silver filigree. In consequence the mace when carried is borne upside-down with the large hand-grip resting over the shoulder and the smaller battering end held by the bearer. The mace is carried as a symbol of Crown authority.

Its use was popularised by Cardinal Wolsey who by all accounts was the father of ostentation. The present mace was made in the reign of King Charles II but has only been in continuous use since the late 1820s. In 1677 it was stolen from the house of Lord Chancellor Finch by a rogue called Thomas Sadler. Happily it was soon recovered though regrettably the rogue Sadler was hanged for his efforts. Since at least the time of this theft a reserve mace has always been kept available.

34 See Lord Macmillan, *A Man of Law's Tale* (Macmillan Press, 1952), p. 156.

35 The vote was reasonably close. The Lord Chancellor's request was approved by 145 peers and opposed by 115. It was also agreed following the debate about the Lord Chancellor's clothes that in future the Lord Chancellor may address the House from the government despatch box more often than has been in the case in the past – hitherto it had been usual for Lord Chancellors to address the House from the Woolsack. Although this aspect of what the House of Lords decided has not attracted a great deal of attention it will almost undoubtedly lead to an enhancement of the perception of the Lord Chancellor as a government minister rather than the speaker of the House of Lords or indeed a judge.

36 By contrast since the Second World War the three longest-serving Lord Chancellors have been Lord Hailsham of St Marylebone (12 years), Lord Mackay of Clashfern (10 years) and Viscount Kilmuir (8 years). Moreover the average term in office for Lord Chancellors in the past half-century has been a mere 5 years. The shortest-serving Lord Chancellor in this time has been Lord Havers of St Edmundsbury who had to retire after 4 months in office because of poor health.

37 See, for example, anon., "His Hybrid Lordship", *The Guardian*, 19 May 1999, p. 19.

38 See Lord Steyn, "The Weakest and Least Dangerous Arm of Government", *Public Law*, Spring 1997, p. 84.

39 See *inter alia* Dyer, C., "Irvine argues for privacy restraint on press", *The Guardian*, 5 Feb. 1998, p. 1, "Woman solicitor's sex bias claim puts Irvine back in firing line", *The Guardian*, 7 Feb. 1998, p. 3, "Irvine climbdown on legal aid", 5 March 1998, p. 11; Hoggart, S., "It's just like VE Day all over again: The last roll of paper is pasted on Lord Irvine's wall, and a nation rejoices", *The Guardian*, 4 March 1998, p. 1; MacAskill, E., "Irvine blocks plan for women", *The Guardian*, 3 March 1998, p. 1; MacAskill, E., K. Ahmed and L. Ward, "Anger over 'Irvine's 'blunders'", *The Guardian*, 6 Feb. 1998, p. 1. The details of other articles of relevance are set out in the bibliography.

40 At the moment the Lord Chancellor is represented in the House of Commons by two MPs, David Lock and Jane Kennedy, who each hold the position of Parliamentary Secretary, a junior ministerial position at the Lord Chancellor's Department. Both Mr Lock and Ms Kennedy play a central role in all the work of the Department save for the appointment of judges and relations between the Lord Chancellor and the judiciary – these are matters for which the Lord Chancellor as head of the judiciary is exclusively responsible and in respect of which he alone answers any questions. Of the two Parliamentary Secretaries Mr Lock is the more senior. However Ms Kennedy's appointment is perhaps the more interesting. Appointed in the late autumn of 1999 she is the first woman and the first non-lawyer to

be appointed to ministerial rank within the Lord Chancellor's Department. Ms Kennedy has replaced Mr Keith Vaz, MP, who left the Lord Chancellor's Department to assume the more senior role of Minister for Europe. As with Ms Kennedy the appointment of Mr Vaz to be a Parliamentary Secretary within the Lord Chancellor's Department in May 1999 represented a small but significant piece of political history, in that it was the first time an elected Member of Parliament of Asian origin had been appointed to serve as a UK government minister. (Making this achievement even more noteworthy was the fact that Mr Vaz was not actually born in the United Kingdom but hails from Aden – now a part of Yemen – where he received his earliest education before coming to England.)

41 The transformation of Lord Irvine into a Chancellor who seems more at ease with the media than when he took office, has been credited to a gentleman called Garry Hart. Mr Hart, who is the godfather to Tony Blair's daughter, used to be senior partner at Herbert Smith, a leading firm of London solicitors whose other partners include Tony Blair's brother-in-law. In March 1998 Mr Hart left his job as senior partner in order to become Lord Irvine's 'Special Adviser', an appointment which the Lord Chancellor was apparently urging Tony Blair to authorise for some considerable time before Blair finally agreed. The press briefing issued around the time of Mr Hart's appointment described his primary role as being "to assist the Lord Chancellor with advice on the development of policy and its effective presentation." Unfortunately Mr Hart's appointment was to occasion some controversy. After the appointment was announced two women who supported the Labour Party brought sex discrimination claims against the Lord Chancellor in which they alleged that because the job of Special Adviser had never been advertised they had been denied any opportunity to apply for the position and this constituted discrimination. One of the women was of colour and claimed that the manner in which Mr Hart had been appointed by the Lord Chancellor also constituted race discrimination. The claims were vehemently denied by the Lord Chancellor but in March 1999 a tribunal found that the Lord Chancellor had been guilty of discrimination in the manner in which he had set about recruiting Mr Hart. The Lord Chancellor's Department indicated that Lord Irvine would be appealing the finding.

42 See Lord Steyn, "The Weakest and Least Dangerous Arm of Government", *Public Law*, Spring 1997, p. 91.

43 The first Lord Russell of Killowen seems to have suffered greatly for his religion. At the outset of his political career he stood as Liberal candidate for Parliament in Durham City but was forced to withdraw his candidature when it became apparent that the voters simply would not elect a Catholic MP. The man who replaced him as Liberal candidate (and who did succeed in becoming Liberal MP for Durham City) was the future Lord Chancellor, Lord Herschell, a devout Protestant who taught Sunday school classes for much of his adult life, even after he had become a judge.

44 See A. Horne, *Macmillan* (Papermac, 1991), vol. II, p. 346.

45 Ibid., at p. 345.

46 See Lord Hailsham of St Marylebone, *A Sparrow's Flight* (Collins, 1990), p. 383.

47 See A. Howard, ed., *The Crossman Diaries* (Mandarin Paperbacks, 1991), p. 588.

48 See A. Horne, *Macmillan* (Papermac, 1991), vol. II, p. 555.

49 For Lord Hailsham's account of the events of October 1963 (from which the quotes attributed to him in this section are extracted) see *A Sparrow's Flight*, ch. 41.
50 See G. Howe, *Conflict of Loyalty* (Pan Books, 1995), p. 527.
51 For Lord Howe's account of the succession to Lord Havers and the possibility that Lord Howe, and not Lord Mackay of Clashfern, might have been elevated to the Woolsack in the autumn of 1987 see ibid. at p. 528.
52 The real-life counterparts of these fictional Indians subsequently became rather disenchanted with this 'god'. A little more than a quarter-century after Lord Haldane's speech India assumed independence and thereafter abandoned the right of appeal to the Privy Council.
53 Why was it that so many Indian litigants proved happy to seek justice in a small, far-away country of which many of them must have known little? A possible answer is that many Indian appellants considered it lent a certain lustre to their names for them to bring appeals the whole way to London. However while that may (and only may) have been a relevant factor it does not really seem enough to explain why such an enormous tide of Indian cases rushed in upon the Appeals Committee at the onset of the 1800s. A more convincing explanation lies in the fact that by launching an appeal which had to travel to London and back Indian appellants managed to defer for a couple of years the awful moment when they would have to comply with whatever judgment it was that they were appealing, and bought themselves the chance that – however hopeless their case – they might just succeed in having that judgment overturned or varied. This of course was very similar to the reasoning which, in the years that followed the unification of Scotland and England in 1707, led Scottish litigants to appeal even the most dubious of cases to the House of Lords with the result that until well into the nineteenth century the House in its judicial capacity functioned almost exclusively as a court of last resort for Scottish cases.
54 At the time of writing the Lord President of the Privy Council is Baroness Jay of Paddington, the daughter of the former Labour Prime Minister James Callaghan (now Baron Callaghan of Cardiff).
55 For an exhaustive account of the evolution of the Judicial Committee and the enactment of the Judicial Committee Act 1833, see P. Howell, *The Judicial Committee of the Privy Council 1833–1876* (Cambridge University Press, 1979).
56 Exactly why this should have been a problem is not at all clear. There is no doubt that Sovereigns have in the past been offered conflicting advice by their Privy Councillors and have had to decide which course of action to follow.
57 There are a couple of exceptions. Britain's scientific base in Antarctica and its military bases in Cyprus fall into a special category of places that have not chosen to accept but are not free to reject the Judicial Committee's jurisdiction.
58 See C. Dyer, "Pinochet Judge is Forgiven", *The Guardian*, 9 Feb. 1999, p. 8.
59 Not all Lords of Appeal have confined themselves to speaking in debates concerning legal and judicial matters. Indeed up to and during the interwar period it was not highly unusual to see a Lord of Appeal speaking on matters of general public interest. Lord Carson, for example, continued to voice

his Unionist views in the House of Lords after he became a Lord of Appeal. However, since at least the time of the Second World War there has been a definite tendency for Lords of Appeal to participate only in those House of Lords debates that touch upon the legal system and the courts system. This possibly springs from a desire on the part of the Lords of Appeal not to become unduly involved in the political process and so perhaps colour their reputation for impartiality.

60 As was mentioned previously in the text such political considerations do not appear to have been a factor in the appointment of Lords of Appeal since at least the end of the Second World War. However with the Appellate Committee set to assume an even more powerful role in the future than it has enjoyed in the past there is a chance that this may change and that Prime Ministers may begin to pay closer attention to the voting records of those whom they are proposing to appoint as Lords of Appeal.

61 The fact that in the future Lords of Appeal will, as members of the Judicial Committee of the Privy Council, have the politically significant and sensitive responsibility of resolving disputes that may arise between the Westminster Parliament and the new Welsh and Scottish national asemblies over the precise ambit of power that each of those bodies enjoy could be viewed as lending credence to the argument that a some what more accountable way of selecting a more diverse and representative array of Law Lords is both desirable and necessary.

Bibliography

The following is a list of *some* of the materials that I found to be of use when preparing this book. In addition to the list below, I found various volumes of *Debrett's Distinguished People of Today*, the *Dictionary of National Biography*, *Keesing's Contemporary Archives*, *Who's Who*, *Who's Who in Scotland*, and *Who was Who* to be helpful. Newspaper obituaries of deceased Lords of Appeal and Lord Chancellors were also a useful source of information.

Ackner, Lord, "The erosion of judicial independence", *New Law Journal*, 6 December 1996, p. 1789.

Allende, I., "Why I don't hate Pinochet", *The Observer*, 24 January 1999, *Review*, p. 1.

Anon., "An Empire Court", *The Times*, 14 August 1933, p. 11.

Anon., "Back to the beginning, says Chile", *The Times*, 18 December 1998, p. 9.

Anon., "Bagehot, A recipe for failure", *The Economist*, 12 July 1997, p. EU30.

Anon., "Bagehot, A wigging for Lord Irvine", *The Economist*, 25 October 1997, p. EU54.

Anon., "Convention overrides state immunity", *The Times*, 25 March 1999, p. 47.

Anon., "Derry's den", *The Guardian*, 5 March 1998, p. 19.

Anon., "Ex-dictators are not immune", *The Economist*, 28 November 1998, p. 13.

Anon., "Extraditing Pinochet", *Irish Times*, 25 March 1999, p. 17.

Anon., "Fast track for judges", *New Law Journal*, 6 July, p. 950.

Anon., "Harman J., A judge of controversy", *Legal Business Magazine*, May 1992, p. 22.

Anon., "Headlines save Lord Irvine", *The Times*, 23 February 1999, p. 41.

Anon., "High Court quality is not high enough", *Legal Business*, April 1994, p. 9.

Anon., "His hybrid lordship", *The Guardian*, 19 May 1999, p. 1.

Anon., "In defence of the judiciary", *New Law Journal*, 4 December 1992, p. 1673.

Anon., "Irvine's 'closed' circle criticised by job tribunal", *The Guardian*, 21 May 1999, p. 12.

Anon., "Judge not, lest ye yourself be judged...", *Legal Business Magazine*, December 1991, p. 27.

Anon., "Judged – The Legal Business Survey", *Legal Business Magazine*, May 1992, p. 25.

Anon., "Judicial turkey", *The Guardian*, 18 December 1998, p. 21.

Anon., "Law Society clashes with the Lord Chancellor", *New Law Journal*, 2 August 1991, p. 1062.

Anon., "Lay Peers in Appeals to the House of Lords", 65 *Law Quarterly Review*, January 1949, p. 22.

Anon., "Lord Macmillan and Lord Wright", 63 *Law Quarterly Review*, July 1947, p. 259.

Anon., "Lords' dread challenge", *The Guardian*, 15 December 1998.

Anon., "Modernising Parliament, Reforming the House of Lords" (The Stationery Office, 1998) (Cmnd 4183).
Anon., "No hiding place", *Financial Times*, 25 March 1999, p. 19.
Anon., "Not proven verdict on Scots judiciary", *New Law Journal*, 26 January 1990, p. 78.
Anon., "Passions over privacy", *The Guardian*, 6 February 1998, p. 18.
Anon., "Peer pressure", *The Times*, 18 December 1998, p. 23.
Anon., "Pinochet again; But who else is on trial?", *The Guardian*, 13 January 1999, p. 17.
Anon., "Pinochet loses", *The Guardian*, 25 March 1999, p. 19.
Anon., "Solicitors in court", *New Law Journal*, 26 January 1990, p. 79.
Anon., "The Commons Interest; MPs should support radical reform of the Lords", *The Times*, 1 March 1999, p. 21.
Anon., "The lawyer's lawyer", *Legal Business Magazine*, January/February 1991, p. 28.
Anon., "The Lord Chancellor's Department and the judges", *Public Law*, p. 157.
Anon., "The Pinochet Case", *The Economist*, 28 November 1998, p. 23.
Anon., "The truth about Bloody Sunday", *The Guardian*, 30 January 1998, p. 20.
Anon., "Troubled Benches", *New Law Journal*, 26 January 1990, p. 77.
Anon., "Ulster's past, Ulster's future", *The Economist*, 31 January 1998, p. EU37.
Ashenfelter, O., T. Eisenberg and S. Schwab, "Politics and the Judiciary: The Influence of Judicial Background on Case Outcomes", XXIV *Journal of Legal Studies*, June 1991, p. 257.
Askill, E., "Anger over Irvine's blunders", *The Guardian*, 6 February 1998, p. 1.
Bale, J. and F. Gibb, "Judgment on Pinochet sets dilemma for Straw", *The Times*, 25 March 1999, p. 1.
Bale, J., "Law lords overturn decision and allow Pinochet hearing", *The Times*, 18 December 1998, p. 1.
Bamforth, N., "Parliamentary sovereignty and the Human Rights Act 1998" (1998) *Public Law* 572.
Beckman M., "Pomp and circumstance", *New Law Journal*, 22 March 1991, p. 398.
Beloff, M., "Towards a Supreme Court? The British Experience" (1998) 33 *Irish Jurist* 1.
Bennett, R., "Straw has to leave his blundering path", *Financial Times*, 25 March 1999, p. 8.
Berlins, M., "Offshore cowardice", *The Guardian*, 30 January 1998, G2, p. 21.
Berlins, M., "Writ large", *The Guardian*, 1 December 1998, G2, p. 17.
Berlins, M., "Writ large", *The Guardian*, 23 March 1999, G2, p. 14.
Berlins, M., "Writ large", *The Guardian*, 24 February 1998, G2, p. 17.
Berlins, M., "Writ large", *The Guardian*, 28 July 1998, G2, p. 11.
Berlins, M., "Writ large", *The Guardian*, 3 March 1998, G2, p. 17.
Beven, T., "The Appellate Jurisdiction of the House of Lords", LXVIII *Law Quarterly Review*, October 1901, p. 155.
Bingham of Cornhill, Lord, "Speech at Dinner for HM Judges", London, 22 July 1998.
Blom-Cooper, L., "Hanging fire", *The Guardian*, 27 May 1999, p. 22.
Blom-Cooper, L. and G. Drewry, "The House of Lords: Reflections on the Social Utility of Final Appellate Courts", 32 *Modern Law Review*, May 1969, p. 262.

Bond, M. and D. Beamish, "The Lord Chancellor" (House of Lords Information Office, 1977).
Bourne, K. (ed.), *The Blackmailing of the Chancellor: Some Intimate and Hitherto Unpublished Letters from Hariette Wilson to her Friend Henry Brougham, Lord Chancellor of England* (Lemon Tree Press, 1975).
Box, M., *Rebel Advocate: a Biography of Lord Gardiner* (Gollancz, 1983).
Bradney, A., "The Changing Face of the House of Lords" (1985) *The Juridical Review*, Part 2, p. 178.
Bresler, F., *Lord Goddard* (Harrap, 1977).
Browne-Wilkinson, Lord, "The Infiltration of a Bill of Rights", *Public Law*, p. 397.
Burns, J. and M. Mulligan, "Pinochet supporters raise £2m to pay his legal costs", *Financial Times*, 11 February 1999, p. 1.
Burns, J. and M. Mulligan, "The powerful regiment lined up behind the general", *Financial Times*, 11 February 1999, p. 3.
Carmichael, P. and B. Dickson, eds., *The House of Lords* (Hart Publishing, 1999).
Carroll, R. and A. Gooch, "Activists celebrate 'landmark' with cheers and champagne", *The Guardian*, 26 November 1998, p. 3.
Charter 88, "Submission on court dress reform to the Lord Chancellor and the Lord Chief Justice" (Charter 88, 1992).
Clarke, D. and D. Snell, "Revision and Amendment of Legislation by the House of Lords – a Case Study" (1994) *Public Law*, p. 409.
Cook Jr, J., "Dream Makers: Black Judges on Justice", 94 *Michigan Law Review*, May 1996, p. 1479.
Dismore, A., "Silks' purse", *The Guardian*, 23 March 1999, p. 14.
Dodd, V., "Irvine ordered to testify in lawyers' sex bias case", *The Guardian*, 5 November 1998, p. 9.
Dyer, C., "Commercial lawyers to judge human rights", *The Guardian*, 18 July 1998, p. 1.
Dyer, C., "Formidable and witty judge with hint of political naivety", *The Guardian*, 8 December 1998, p. 4.
Dyer, C., "Hoffmann silence dismays judges", *The Guardian*, 18 December 1998, p. 7.
Dyer, C., "Irvine argues for privacy restraint on the press", *The Guardian*, 5 February 1998, p. 1.
Dyer, C., "Irvine climbdown on legal aid", *The Guardian*, 5 March 1998, p. 11.
Dyer, C., "Key decision rests with Straw as defence lawyers prepare appeal", *The Guardian*, 25 March 1999, p. 6.
Dyer, C., "Law lords condemn Hoffmann", *The Guardian*, 15 January 1999, p. 1.
Dyer, C., "Law Lords reject right to light up on trains", *The Guardian*, 3 April 1998, p. 8.
Dyer, C., "Law Lords", *The Guardian*, 5 August 1998, p. 13.
Dyer, C., "Lord Chancellor bares soul", *The Guardian*, 3 December 1998.
Dyer, C., "Lord Denning, controversial 'people's judge', dies aged 100", *The Guardian*, 6 March 1999, p. 1.
Dyer, C., "Lords grant Chile role at Pinochet hearing", *The Guardian*, 14 January 1999.
Dyer, C., "New bias claim against Irvine", *The Guardian*, 26 February 1998, p. 1.
Dyer, C., "Peers question Irvine's judicial rights in Lords", *The Guardian*, 28 May 1999, p. 14.

Dyer, C., "Pinochet 'denied fair trial' by lords", *The Guardian*, 16 December 1998, p. 2.
Dyer, C., "Pinochet 'led Chile tortures'", *The Guardian*, 19 January 1999, p. 1.
Dyer, C., "Pinochet fightback before law lords", *The Guardian*, 15 December 1998, p. 3.
Dyer, C., "Pinochet judge is forgiven", *The Guardian*, 9 February 1999, p. 8.
Dyer, C., "Pinochet ruling set aside links over Amnesty", *The Guardian*, 18 December 1998, p. 1.
Dyer, C., "Pinochet's crimes 'may pre-date' immunity", *The Guardian*, 20 January 1999, p. 7.
Dyer, C., "Women solicitor's sex bias claim puts Irvine back in firing line", *The Guardian*, 7 February 1998, p. 3.
Dyer, C., M. White and W. Woodward, "Law lords back Pinochet extradition", *The Guardian*, 25 March 1999, p. 1.
Edwards, J., "The good, the bad, and the bench", *Legal Business*, April 1994, p. 51.
Egan, D., "Roll model", *Legal Business*, March 1994, p. 44.
Egan, D., "The men who would be kings", *Legal Business*, April 1997, p. 27.
Egan, D., K. Mills and D. Cobb, "40 under 40 at the Bar", *Legal Business*, July/August 1997, p. 36.
Feldman, D., "Public law values in the house of Lords", 106 *Law Quarterly Review*, April 1990, p. 246.
Fitz-James, M., "Free expression and the judges", *New Law Journal*, 30 April 1993, p. 622.
Flintoff, J., "new_judge@parliament.uk", *Legal Business*, December 1997/January 1998, p. 30.
Franklin, J., "Chile: calm in all quarters", *The Guardian*, 25 March 1999, p. 7.
Freeman, I., *Lord Denning: a Life* (Arrow Books, 1994).
Fyfe, D., *Political Adventure: the Memoirs of the Earl of Kilmuir* (Weidenfeld and Nicholson, 1964).
Gamina, G., "Both sides celebrate a victory", *The Times*, 25 March 1999, p. 11.
Gibb, F. and J. Bale, "Law lords' ruling set to boost Pinochet's hopes", *The Times*, 24 March 1999, p. 1.
Gibb, F., "Bar could pay taxpayer's bill for new QCs", *The Times*, 11 February 1999, p. 10.
Gibb, F., "Coup de grace for death penalty", *The Times*, 28 January 1999, p. 1.
Gibb, F., "Judge's lapse could lead to bench 'vetting'", *The Times*, 18 December 1998, p. 9.
Gibb, F., "Law lords' log-jam delays key-rulings", *The Times*, 26 February 1999, p. 2.
Gibb, F., "Make 'em laugh, milord", *The Times*, 17 November 1999, p. 43.
Gibb, F., "Pinochet rebuke may end law lord's career", *The Times*, 15 January 1999, p. 1.
Gibb, F., "Straw must clear new legal hurdles", *The Times*, 25 March 1999, p. 10.
Gibb, F., "Strong-willed maverick was poised to be a legend", *The Times*, 18 January 1998, p. 9.
Gibb, F., "The people's judge: Lord Denning celebrates his centenary", 26 January 1999, p. 43.

Gilligan, A. and R. Evans, "Revealed: pleadings behind Lord Irvine's dealings with Blair", *The Sunday Telegraph*, 30 May 1999, p. 5.
Gooch, A., "Spain: clamour for prosecution", *The Guardian*, 25 March 1999, p. 7.
Graves, D., "Allende aide accused of masterminding Spain's extradition moves", *The Daily Telegraph*, 18 January 1999, p. 11.
Greenslade, D., "Objections to Woolf", *New Law Journal*, 2 August 1998, p. 1147.
Griffiths, C. and D. Egan, "Closed Shop", *Legal Business*, May 1995, p. 50.
Hailsham of St Marylebone, Lord, *A Sparrow's Flight: the Memoirs of Lord Hailsham of St. Marylebone* (Collins, 1990).
Hailsham of St Marylebone, Lord, *The Problems of a Lord Chancellor* (Holdsworth Club, University of Birmingham, 1972).
Haldane of Cloan, Lord, "The Work for the Empire of the Judicial Committee of the Privy Council" (1923) 1 *Cambridge Law Journal*, p. 143.
Hall, J. and D. Martin, "The future of the Judicial Committee of the Privy Council", *New Law Journal*, 19 November 1993, p. 1652.
Halligan, L., "A lament for the end of pomp as Lord Irvine ditches his wig", *Financial Times*, 7 November 1998.
Hamilton, A., "A rather uncomfortable day on the Woolsack", *The Times*, 18 December 1998, p. 9.
Harvey, R., *Diplock and the Assault on Civil Liberties: Time to Repeal Northern Ireland's Emergency Legislation* (Haldane Society, 1980).
Hayes, J., "Appointment by invitation", *New Law Journal*, 11 April 1997, p. 520.
Hencke, D., "Blair picks Tory fixer to decide what comes next for Lords", *The Guardian*, 21 January 1999.
Heuston, R., *Lives of the Lord Chancellors 1940–1970* (Clarendon Press, 1987).
Hoggart, S., "It's just like VE Day all over again. The last roll of paper is pasted on Lord Irvine's wall, and a nation rejoices", *The Guardian*, 4 March 1998, p. 1.
Holland, T., "The JUSTICE Report", *New Law Journal*, 11 December 1992, p. 1716.
Holloway, I., "O'Connell v. The Queen; A Sesquicentennial Remembrance" (1995) 46(1) *Northern Ireland Law Quarterly*, p. 63.
Home Department, "Rights Brought Home: The Human Rights Bill" (1997, Cmnd 3782).
Hoon MP, G., "Appearance before the Legal Affairs Committee of the European Parliament in Brussels, Opening Statement", Brussels, 2 February 1998.
Hopkins, N., "Pinochet allies and enemies prepare for Lords ruling", *The Guardian*, 23 March 1999, p. 8.
Hopkins, N., "Pinochet goes on attack with Allende in firing line", *The Guardian*, 19 January 1999, p. 6.
Howell, P., *The Judicial Committee of the Privy Council 1833–1876* (Cambridge University Press, 1979).
Irvine of Lairg, Lord "Speech at the presentation of the 1997 Campaign for Freedom of Information Awards", London, 28 April 1998.
Irvine of Lairg, Lord, "Address at the Presentation of Silk Ceremony", Westminster, 1 May 1998.
Irvine of Lairg, Lord, "Address to the Third Clifford Chance Conference on The Impact of a Bill of Rights on English Law", London, 28 November 1997.

Irvine of Lairg, Lord, "Constitutional Change and Modernisation of the Law in Britain", Paris, 26 February 1998.

Irvine of Lairg, Lord, "Constitutional Change in the United Kingdom: British Solutions to Universal Problems", Washington, DC, 11 May 1998.

Irvine of Lairg, Lord, "Creating a Nation of Real Citizens: Partnership between the People and the State", Speech to the Citizenship Foundation, 27 January 1998.

Irvine of Lairg, Lord, "Improving youth justice", Letter to the Chairmen of all Youth Panels in England and Wales, 28 September 1998.

Irvine of Lairg, Lord, "Keynote address to the Conference on a Bill of Rights for the United Kingdom", London, 4 July 1997.

Irvine of Lairg, Lord, "Opening Address to the Conference on Constitutional Reform in the UK", Cambridge, 17 January 1998.

Irvine of Lairg, Lord, "Oral Statement to the House of Lords, Publication of a Consultation Paper 'Access to Justice with Conditional Fees' ", Westminster, 4 March 1998.

Irvine of Lairg, Lord, "Principle and Pragmatism: The Development of English Public Law under the Separation of Powers", Speech made in Hong Kong, 18 September 1998.

Irvine of Lairg, Lord, "Review of the Court of Appeal", Speech to the London Common Law and Commercial Bar Association, London, 3 December 1997.

Irvine of Lairg, Lord, "Sentencing for assaults on NHS staff", Speech made at Winchester, 19 June 1998.

Irvine of Lairg, Lord, "Speech for the closing session of the Fourth European Conference on Family Law", Strasbourg, 2 October 1998.

Irvine of Lairg, Lord, "Speech to Justice and Legal Aid Group Conference", Westminster, 3 July 1998.

Irvine of Lairg, Lord, "Speech to Relate's Diamond Jubilee Annual Conference", Oxford, 28 June 1998.

Irvine of Lairg, Lord, "Speech to the 1998 Women Lawyer Conference", London, 25 April 1998.

Irvine of Lairg, Lord, "Speech to the Annual Conference of the Association of Personal Injury Lawyers", London, 7 May 1998.

Irvine of Lairg, Lord, "Speech to the Annual General Meeting of the Magistrates' Association", Salford, 17 October 1998.

Irvine of Lairg, Lord, "Speech to the Association of Women Barristers' Annual Dinner", London, 11 February 1998.

Irvine of Lairg, Lord, "Speech to The Institute of Personnel and Devlopment Conference", London, 9 July 1998.

Irvine of Lairg, Lord, "The Development of Human Rights in Britain under an Incorporated Convention on Human Rights", London, 16 December 1997.

Jacob, H., E. Blackenburg, H. Kritzer, D. Privine and J. Sanders, *Courts, Law, and Politics in Comparative Perspective* (Yale University Press, 1996).

Jowell, J., "Age of revolution?", *The Guardian*, 10 November 1996, G2, p. 17.

Jowell, J., *Lord Denning: the Judge and the Law* (Sweet and Maxwell, 1984).

Kavanagh, J., "Chilean military leader warns of the 'threat to democracy' ", *Irish Times*, 25 March 1999, p. 19.

Kelly, B., *Famous Advocates and their Speeches: British Forensic Eloquence from Lord Erskine to Lord Russell of Killowen* (Sweet and Maxwell, 1921).

Landale, J., "Lord Chancellor told he may abandon breeches", *The Times*, 17 November 1998, p. 1.

Landale, J., "Lords commission expected to stumble over tight deadline", *The Times*, 1 March 1999, p. 2.

Lester of Herne Hill, Lord, "Pros and cons of bills", *The Guardian*, 7 February 1998, p. 13.

Letts, Q., "Peers to see the man in tights stripped of dignity and tradition", *Daily Telegraph*, 17 November 1998, p. 16.

Lord Chancellor's Department Press Release 108/98, 25 April 1998.

Lord Chancellor's Department, " 'Creating a Nation of Real Citizens Partnership between the People and the State' The Lord Chancellor's Speech to the Citizenship Foundation", Lord Chancellor's Department Press Release 25/98, 27 January 1998.

Lord Chancellor's Department, " 'It is essential that government be able to speak to the Judiciary and the Judiciary to government' – The Lord Chancellor's Speech to the Lord Mayor's Dinner for Her Majesty's Judges", Lord Chancellor's Department 163/97, 23 July 1997.

Lord Chancellor's Department, " 'Judicial Independence' – The Lord Chief Justice gives Inaugural Lecture of the Judicial Studies Board", Lord Chancellor's Department Press Release 322/96.

Lord Chancellor's Department, " 'Our Parliament, our courts, our rights' says Lord Chancellor", Lord Chancellor's Department Press Release 287/97, 28 November 1997.

Lord Chancellor's Department, "'We should be leading in the development of human rights in Europe', says Lord Chancellor", Lord Chancellor's Department Press Release 141/97, 4 July 1997.

Lord Chancellor's Department, "1998 Silk Presentation Ceremony", Lord Chancellor's Department 122/98, 1 May 1998.

Lord Chancellor's Department, "Access to Justice with Conditional Fees", Lord Chancellor's Department Press Release 57/98, 4 March 1998.

Lord Chancellor's Department, "Assistant Recordership Competition 1998/99", Lord Chancellor's Department Press Release 85/98, 6 April 1998.

Lord Chancellor's Department, "Biographical details – Baron Irvine of Lairg, QC", Lord Chancellor's Department Press Release 7/97, May 1997.

Lord Chancellor's Department, "Biographical Details – Geoffrey Hoon MP Parliamentary Secretary at the Lord Chancellor's Department", Lord Chancellor's Department Press Release 8/97, 6 May 1997.

Lord Chancellor's Department, "British Law Lords for the Court of Final Appeal", Lord Chancellor's Department 199/97, 8 September 1997.

Lord Chancellor's Department, "British Law Lords' Appointments endorsed by Hong Kong Court of Final Appeal", Lord Chancellor's Department Press Release 10/98, 9 January 1998.

Lord Chancellor's Department, "Criminal Sentencing and Public Opinion", Lord Chancellor's Department Press Release 148/9, 10 July 1997.

Lord Chancellor's Department, "Director of Communications", Lord Chancellor's Department Press Release 83/98, 6 April 1998.

Lord Chancellor's Department, "Extending civil judicial cooperation within the EU", Lord Chancellor's Department Press Notice 27/98, 2 February 1998.

Lord Chancellor's Department, "Government to Control Media Payments to Witnesses", Lord Chancellor's Department Press Release 48/98, 27 February 1998.
Lord Chancellor's Department, "Judicial Appointments Commission", Lord Chancellor's Department Press Release 125/97, 23 June 1997.
Lord Chancellor's Department, "Judicial Retirement", Lord Chancellor's Department Press Release 58/97, 25 March 1997.
Lord Chancellor's Department, "Judicial Retirements", Lord Chancellor's Department Press Release 236/98, 27 July 1998.
Lord Chancellor's Department, "Judicial Retirements", Lord Chancellor's Department Press Release 271/98, 8 September 1998.
Lord Chancellor's Department, "LCD upgrades its Internet website", Lord Chancellor's Department Press Release 35/98, 18 February 1998.
Lord Chancellor's Department, "Lord Chancellor and Cherie Booth to Judge in Magistrates' Court", Lord Chancellor's Department Press Release 165/98, 5 June 1998.
Lord Chancellor's Department, "Lord Chancellor Announces New Measures for Judicial Appointments", Lord Chancellor's Department Press Release 220/97, 9 October 1997.
Lord Chancellor's Department, "Lord Chancellor appoints additional Parliamentary Secretary", Lord Chancellor's Department Press Release 308/97, 16 December 1997.
Lord Chancellor's Department, "Lord Chancellor Appoints Parliamentary Private Secretary Dr Tony Wright MP", Lord Chancellor's Department Press Release 98/97, 14 May 1997.
Lord Chancellor's Department, "Lord Chancellor invites judicial office-holders to declare Masonic status", Lord Chancellor's Department Press Release 217/98, 24 July 1998.
Lord Chancellor's Department, "Lord Chancellor opens new judicial training centre", Lord Chancellor's Department Press Release 11/98, 14 January 1998.
Lord Chancellor's Department, "Lord Chancellor praises personal injury lawyers for adapting to change", Lord Chancellor's Department 129/98, 7 May 1998.
Lord Chancellor's Department, "Lord Chancellor seeks more women judges",
Lord Chancellor's Department, "Lord Chancellor seeks to appoint more women judges", Lord Chancellor's Department Press Release 36/98, 11 February 1998.
Lord Chancellor's Department, "Lord Chancellor to deliver lecture in US Supreme Court", Lord Chancellor's Department Press Release 134/98, 11 May 1998.
Lord Chancellor's Department, "Lord Chancellor to meet senior French judges and to visit the French Ministry of Justice", Lord Chancellor's Department Press Release 47/98, 23 February 1998.
Lord Chancellor's Department, "Lord Chancellor to visit Hong Kong", Lord Chancellor's Department Press Release 193/97, 2 September 1997.
Lord Chancellor's Department, "Lord Chancellor to visit New Zealand, Australia and Hong Kong", Lord Chancellor's Department Press Release 269/98, 4 September 1998.
Lord Chancellor's Department, "Lord Chancellor visits European Court of Justice", Lord Chancellor's Department Press Release 112/98, 28 April 1998.

Lord Chancellor's Department, "Lord Chancellor wants new advice and assistance scheme in place next year", Lord Chancellor's Department Press Release 12/98, 15 January 1998.

Lord Chancellor's Department, "Lord Chancellor welcomes report on Review of the Court of Appeal, Civil Division", Lord Chancellor's Department Press Notice 251/97, 6 November 1997.

Lord Chancellor's Department, "Lord Chancellor's Official Residence", Lord Chancellor's Department Press Release 117/97, 11 June 1997.

Lord Chancellor's Department, "Lord Chancellor's Official Residence, Statement by Lord Irvine", Lord Chancellor's Department Press Release 45/98, 23 February 1998.

Lord Chancellor's Department, "Lord Chancellor's Special Adviser", Lord Chancellor's Department Press Release 55/98, 4 March 1998.

Lord Chancellor's Department, "Lord Chief Justice to sit at Cardiff", Lord Chancellor's Department Press Release 310/98, 8 October 1998.

Lord Chancellor's Department, "Lord Saville of Newdigate", Lord Chancellor's Department Press Release 2/98, 29 January 1998.

Lord Chancellor's Department, "Lord Taylor of Gosforth – Tribute by the Rt Hon Lord Bingham of Cornhill The Lord Chief Justice of England", Lord Chancellor's Department Press Release 91/97, 29 April 1997.

Lord Chancellor's Department, "Lord Woolf to 'blitz' Court of Appeal backlog", Lord Chancellor's Department Press Release 336/96, 28 November 1996.

Lord Chancellor's Department, "Macmillan Charity – Brixton Prison", Lord Chancellor's Department Press Release 286/98, 17 September 1998.

Lord Chancellor's Department, "New proposals due on rights of audience", Lord Chancellor's Department Press Release 50/98, 24 February 1998.

Lord Chancellor's Department, "Press Notice Issued on Behalf of the Lord Chief Justice by the Lord Chancellor's Department Press Office", Lord Chancellor's Department Press Release 224/96, 17 July 1996.

Lord Chancellor's Department, "Queen's Counsel 1998", Lord Chancellor's Department Press Release 86/98, 9 April 1998.

Lord Chancellor's Department, "Reform of the Court of Appeal will result in a more efficient, faster, better focused appeal system", says Lord Chancellor", Lord Chancellor's Department Press Release 295/97, 3 December 1997.

Lord Chancellor's Department, "Refurbishment of Lord Chancellor's Residence", Lord Chancellor's Department 154/97, 16 July 1997.

Lord Chancellor's Department, "Senior Civil Service Appointments", Lord Chancellor's Department Press Release, 27 February 1998.

Lord Chancellor's Department, "The LCD Strategic Plan 1996/97–1998/99", (Lord Chancellor's Department, 1996).

Lord Chancellor's Department, "Three Additional Lords Justices to be Appointed", Lord Chancellor's Department Press Release 79/96, 26 March 1996.

Lord Chancellor's Department, "We will deliver a Freedom of Information Act and it will deliver", Lord Chancellor's Department Press Release 114/98, 28 April 1998.

Love, E., "Judges' verdict opens Chile's old wounds", *The Guardian*, 26 November 1998, p. 3.

MacAskill, E., "Irvine blocks plan for women", *The Guardian*, 3 March 1998, p. 1.
MacAskill, E., "Irvine indicates opening hours after £650,000 apartment refit", *The Guardian*, 5 March 1998, p. 11.
MacAskill, E., "Ministers discuss reform of Lords with Conservatives", *The Guardian*, 5 March 1998, p. 11.
Mackay of Clashfern, Lord "Underpinning justice", *New Law Journal*, 21 February 1992, p. 238.
Mackay of Clashfern, Lord, "Litigation in the 1990s", 54(2) *Modern Law Review*, March 1991, p. 171.
Mackay of Clashfern, Lord, *The Role of the Lord Chancellor* (Society of Solicitors in the Superior Courts of Scotland, 1989).
MacLean, A., "The House of Lords and Appeals from the High Court of Justiciary, 1707–1887" (1985) *The Juridical Review*, Part 2, p. 192.
Macmillan, Lord, *A Man of Law's Tale* (Macmillan, 1952).
Macmillan, Lord, "The Last Court of Appeal", *The Times*, 14 August 1933, p. 11.
Mansfield QC, M., "More time with his wallpaper", *Independent on Sunday*, 1 March 1998.
Mark, I., "Chilean rulers weary of legal twists", *Financial Times*, 18 December 1998, p. 5.
Markesinis, B. and S. Deakin, "The Random Element of their Lordship's Infallible Judgment: An Economic and Comparative Analysis of the Tort of Negligence from Anns to Murphy", 55(5) *Modern Law Review*, September 1992, p. 619.
Mason, J., "British law lords overturn Pinochet immunity ruling", *Financial Times*, 18 December 1998.
Mason, J., "Criticised law lord decides to reserve judgment over his future in the House", *Financial Times*, 16, 17 January 1999, p. 5.
Mason, J., "Law lord in Pinochet case is criticised", *Financial Times*, 18 December 1998, p. 1.
Mason, J., "Law lords restrict grounds for Pinochet extradition", *Financial Times*, 25 March 1999, p. 20.
Mason, J., "Pinochet should lose immunity", *Financial Times*, 6 November 1998, p. 5.
Mason, J., "Red faces in UK after reversal of Pinochet ruling", *Financial Times*, 18 December 1998, p. 5.
Mason, J., "Twice damned", *Financial Times*, 25 March 1999, p. 18.
McCaughan, M., "Citizens of Santiago react to decision with calm", *Irish Times*, 25 March 1999, p. 19.
McConnell, B., "What the judges read", *New Law Journal*, 3 April 1991, p. 468.
McLachlin, B., "The Role of Judges in Modern Commonwealth Society", 110 *Law Quarterly Review*, April 1994, p. 260.
Middap, C. and V. Elliott, "Irvine found guilty of job discrimination", *The Times*, 27 March 1999.
Millar, F., "Straw obliged to rethink Pinochet case after ruling", *Irish Times*, 25 March 1999, p. 19.
Millar, S., "Irvine accused of discrimination in appointing 'crony'", *The Guardian*, 24 March 1999, p. 9.
Mills, K., "The silk cut", *Legal Business*, May 1997, p. 30.

Pallister, D., "Lords rule torture is extradition crime", *The Guardian*, 25 March 1999, p. 8.

Pannick, QC, D., "Does it matter if 247 judges are Masons?", *The Times*, 17 November 1998, p. 41.

Pannick, QC, D., "Principles of interpretation of Convention rights under the Human Rights Act and the discretionary area of judgment" (1998) *Public Law* 545.

Pannick, QC, D., "When legal and judicial functions no longer mix", *The Times*, 9 February 1999, p. 35.

Parker, A. and D. White, "Extradition process goes on pending new court ruling", *Financial Times*, 18 December 1998, p. 5.

Parker, A. and J. Burns, "Months of legal battle for Pinochet", *Financial Times*, 25 March 1999, p. 4.

Parker, A., "Commission to overhaul Lords unveiled", *Financial Times*, 9 February 1999, p. 7.

Parker, A., "Doubts cast on timetable for Lords reform", *Financial Times*, 23 February 1999, p. 8.

Parker, A., "Ejected peers may become 'substitutes' ", *Financial Times*, 16 February 1999, p. 8.

Parker, A., "Peer calls for mainly elected upper house", *Financial Times*, 24 February 1999, p. 8.

Parker, A., "Tory review of Lords set to back Labour line", *Financial Times*, 11 February 1999, p. 8.

Paterson, A., "Scottish Lords of Appeal, 1876–1978" (1988) *The Juridical Review*, Part 2, p. 235.

Paterson, A., *The Law Lords* (Macmillan, 1982).

Perkins, A., "The battles of Derry", *The Guardian*, 2 March 1999, G2, p. 3.

Perkins, A., "When I grow up I want to be..." *The Guardian*, 17 May 1999, G2, p. 2.

Purchas, F., "The constitution in the market place", *New Law Journal*, 12 November 1993, p. 1604.

Quinn, S., "Torture a state function – Pinochet defence", *The Guardian*, 26 January 1999, p. 4.

Robertson, G., "Judgment day", *The Guardian*, 6 March 1999, p. 21.

Robertson, G., "Not so divine intervention", *The Guardian*, Law and Society Supplement, 24 February 1998, p. 17.

Routledge, P., "Irvine's refurb bill hits £650K", *Independent on Sunday*, 22 February 1998.

Rozenberg, J., *The Search for Justice* (Hodder and Stoughton, 1994).

Rusbridger, A., "Privacy rights and a free press", *The Guardian*, 7 February 1998, p. 12.

Scrivener QC, A., "Lord Denning at 100", *The Observer*, 24 January 1999, p. 29.

Shaw, T., "Pinochet's Spanish tormentor at appeal", *The Daily Telegraph*, 19 January 1999, p. 11.

Shaw, T., "Seven may be the general's lucky number", *The Daily Telegraph*, 18 January 1999, p. 11.

Shell, D., "The House of Lords: time for a change?" (1994) 47(4) *Parliamentary Affairs* 721.

Simpson, A., "The Judges and the Vigilant State", *Denning Law Journal post-1989*, p. 145.

Slynn of Hadley, "What is a European Community Law Judge?" 53(2) *Cambridge Law Journal*, July 1993, p. 234.

Sparrow, A., "Lord Irvine wins the right to take off his breeches", *Daily Telegraph*, 17 November 1998, p. 16.

Steele, J., "Torture trail", *The Guardian*, 20 January 1998.

Stevens, R., *Law and Politics – The House of Lords as a Judicial Body 1800–1976* (Weidenfeld and Nicholson, 1979).

Stevens, R., "The case for banishing M'Lud from the Lords", *The Times*, 22 December 1998, p. 30.

Stevens, R., "The Final Appeal: Reform of the House of Lords and Privy Council 1867–76", 80 *Law Quarterly Review*, July 1964, p. 343.

Steyn, Lord, "Does Legal Formalism Hold Sway in England?" (1996) 49(2) *Current Legal Problems*, p. 43.

Strong, R., "Just hang on to your breeches, Lord Irvine", *Daily Mail*, 13 August 1998, p. 10.

Styles, S., "The Scottish Judiciary 1919–1986", (1988) *Juridical Review*, Part I, p. 41.

Swinfen, D., "Henry Brougham and The Judicial Committee of the Privy Council", 90 *Law Quarterly Review*, July 1974, p. 396.

Swinfen, D., "The Single Judgment in the Privy Council 1833–1966", (1975) 20 *Juridical Review*, p. 153.

Sylvester, R., "Wallpaper wins over Irvine's guests", *Daily Telegraph*, 20 March 1998, p. 2.

Templeman, Lord, "The appellate mosaic" (Holdsworth Club, University of Birmingham, 1984).

Templeman, Lord, "The House of Lords", (1993) 25 *Bracton Law Journal*, p. 11.

Timmis, C., "Off with their wigs", *Legal Business*, February 1998, p. 28.

Timmis, C., "QC quandaries: elite or obsolete?", *Legal Business*, May 1998, p. 20.

Topping, I., "Police officers and membership of organisations", *New Law Journal*, 17 January 1997, p. 63.

Travis, A., "Irvine to spend £2.5m on think tank", *The Guardian*, 23 February 1998, p. 2.

Travis, A., "The usual suspects", *The Guardian*, 25 February 1998, p. 13.

Travis, A., "Trying time for minister", *The Guardian*, 25 March 1999, p. 6.

Underhill, *The Lord Chancellor* (T. Dalton, 1978).

Walker, J., "'Satisfied' Garzon now set to present new details", *Irish Times*, 25 March 1999, p. 19.

Ward, L., "Elected peers may lose some powers", *The Guardian*, 21 January 1999, p. 8.

Watkins, A., "Ease up Derry and stare at those fine walls", *Independent on Sunday*, Section 2, 15 March 1998.

Webster, P. and V. Elliott, "The Lords in their hands", *The Times*, 9 February 1999, p. 10.

White, B., "Revolution for the Lords", *The Guardian*, 21 January 1999, p. 1.

White, D., "A pyrrhic victory for unhappy Madrid", *Financial Times*, 25 March 1999, p. 4.

White, M., "Irvine attempts to turn the tide", *The Guardian*, 24 February 1998, p. 3.

White, M., "Irvine denies guilt in hanging offence", *The Guardian*, 21 February 1998, p. 3.

White, M., "Leaked letter shows Irvine wanted only the best in flat refit", *The Guardian*, 25 February 1998, p. 6.

Wilson, J. and B. Wazir, "Pinochet challenges Law Lord", *The Guardian*, 5 December 1998, p. 1.

Wilson, J. and N. Hopkins, "Pinochet law lord linked to Amnesty", *The Guardian*, 8 December 1998, p. 1.

Wilson, J., "Law lords pave way for hangings as Trinidad death row appeals fail", *The Guardian*, 27 May 1999, p. 3.

Wilson, J., "Pinochet's foe to witness Lords fate", *The Guardian*, 18 January 1999, p. 11.

Wilson, J., "Protesters march in white masks as friends come to defence", *The Guardian*, 18 January 1999, p. 11.

Wilson, J., N. Hopkins and E. MacAskill, "You can hide, general, but you can't run", *The Guardian*, 10 December 1998, p. 1.

Woodhouse, D., "The Office of Lord Chancellor" (1998) *Public Law* 617.

Woolf, Lord, "Civil justice is important as well", *New Law Journal*, 22 November 1996, p. 1701.

Wright, Lord, "In Memoriam Lord Atkin of Aberdovey", 60 *Law Quarterly Review*, October 1944, p. 332.

Young, H., "Lords Justices Hobhouse and Millett, who they?", *The Guardian*, 18 July 1998, p. 1.

Young, H., "Pinochet may, or may not, clear off. But Hoffmann certainly should", *The Guardian*, 19 January 1999, p. 16.

Young, H., "The danger looms of these judges looking like a pack of squabblers", *The Guardian*, 14 January 1999.

Young, H., "The folly, negligence and lack of judgment of the brilliant Hoffmann", *The Guardian*, 15 December 1998.

Young, H., "Tortuous questions", *The Guardian*, 25 March 1999.

Index